CURRENCY SUBSTITUTION AND LIBERALIZATION

to R.D. and G.J.

Currency Substitution and Liberalization

The Case of Argentina

UGO FASANO-FILHO
*Economist, Developing Countries Department,
Kiel Institute of World Economics*

Gower

Published by
Gower Publishing Company Limited,
Gower House, Croft Road, Aldershot, Hants GU11 3HR,
England

Gower Publishing Company,
Old Post Road, Brookfield, Vermont 05036,
U.S.A.

ISBN 0 566 05234 2

Printed and bound in Great Britain by
Paradigm Print, Gateshead, Tyne and Wear

Contents

List of tables

STATISTICAL APPENDIX II

List of figures

Preface

This book is a revised version of my PhD dissertation submitted to the University of Illinois at Urbana-Champaign in March 1984. I would like to thank my PhD committee; in particular, the chairman, Professor Werner Baer, for his useful suggestions and criticisms and also for his endless encouragement. The help and guidance from Professors Donald Hodgman and Stephen Turnovsky, the other two members of my committee, were very much appreciated and important to me. I am also in debt to Professor Don Roper with whom I had the opportunity to discuss relevant issues relating to currency substitution during his stay in Illinois as a visiting professor in 1982. I also have to mention that during my summer-internships at the World Bank (Brazil Division) in 1982, and at the International Monetary Fund (Stand-by Operations Division) in 1983, I benefited from their excellent research facilities and from discussions with some economists in such organizations.

Throughout the process of rethinking and subsequent revisions since 1984, I have received important comments from my colleagues at the Kiel Institute of World Economists. I also presented three working papers about some of the ideas introduced in this study in seminars at the Advanced Studies in International Economic Policy Research Program (August 1984-May 1985 at the Kiel Institute). Suggestions from participants in the seminars and in particular from Dr. Peter Tapp, are greatly acknowledged.

I am very thankful as well to Christiane Schröder for her meticulous typing work and Julia Feldmeier for her editing help. I should finally emphasize that I am solely responsible for any errors and omissions.

Kiel, Federal Republic of Germany

Ugo Fasano-Filho

1 Argentina: a case study of currency substitution

1.1 INTRODUCTION

"In Argentina, where the local money is worth less almost by the hour, it is sometimes cheaper to cover your wall with pesos than wallpaper.... What that means is that everyone buys dollars, as many as possible as often as possible .... All of [our] savings, what little we can save goes into dollars, and no one dares put them in the bank. They go in the mattress. The plain fact is that the peso has dropped out of sight in Argentina, because one government after another printed too much of them and because no one has any confidence in its value."
[1]

The theoretical importance and empirical evidence of currency substitution (CS) is still being debated. It is often suggested that the CS literature has added no new insights because its implications are similar to (perfect) capital mobility or capital flight; topics extensively studied. In addition, the distintion between direct and indirect CS, using McKinnon's terminology, seems to arise theoretical confusion. Empirically, since almost all the research has been based on the experience and framework within institutional aspects of developed countries, it is another reason why the relevance of CS and its policy implications are still not widely recognized.

There is a very important gap in the CS literature because practically no research has focused on the case of developing countries where the casual evidence suggests that this phenomenon is much more relevant and older than in industrialized economies [2]. In particular, the use of the US dollar for transaction purposes or as a store of value in many Latin American countries and even in Israel (classified as a developed country by the U.N.) is known to their policy-makers. Therefore, the purpose of this study is to (partially) fill up such a gap.

Our analysis is based on the case of Argentina. Argentinians have been encouraged to shift into foreign currency due to a relatively high domestic inflation rate, ceilings on nominal interest rates, and the certainty that the nominal exchange rate would be always adjusted. Besides, it is often mentioned the evidence of such a phenomenon in the Argentine central bank annual reports. Empirically, the period 1959-81 was covered. However, the last five years received our main attention. In March 1976, a military government implemented an economic program characterized by free-market oriented policies, particularly in the financial sector, to reverse a long period of low growth and high inflation. The analysis of such a program and its consequences represents an important case study to determine whether liberalization policies can solve the CS phenomenon.

1.2 OUTLINE OF THE STUDY

The objective of chapter 2 is to survey the contributions of the theory of substitutable monies. It is considered that the development of this literature has mainly raised new empirical and policy issues in the following topics: the conduct of monetary policy; determinants of the money demand in an open-economy; exchange rate determination; the difference between bond substitution and currency substitution; and stabilization policy in the presence of CS. In sum, we conclude that CS has mainly raised more relevant empirical and policy issues rather than new theoretical ones. In the last section of this chapter it is examined the importance and policy implications of CS for high-inflation developing countries. It is stressed here the important link, most of the time neglected by policy-makers in developing countries, between the exchange rate and the interest rate.

The purpose in Chapter 3 is to relate in the analysis the exchange rate and interest rate policies implemented in Argentina from 1959 to 1975, the demand for local and foreign currency, and their impact on the balance of payments. This help us to gain a historical perspective of why CS turned out to be a significant phenomenon in Argentina. In the last section, the CS effect is incorporated in estimations of money demand functions in the period 1960-76. Such an effect is captured by the expected rate of devaluation. The stability of these functions is also tested because it is generally argued that the demand for money becomes unstable in the presence of CS.

The stabilization-liberalization program implemented from April 1976 until March 1981 is described in Chapter 4. Two main phases are analyzed: first phase April 1976-December 1978, and second phase January 1979-March 1981. The stabilization objectives were to strengthen the balance of payments and to prevent hyper-inflation. Through a liberalization of the economy, it was sought to force the economy, particularly the industrial sector which benefited for many years from high tariff protection, to become more efficient. Therefore, it is important to distinguish between structural and temporary changes brought about by such a program. It is shown that the authorities failed to achieve the program's objectives.

Chapter 5 tries to answer the following question: why did the stabilization-liberalization fail? The main focus is on the second phase of the economic program. After reviewing the arguments of some authors, it still remains quite debatable the reasons behind its failure. However, we stress that there was nothing new and surprising in the failure of such a program when the past Argentine experience is brought into the analysis. The relationship between the real exchange rate and real wages is emphasized here. Nevertheless, there were new institutional aspects that were not present before in the Argentine economy and must be taken into account. In sum, the failure of the program is not considered to be related to the open-up of the capital and the trade accounts per se; although, this may have speeded up its collapse. The causes of such a collapse were the traditional combination of high real wages and real appreciation. This also suggests that no important structural changes took place in 1976-81 (with the exception of the liberalization of the domestic financial sector).

Finally, Chapter 6 presents a comparison of macroeconomic events in the Southen Cone countries during the time when these countries were embarked in similar economic policies.

1.3 BRIEF BACKGROUND ON THE ARGENTINE ECONOMY

Argentina's economic performance between the early 1960s and mid-1970s was characterized by high and volatile rates of inflation, recurrent balance of payments difficulties, and very low real GDP growth (see Table 1 in Statistical Apppendix I). This mediocre performance is generally explained through the "stop-go" process which describes the existence of a trade-off: either the economy attempts to reach a full-employment level or an external equilibrium, but it cannot achieve both simultaneously. The reference to such a false trade-off was very common during the period of the highly praised import-substitution approach. Thus, the reason for the presence of a stop-go pattern in Argentina must be found in the development strategy chosen and in the characteristics of Argentine exports and imports.

The Argentine authorities resorted to a policy of import-substitution as the main growth strategy, particularly since the 1940s [3]. Therefore, private and public consumption became the dynamic components of aggegate demand (e.g. total consumption generally represented more than 80 percent of GDP at market prices) under this strategy. The main variables used to influence economic activity were the domestic credit policy and real wages. The first one was relevant due to the need to finance increasing government deficits and the private sector working capital and/or investments. One also has to bear in mind that credit rationing was often in effect because the government imposed ceilings on interest rates, resulting in negative rates. Decree-increases in wages benefited urban groups and this encouraged higher consumption (economic activity).

Since production was mainly directed towards the domestic market due to a high anti-export bias, exports became a residual of domestic consumption. On the other hand, more than 80 percent of imports consisted of raw materials, intermediate and capital goods demanded by the industrial sector as inputs into the production process. Thus an overvalued exchange rate had positive (short-run) effects on the economy: e.g. the cost of imported goods decline and more goods were available for domestic consumption at a lower price (in local currency).

Therefore, periods of growth and lower inflation were brought about by a real appreciation of the exchange rate and higher real wages. Figure 1.1 shows a clear positive relationship between the change in real wages and real GDP growth rate. Figure 1.2 depicts a positive relationship between the real exchange rate and inflation, that is, real appreciation (the real exchange rate index curve goes down) was accompanied by a lower inflation rate. Figure 1.3 shows that a higher growth rate was accompanied by a lower inflation rate (by a real appreciation). However, as expected, this policy was short-lived (one or two years) because of a foreign exchange crisis. Higher domestic consumption and the real appreciation (domestic inflation still remained high relative to an international standard) discouraged exports, increased imports but principally fostered expectations of a future devaluation which encouraged people to buy foreign currency or engaged in capital flight. Thus, most of Argentina's balance of payments crises originated in the capital account rather than in the trade balance (e.g., in the period 1958-80, Argentine only experienced seven years of a trade deficit. See Table 3 in Statistical Appendix I).

To solve the balance of payments crisis, the authorities generally switched to a policy of real exchange depreciation and lower real wages. Consequently, the crisis was solved but at the expense of economic activity. Diaz-Alejandro (1970, p.390) has pointed out:

> It is a well-known result of trade theory that a devaluation (in a small country) will result in upward pressure on real output, by first stimulating production of exportable and import-competing goods. But the argument stresses that with a wage lag, devaluation will also lead to a redistribution of income toward nonwage earners who in the short run will have a lower propensity to spend, especially on domestic products. Unless supply responses of exportable and import-competing goods are very price-elastic, a drop in real output may result.

The above statement describes the natural outcome of a devaluation within a growth strategy based on indiscriminate import-substitution and on negligence in promoting exports. Argentina has never implemented specific and consistent policies that would have made the economy followed a more export oriented growth despite the small domestic market, as many other developing countries did in the 1960s. Total exports hardly accounted for more than 10 percent of GNP before 1975.

However, there is nothing surprising in the Argentine experience because it is a generally accepted result of open macroeconomic theory that the cost of a successful devaluation is a reduction in real wages. But since Argentina was relatively closed, this also meant lower domestic consumption (higher exports), and a drop in output (and imports), thus a trade balance surplus (or lower deficit). Note that the trade balance always experienced a surplus in the period 1963-74. That is, the amount of exports were more than enough to finance imports even in years of higher than average GDP growth (e.g., 1964, and 1969).

FIGURE 1.1

ARGENTINA – REAL WAGES AND REAL GDP GROWTH RATE, 1961–75

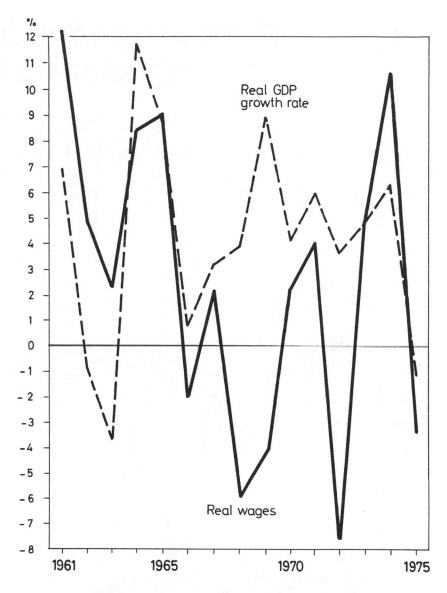

Source: Table 1 and Banco Central de la Repúblic Argentina,
        Sistema de Cuentas del Producto e Ingreso de la
        Argentina, Vol. 2 (1975).

FIGURE 1.2

ARGENTINA – REAL EXCHANGE RATE INDEX, AND WHOLESALE
PRICE INFLATION RATE, 1959–81

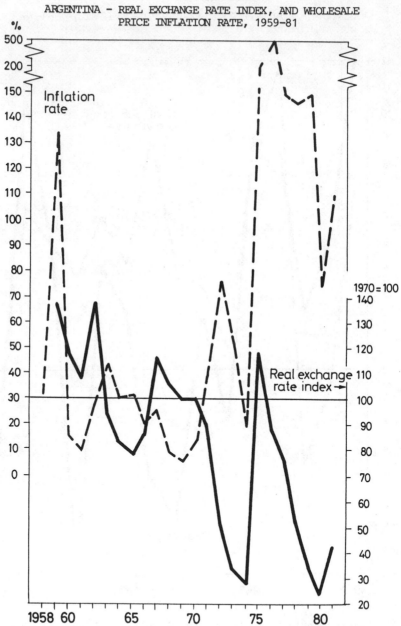

Source: Table 1.

FIGURE 1.3

ARGENTINA – REAL EXCHANGE RATE INDEX AND REAL GDP
GROWTH RATE, 1958–81

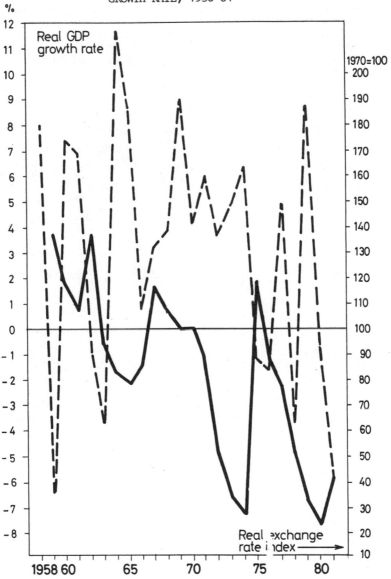

Source: Table 1.

Argentina did not experience high growth in the period 1960-75; according to the World Bank Atlas, real GNP per capita grew by 3.1 percent average a year. During the same period, Brazil experienced a 4.3 percent and South Korea a 7.1 percent per capita real GNP growth. However, there was a clear deterioration in the Argentine economic performance during the 1970s: real GNP per capita increased 0.7 percent average a year during 1970-80 (Brazil grew at 5.9 percent and South Korea at 7.5 percent). In addition, the high inflation rate and the instability of Argentine growth confirmed the serious inbalances in the economy and in the strategy pursued. It is this background that must be kept in mind to understand the policies implemented after 1975 and the reason of their failure.

NOTES

[1] This quotation was taken from an article written by George de Lama which appeared in the Chicago Tribune newspaper (section 1, p.8) on March 7, 1984.

[2] Only two articles were found that addressed the currency substitution issue for developing countries: one by Ortiz (1983) who studied the case of Mexico, and the other by Canto (1985) who studied the case of the Dominican Republic.

[3] See Baer (1972) for a further analysis on the effects of import substitution policies in Latin America.

2 Currency substitution: some major issues

2.1. INTRODUCTION

Monetary theory has traditionally assumed that only the local currency circulates within a country. However differential inflation rates among countries can create an incentive for money-owners to hold their money balances in the currency that depreciates least rapidly. Under this circumstance, the possibility of CS arises. Therefore, CS refers to the fact that people also hold foreign currency balances as a response to differential inflation rates among countries. Thus, what matters for its emergence is a relative higher domestic rate of inflation which will be reflected in a depreciating (black or parallel) market exchange rate. In other words, CS is encouraged due to the relative low value of the local currency and the certainty that the (nominal) exchange rate will have to be adjusted due to balance of payments considerations.

Theoretically, it is only under a flexible exchange rate regime that a country can choose its own rate of inflation. Since this regime has been mainly implemented by developed countries, much of the CS empirical research has focused on their experience. Although, expectations about the future behaviour of exchange rates have become more volatile with the implementation of flexible rates, under any exchange rate regime, it is always relevant to determine for how long the government will keep (or the market will sustain) a given parity. Thus, in practice CS can become a significant phenomenon in any type of country (developed or developing) and under any exchange rate regime [1].

The theoretical importance and empirical evidence of CS is still being debated. Several researchers have studied this phenomenon[2]. Among others, Miles, Girton and Roper, McKinnon have emphasized its importance; while Cuddington (1983, p. 58) has concluded that "the inclusion of foreign money in the usual menu of available assets introduces virtually no new insights." He drew this conclusion after introducing the choice of foreign money in a standard portfolio balance. However, his findings were based on two main assumptions: gross substitutability and no risk. Furthermore, he criticized the empirical results of existing CS models because they failed to distinguish CS per se from high international capital mobility. After this distinction was introduced, his own results did not strongly support the presence of CS in several developed countries. In general, he stressed that the macroeconomic implications of CS are qualitatively not different from high capital mobility. On the other hand, the experience of developing countries suggests that CS has relevant policy-implications that must be fully recognized even though its importance is not easy to model.

The objective of this chapter is to survey the contribution of the theory of substitutable monies. We consider that the development of this literature since the mid-1970s has mainly added new insights to empirical and policy issues in the following topics: (1) the conduct of monetary policy; (2) determinants of the money demand in an open-economy; (3) exchange rate determination; (4) the differences between bond substitution and currency substitution; and (5) stabilization policy. Section 2 will discuss the contributions of CS for each one of these areas. As mentioned before, much of the literature has been developed around the experience of developed countries (Western Europe, the U.S., Canada) under a flexible exchange rate regime. Researchers have paid little attention to the importance and policy implications of CS for (high) inflationary developing countries. The last section will present an analysis on this topic.

2.2.   THE ISSUES

2.2.1. Monetary Policy

The development of the theory of substitutable monies has given a new reason for not differentiating the conduct of monetary policy under fixed and flexible exchange rates[3]. The conclusion of traditional international economic models based on perfect capital mobility and the law of one price assumptions, is that an autonomous monetary policy cannot take place under fixed exchange rates; in other words, the domestic inflation rate cannot depart from the international one without causing disruptive consequences to the balance of payments. On the other hand, it is argued, if exchange rates are flexible, each country can set its own monetary policy and therefore, its own rate of inflation.

Brillembourg and Schadler (1979, pp. 515-516) pointed out that:

When currencies are substitutes, monetary authorities face similar types of constraints under flexible rates and under fixed rates. Under fixed exchange rates and unimpeded trade in capital and goods, excessive domestic credit creation results in a balance of payments deficit that eventually leads to a reversal of the expansionary policy. When exchange rates are permitted to change, monetary authorities may have more flexibility in the short-run. In the long-run, however, a continuing attempt to expand the money supply faster than demand for it steadily erodes demand and increases the rate of depreciation of the currency as money holders attempt to switch into other currencies. Thus even with flexible exchange rates, there are limits to the policies available to monetary authorities. In the long-run, excessively expansionary policies must be reversed or capital and trade restrictions will have to be imposed.

Once CS is accepted as an empirically significant phenomenon, then the central bank cannot set an "independent" or "autonomous" monetary policy even under a flexible exchange rate regime. The coordination of monetary policy among central banks whose currencies are close substitutes becomes necessary to avoid shifts in currency demand [4].

However, Brillembourg-Schadler's statement is also a valid in a world of perfect capital mobility. Under this circumstance, the domestic interest rate cannot differ from the foreign one and a monetary expansion becomes ineffective in changing real income. Such an expansion is reflected in an equal increase in prices and the exchange rate. Therefore, the monetary authorities face, qualitatively, the same constraints of an expansionary monetary policy under a flexible exchange rate regime in the presence of CS or perfect capital mobility[4].

2.2.2. The Demand for Money

Two related issues are relevant here: (1) the stability of the demand for money in the presence of CS, and (2) a reconsideration of money demand specification in open economies.

The work done by Brittain (1981), Miles (1978, 1980), Melvin (1982), and McKinnon (1982) emphasized money demand instability in the presence of CS. McKinnon (1982, pp. 320-321) said that:

> The monetarists have a strategy for exercising monetary autonomy: each country pursues its own fixed monetary growth rule as if the demands for national monies were stable and independent of one another ... The casual empirical evidence ... suggests a radically different view: the national (convertible) monies of an inner group of industrial countries are highly substitutable in demand in response to expected exchange rate movements. This international currency substitution destabilizes the demand for individual national monies.

Brittain presented empirical evidence that CS could explain the instability of income velocity in a number of industrial countries. Joines (1985) has also empirically studied the degree to which international CS destabilizes the demand for money of several Western European countries and Canada. He did not find support for Brittain's results and stressed that just a high elasticity of international CS is insufficient to make the demand for local money unstable. The ratio of foreign to domestic money balances held by domestic residents should be also substantial in order to destabilize such a demand.

In general, stability of the demand for money function refers to the idea that it must be highly predictable and is related to a small set of key variables [Jodd and Scadding (1982)]. But this implies that its arguments are highly predictable. Thus, the demand for money is unstable in the sense that it becomes more difficult to predict ex-ante. For stability it is also understood that two complementary conditions must hold: the arguments must be highly predictable and the value of the coefficients, over time, must remain constant. On the other hand, Friedman has said that (1956, p. 16) "... there is indeed little if any difference between asserting that the demand for money is highly unstable and asserting that is a perfectly stable function of an indefinitely large number of variables." Friedman is also supporting the argument that it must be a function of a few variables. CS is thus adding an extra variable to explain the variance in the demand for local currency.

The other main problem is which variable can capture the CS effect (in the demand for money) without misleading interpretations. Although, there is no final agreement on this issue, articles by Calvo and Rodriguez (1977), Boyer (1978), Miles (1978), Girton and Roper (1981), and Bordo and Choudhri (1982), identified CS with the effect of the expected rate of depreciation on the demand for local currency. Frenkel (1977, p. 668) wrote that "to the extent that domestic money is held as a substitute for foreign exchange, the specification of the demand for money should include the anticipated change in the exchange rate."

Cuddington (1981, p. 18) proposed the following money demand function:

$$\log (M/P) = \beta_o + \beta_1 \log Y + \beta_2 r + \beta_3 (r^*+x) + \beta_5 x \qquad (2.1)$$

where:

    M = domestic money demand
    P = domestic price level
    Y = real domestic income
    r = nominal interest rate on the local bond
    r* = foreign nominal interest rate on the foreign bond
    x = expected exchange rate depreciation

He emphasized the importance of distinguishing the effect of changes in the (net) return of foreign bonds: $(r^* + x)$ which reflects the presence of "capital mobility" from changes in the return on foreign currency: x (CS per se) on the demand for local currency. According to his equation, CS is not important under the null hypothesis that β_5 is zero. In the presence of CS, β_5 must be a significantly negative coefficient. That is, the higher the expected exchange rate depreciation the lower the domestic money demand. If domestic and foreign bonds are perfect substitutes, then β_3 can be set equal to zero and still identify CS with $\beta_5 < 0$, since r will capture now the capital mobility effect.

Cuddington criticized some of the empirical studies done because the authors assumed that the Fisher open condition holds without empirically testing it. If domestic and foreign bonds were not perfect substitutes, then $\beta_5 < 0$ indirectly shows CS because at the same time it is capturing the effect of the change on the bond yield. Only the work done by Bordo and Choudhri (1982) has tested the relationship between the domestic and the foreign interest rate plus the expected rate of depreciation and found that setting $\beta_3 = 0$, was a valid assumption; therefore correctly identifying CS with $\beta_5 = 0$. In the case of developing countries where domestic investors do not have access to, or for liquidity preference or transaction costs, do not hold foreign assets like bonds, stocks or time deposits but foreign currency, the expected rate of devaluation can "correctly" identify the effect of CS on the demand for local currency (in this case r* would be equal to zero).

Therefore, the introduction of CS can be an important explanation to the international shift of the demand for money. This insight is not so clear from a model that only assumes perfect capital mobility, even less, if money (narrowly defined) is considered just a function of (permanent) income, excluding the interest rate.

2.2.3. Exchange Rate Determination

Several models have been developed to analyze exchange rate determination[5]. CS comes to complement the predictions of the monetary or the asset market approach which considere the exchange rates being determined by the relative supplies and demands of two national monies.

The common exchange rate determination equation introduced by the asset approach is shown below:

$$S = M \ K^* \ (i^*, Y^*)/M^* \ K \ (i, Y) \qquad (2.2)$$

where:

*	= represents foreign country,
M	= the money supply,
S	= the spot exchange rate,
Y	= level of real income,
i	= nominal interest rate,
$K(i,Y)$	= demand for money is a negative function of "i" and a positive function of "Y".

This equation implies that the exchange rate (S) will depreciate (S will rise) whenever the supply of local currency (M) or the demand for foreign currency (K*) goes up. These changes will have a proportional impact on S. Note that the demand for money specified in this model is not being influenced by any foreign component: e.g., foreign interest rate, income, and/or forward premium on foreign exchange. The latter would indirectly affect the domestic demand for money only if the interest parity condition holds. Therefore, equation (2.2) does not capture the CS effect.

Girton and Roper (1981) presented the first comprehensive analysis of exchange rate determination in the presence of CS. They showed that exchange rate volatility or instability increases with the degree of CS up to the point that when two currencies are perfect substitutes, the exchange rate becomes indeterminate.

According to the model introduced by these authors, the exchange rate is determined as follows:

$$e = \tilde{e} - \eta(i_1 - i_2 - x) \qquad (2.3)$$

where:

E = exchange market price;
e = Ln E
$\tilde{e}$ = captures exogenous money-supply and demand factors;
$\eta = \alpha + 2\sigma$
σ = coefficient of substitution between monies one and two;

α = coefficient of substitution between domestic money
   and the nonmonetary asset;
x = anticipated rate of change of the exchange rate;
i_i= nominal interest rate on money, i = 1,2

Changes in the supplies of monies have a proportional impact on "e" for all finite degrees of CS as the asset approach would have predicted according to (2.4).

$$\partial e / \partial \tilde{e} = 1 \qquad\qquad (2.4)$$

$$\partial e / \partial x = \alpha + 2\sigma = \eta \qquad\qquad (2.5)$$

If σ = 0, meaning that CS does not exist, the exchange rate is determined by the stock of the two currencies and a new equilibrium is attained when the existing stocks of the two monies are willingly held. On the other hand, it can be seen from (2.5) that the impact of a shift in the anticipated rate of change of the exchange rate (x) on the exchange rate will be larger the greater the degree of CS. That is, equation (2.3) shows that CS is introducing a new element, the relationship between the expected rate of devaluation and the spot exchange rate. The value of the coefficient that relates both variables (σ) can vary between 0 and ∞; when σ = 0 , domestic investors do not hold foreign currency, and if $\sigma = \infty$, they are indifferent at which one to hold since domestic and foreign monies are perfect substitutes. Therefore, under flexible exchange rates, the exchange rate becomes indeterminate if both currencies were perfect substitutes[6]. Note that this extra argument may explain why during the 1970s, the exchange rates of developed countries have shown a variability that cannot be explained by just the relative changes in the money supply of every country.

Girton and Roper assumed that the interest rate on money "one" and "two", was equal to zero. Later, they suggested that if they were different from zero, the explicit policy of altering the interest rate paid on each money would change the real rate of return on money. Therefore, this may induce the necessary changes in the demand for money to eliminate or at least to dampen fluctuations in the exchange rate. Consequently, if CS is a relevant phenomenon and monetary authorities do not want severe fluctuations in the exchange rate, they should better alter their monetary policy to accommodate foreign monetary policies. If, for example, the rest of the world tightens up, then the domestic banking system had better match the rise in foreign interest rates; otherwise, the domestic currency will depreciate, and depreciate a lot if currencies are strong substitutes. This suggests that it is a better policy to control the world money supply rather than individual countries money supply as emphasized by McKinnon.

Former models that have included foreign bonds as the only alternative foreign asset, did not bring the same results as the Girton-Roper model. In general, we can conclude that to the extent that the alternative to holding domestic money is, besides domestic bonds and goods and foreign bonds, also foreign exchange, a re-specification of the demand for money must follow to include all the spectrum of alternative assets[7].

2.2.4. Bond Substitution and Currency Substitution

The CS theory also emphasizes the difference in substitution between bonds and between currencies. Suppose that domestic investors hold local and foreign currencies as well as domestic and foreign bonds in their portfolio. If asset-holders suddenly expect a change in the expected rate of depreciation, they now want to hold relatively more foreign assets (including foreign currency) in their portfolio than domestic assets (including domestic currency). Therefore, their effort to sell the domestic bond and purchase the foreign one, increases the yield on the first one and reduces the yield on the second one. After this adjustment has taken place, the interest parity condition again holds and both bonds remain perfect substitutes. At this point, asset-holders are satisfied with the existing quantities of both bonds because they offer the same expected yield. This is a typical example of capital mobility, in this case perfect capital mobility. Note that as long as there exists a disparity between the yield on the domestic bond and the yield on the foreign bond, a capital flow will continue but once the yield difference disappears, the capital movement must stop. However, since we have also assumed that foreign currency is part of the portfolio choice, we can still see capital flow or "currency mobility" since wealth-holders are shifting from local into foreign currency because the expected value on the first one is decreasing. McKinnon (1982, p. 237) pointed out that "... massive capital flows can easily be induced even when the interest differential remains "correctly" aligned to reflect accurately the change in expected exchange depreciation."

The above implies that it is possible that capital flows still occur although interest rate parity on bonds holds. If we assume that the interest rate on money is freely determined and/or that the authorities do not intervene in the foreign exchange black (parallel) market under a fixed exchange rate regime or follow clean floating under a flexible exchange rate, then, with perfect CS, there is a money interest rate parity condition just as there is with perfect bond substitution. As perfect bond substitution says that the nominal interest rate differential between two similar bonds must equal the expected rate of change of the exchange rate, perfect CS says that the nominal interest differential on monies must equal the expected rate of change of the exchange rate. Looking back at equation (2.3), the term $(i_1 - i_2 - x)$ becomes zero if interest rate parity on monies continuously holds, then the exchange rate will only be affected by the first term. Thus, as long as the interest parity on monies does not hold, money flows will continue, and the effect of a change in the expected rate of devaluation will be more serious on the level of international reserves of the central bank than by just considering bond substitution. Note that CS has here a quantitative effect that can be relevant to consider during a stabilization or adjustment program.

McKinnon (1982) considered a first channel or direct route and a second channel or indirect route through which CS manifests itself. Assuming that the Fisher open condition holds and that domestic investors hold foreign currency and bonds as well as domestic currency and bonds, the first impact of a change in the expected rate of depreciation is to substitute non-interest bearing working balances of the depreciating currency for the foreign one to reduce direct losses from anticipated local currency devaluation. This is done by large commercial banks, some non-financial multinationals and trade-oriented institutions. He stated that this direct form of currency substitution, channel one, may well be significant without being dominant in developed countries. The indirect route uses the strong assumption of perfect capital mobility: the yield on the domestic bond and the foreign one will quickly adjust to new exchange-rate expectations. Asset-holders will move out of local bonds into foreign bonds and this causes interest rates to adjust. Once the yield differential disappears, capital outflows need not occur since there is no more reason for arbitrage in international tradeable bonds. He pointed out that currency substitution induced by these interest-rate changes occurs indirectly. The rise in the domestic bond interest rate increases the opportunity cost of holding local currency while the decline in the foreign interest rate decreases the opportunity cost of holding foreign currency, which is translated as a decline in the demand for domestic currency and an increase in the demand for foreign currency.

Therfore, it would be wrong to aggregate foreign bonds and currencies into one category as foreign assets as advocated by Cuddington. It is thus relevant to compare the adjustment of portfolios that include foreign currency balances as an alternative asset from those that do not, after, for instance, there has been a change in the rate of return of foreign money. At the same time, an extra condition is necessary to stop or to reduce capital flows in the presence of CS, that is, the interest rate parity on monies should also hold together with the interest rate parity on bonds. The lack of recognition of this quantitative effect can pose serious stabilization problems.

2.2.5. Stabilization Policy in the Presence of CS

Vaubel (1980, p. 25) wrote that:

> When residents change their demand for the domestic money at the expense or in favor of foreign currencies, this affects, ceteris paribus, the domestic income velocity of the circulation of money ... Thus, in principle, international shift in the demand for money raise the same policy problems, as instability of the velocity of circulation would in a closed economy.

This instability of the velocity of circulation implies for a closed economy [as stated by Poole (1970)] that the authorities should implement a fixed interest rate rule rather than a money growth rate rule to reduce the variance of domestic income. For an open economy and assuming perfect capital mobility, the implication is that the authorities should implement a fixed exchange rate.

Boyer (1978, p. 197) noted that "both the growth of currency mobility and the diminution of money illusion argue for a substantial degree of exchange rate fixity in the real world." Miles (1978) and McKinnon also advocated fixed exchange rates in the presence of (direct) CS. Fasano-Filho (1984) introduced CS into a standard stochastic macro-model of optimal intervention policy that is an extension of the one presented by Roper and Turnovsky (1980). The model follows a Poolean-type analysis and is more policy oriented than other optimal intervention policy papers [see for instance Boyer (1978), Henderson (1979)]. Not surprisingly, he concluded that the implementation of a fixed exchange rate regime assures domestic real income stabilization in the presence of CS. This was based on two main assumptions: the disturbance terms in the real and monetary sectors were uncorrelated and the disturbance only originated in the domestic monetary sector.

Fasano-Filho and Horta-Correia (1985) showed that traditional results on income and prices after a monetary and a real shock took place, were obtained in a model that introduces CS. This seems to support Cuddington's argument that CS has added no new insights. However, the authors verified that the higher the degree of CS the less the difference of either disturbance effects in the economy independently of the exchange rate regime. This outcome was already suggested when the implications of CS for the conduct of monetary policy were discussed above. Note that in models that assume perfect capital mobility, this is not an obvious outcome. Fasano-Correia's model is similar to Marston (1983). His model assumed perfect capital mobility, no CS, and as shown below, the real demand for money (m_t-p_t) was expressed as a function of real income (y_t; the income elasticity is set equal to one) and the interest rate:

$$m_t - p_t = y_t - k_1 r_t^f - k_1 (_tEx_{t+1} - x_t)$$ (2.6)

where:

r^f = foreign interest rate

$_t Ex_{t+1}$ = expected exchange rate in the next period

x = domestic currency price of foreign currency

In Fasano-Correia's model r^f is assumed equal to zero and k_1 represents the elasticity of CS: k_1 tends to ∞ as currencies become perfect substitutes. In Marston's model k_1 only takes a finite value; thus in the presence of perfect capital mobility there is no reason to assume that the coefficient k_1 can become infinite and/or unstable. This is the most important difference that arises from introducing CS: the value and stability of the coefficient k_1. This becomes an empirical question that has to be determined for every economy. The fact that a foreign currency is circulating within a country (and being also used for transactions purposes), gives a good reason to question a finite and constant value for the coefficient k_1 which is neglected in models with perfect capital mobility. In sum, CS has raised more relevant empirical and policy issues rather than new theoretical ones.

2.3. CURRENCY SUBSTITUTION IN HIGH-INFLATION DEVELOPING COUNTRIES

Developing countries tend to experience inflation rates much higher than the rest of the world. Therefore, domestic wealth-holders may be encouraged to keep a large portion of their portfolio in foreign currency. For instance, McKinnon (1982b, p. 78) has said that:

In Latin America, dollars typically circulate in parallel with the domestic currency for transactions purposes. They are literally competing monies for buying the same range of goods. In this circumstance, direct currency substitution is important and is highly de-stabilizing. By trying to impose the inflation tax on pesos, people simply switch into dollars. The peso base for the inflation tax erodes, and hyperinflation in pesos becomes an ever-present possi-bility.

This substitution takes place, because of a relatively higher domestic inflation rate the value of non-interest bearing domestic assets is dra-stically declining due to this inflation high that encourages expectations of a future depreciation, and ceilings on nominal deposit interest rates which result in negative real ones. Besides, in an inflationary environ-ment it is paramount to remain as liquid as possible in order to facili-tate fast shifts from one type of asset to another due to uncertainty about rates of return. Thus, cash dollars become the best option.

Therefore, CS is likely to be a much older and significant phenome-non in Latin America than in industrialized countries. But it now be-comes a non-symmetrical phenomenon, "this means that we define CS in the context of a small open economy which has a "weak" or "soft" cur-rency and substitutes it for a "hard" currency, but the domestic cur-rency is not demanded by the hard-currency country," [Rubli (1981), p. 7]. In developing countries where CS is a relevant phenomenon, two currencies (the local and the U.S. dollar) will be generally used as units of account, medium of exchange, and store of value. However, the government has only direct control over the domestic one, meaning that in its presence the government has to accept a loss of seignorage. Consequently, the inflationary tax needed to finance a given budget deficit must be higher, aggravating the already high inflation rate, without CS being the cause behind high inflation but the other way around.

It was already pointed out that most of the research undertaken in the CS literature focused on the demand for non-interest bearing mone-tary assets and the empirical studies were done for Western European countries currencies vis-à-vis each other and to the U.S. dollar and between the U.S. dollar and the Canadian one. In many Latin American countries, however, we must also consider the fact that asset-holders switch from time and savings deposits denominated in local currency into foreign currency rather than into foreign bonds. This is due to a liquidity preference, the presence of exchange and capital flow controls which increases the risk and the transaction costs of such operations, and the ceilings imposed on nominal interest rates. Besides, domestic stocks and bonds may not be widely available. By holding foreign cur-rency, domestic wealth-holders hedge against inflation. They know that the government will sooner or later have to devalue in order to avoid a balance of payments crisis. Referring to this, Tanzi and Blejer (1981, pp. 783-784) wrote that:

> We have emphasized currency substitution affecting the most liquid part of money demand, that is, the fraction held in non-interest-bearing monetary assets and used for immediate transactions. How-ever, part of the monetary needs of individuals and firms is sa-tisfied by less liquid interest-bearing assets. As these balances are not held for immediate transactions, but reflect in part one form of holding wealth, it is likely that the elasticity of substitution be-tween foreign and domestic interest-bearing assets, in response to differentials in their rates of return, will be high even when for-

eign currency (or deposits denominated in foreign currency) has relatively low domestic liquidity ... Investors will substitute foreign-denominated for domestic-denominated interest-bearing assets and, thus currency substitution will occur not just for balances held for immediate transactions but also (and perhaps especially) for balances held (using the Keynesian terminology) as a store of value or for precautionary motives.

It is then important to include less-liquid interest-bearing domestic monetary assets in the analysis. Nevertheless, the use of foreign currency for domestic transactions purposes remains the most relevant implication of CS (for developing countries) even in a world of perfect capital mobility.

At this point, it is relevant to determine how to relate capital-flight to the CS phenomenon. Capital flight refers to the fact that residents of a country shift foreign currency (cash) abroad. Therefore, this has an impact on the balance of payments, particularly through the current account (e.g., underinvoicing of exports, overinvoicing of imports, "tourists" buying foreign currency who are actually local residents). On the other hand, capital flows are understood as flows of international tradeable bonds - which receive an interest payment. Capital-flight is thus the LDC version of capital flows since asset-owners do not hold foreign bonds but currency. Under this circumstance, capital flight or CS and capital flows are all the same phenomenon. But it must be stressed that capital flight is only capturing one aspect of CS: the use of foreign currency as a store of value.

One should also consider the fact that domestic investors may not necessarily send their foreign currency balances abroad. They can keep them in security-boxes at commercial banks or even "under the mattress" because the rate of return on these balances represented by the expected rate of devaluation is much more important (due to the high rate of domestic inflation) than changes in the foreign interest rate. Thus, foreign variables may not affect their holding. Therefore, CS remains an important phenomenon as long as the foreign currency balances stay in the country. If the people manage to take them abroad, this is a capital movement. It is hard to believe that the dollars will be left in a suitcase once they reach Miami; certainly they will be deposited in time deposits at commercial banks or US bonds will be bought.

If one aspect of CS in developing countries is caused by the imposition of interest rate ceilings, then to which extent the liberalization of those rates per se will dampen CS? Assuming that the local interest rate on deposits is freely determined; an increase in the expected rate of devaluation, will encourage domestic trade-oriented institutions, and other international firms or banks, to replace their local currency working balances by foreign currency (direct or first channel), and investors to shift into foreign currency from time and savings deposits denominated in local currency (indirect or second channel). This may cause domestic interest rates to go up by the full-amount of the expected change in the exchange rate. At this stage, significant currency mobility need not occur since local currency time and savings deposits and foreign currency offer the same yield. Local residents also try to sell non-interest bearing domestic currency by depositing them into time deposits. But this arbitrage from local currency into time deposits, may create downward pressure on the nominal interest rate so as to leave the interest rate below the exchange rate change. Again there will be a reduction of local currency time and savings deposits and the demand for US dollar cash balances will increase. This adjustment mechanism is quite similar to the one described before by McKinnon. The only difference is that an interest rate parity on monies rather than on bonds is achieved.

It was emphasized before that the interest rate parity on bonds hold because the value of the bonds is inversely related to its price. In the case of money, this inverse relationship does not exist unless there is a specific policy that relates the interest rate on money to its value, e.g. through indexation. If this were the case, Girton and Roper (1981, p. 21) concluded that "the implications of CS would be similar to the implication of substitution between other financial assets". Therefore, there is no reason to believe beforehand that the interest rate on time and savings deposits will automatically rise by the full-amount of the change in the expected rate of devaluation since the yield on money does not depend directly on its value, as is the case for bonds, and time deposits do not have the characteristics of an international tradeable asset.

It is also possible that when the interest rate is freely determined that it will increase by more than the domestic inflation rate. This larger change in the nominal interest rate can be caused by uncertainty (e.g. exchange rate risk) or when people expect that the monetary-authorities will devalue by more than the difference between the domestic and foreign inflation rates in order to catch up from past overvaluation or to "gain some time". But since industrial and agricultural firms usually borrow from commercial banks to finance their working capital; this increase in their financial cost in real terms may bring about bankruptcies and/or a higher domestic inflation rate. Bankruptcies can occur if the government implements strict price controls which do not allow firms to pass on the higher level of real financial costs to prices. The same may happen if due to a trade liberalization program (e.g. tariff reductions), foreign competition discourages local firms from boosting their prices. Therefore, policy-makers may want to follow an interest rate policy that pegs the nominal interest rate to the domestic rate of inflation in order to keep the real interest rate constant at a predetermined level, and an exchange rate policy that keeps the rate of devaluation as close as possible to the domestic inflation rate. This sort of policy can be implemented during an adjustment or stabilization program.

The aforementioned interest rate policy is consistent with Girton and Roper's (1981, p. 13 and 21) conclusion that:

> The usual fixed-money-growth rule will lead to an inferior, depreciating money if the public is offered competitively produced substitutes ... It is particularly appropriate for an issuer of substitutable money to use the real return on money as the monetary control variable.

The experience of the Southern Cone countries exemplifies this fact. The financial reform implemented by these countries in the mid-1970s was accompanied by extreme variations in the real interest rate on money. For instance, the annual real short-term lending interest rate reached a maximum of 60 (first quarter of 1981), 128.8 (fourth quarter of 1976), and 59.6 percent (fourth quarter of 1981), in Argentina, Chile, and Uruguay, respectively (see Tables A-1.1, C-1, and U-1). These rates were achieved as a result of the local authorities inconsistent monetary, exchange rate, and interest rate policy. The financial reform increased the link between those policies, so that, any inconsistency was easily translated to the whole economy through the changes in the interest rate: the overvaluation of the local currency increased the expected rate of devaluation, pushing up (real) interest rates.

Also note that if the authorities allow domestic financial intermediaries to offer demand and time deposits denominated in foreign currency, the resulting shift into foreign currency will not represent a leakage for the economy as is the case in the presence of international tradeable bonds. That is, foreign currency balances will be kept neither "under the mattress" nor will they be send abroad. The shift will not cause a balance of payments crisis under this institutional arrangement since there will not be capital flight but just a change in the ownership of the foreign currency from the government to the private sector. However, we may have not solved the CS problem completely because there will still be substitution from the non-interest bearing domestic assets into foreign currency. It is important that commercial banks be allowed to offer interest payments on demand deposits as well. Although these policies will not make CS disappear, it may be dampened or reduced to an insignificant level. Consequently, note that there is a relevant difference between a portfolio composed by two perfect substitutable bonds (local and foreign) and another one composed by demand and time deposits denominated in local and foreign currency which are held in local financial intermediaries. An increase in the expected rate of devaluation may not bring about a balance of payments crisis, and therefore a lower level of domestic economic activity, if we consider the last portfolio.

In open-economies the relationship between the interest and exchange rate policies is paramount. As mentioned before, the authorities may peg the nominal interest rate to the expected rate of devaluation. This will keep the real interest rate constant if the expected rate of devaluation were equal to the domestic inflation rate. We are not advocating fixed (nominal) exchange rates, but a policy that target the real exchange rate, and relates it to the interest rate policy in order to avoid sudden shifts in money demand and undesirable capital flight. Obviously, the number of instruments available to, and the targets chosen by the government remain part of a consistent economic program.

Therefore, it is through a consistent exchange rate and interest rate policy that the government may encourage domestic investors to reduce their foreign currency balances and not just by allowing the domestic interest rate to be freely determined. However, this type of policy does not take into account the substitution between non-interest bearing monetary assets. Policy-makers have only one major alternative to resolve the CS problem, that is, to eliminate the main reason behind it: a relatively high domestic inflation rate. With respect to this, the Israeli and the Panamanian experiences with CS are important to mention.

In the fall of 1983 Israel's Minister of Finance proposed a dollarization program in order to cure inflation that was running at more than 14 percent average per month according to the cost of living index. Under this program the U.S. dollar would become the currency and legal tender in Israel, replacing the Israeli snekel. Consequently, prices, wages, contracts, financial transactions and deposits would have been denominated and carried out in dollars. The program was accepting a de facto widespread dollarization of the Israeli economy. Since the persistent of Israel inflation was mainly associated with a high government deficit, as in Latin America, dollarization would force the authorities to reduce expenditures. In other words, the program would prevent the government from printing money. Any budget deficit left would have to be financed by borrowing from the international capital market. The final outcome would be that inflation in Israel would be similar to that in the United States.

The program was going to limit the options that the Israeli government had in determining economic policy and it would also require a sufficient supply of dollars for daily transactions (where would they come from?). Besides, an increase in foreign debt, drastic cut in the government budget, higher unemployment, lower real wages, and a decline in competitiveness due to any potential strengthening of the dollar, would have been certainly brought about by the dollarization program. This outcome did not seem to differ very much from a drastic and orthodox stabilization program. However, once the program was implemented, dollarization would force any government to stick to anti-inflationary policies and the people would be convinced that indeed inflation was being conquered. Nevertheless, it was never carried out.

On the other hand, Panama has kept for more than three decades its exchange rate fixed to the US dollar, accepting a de facto dollarization of the economy since only this currency circulates within the country. This success is not surprising due to the characteristics of the economy. Panama does not export manufactured products and much of its foreign exchange receipts come nowadays from the service sector. Besides, its GNP at current market prices was only US$ 4.0 billion in the early 1980s, that is, small enough to obtain the necessary amount of dollars to carry out daily transactions. Certainly, these characteristics are not those of Argentina or Israel.

In March 1976, a military government implemented in Argentina free-market oriented policies, particularly in the financial sector to reverse a long period of low growth and high inflation. The analysis of this program and its consequences represents an important case study to determine whether liberalization policies can solve the CS phenomenon.

NOTES

[1] Differences in inflation rates are viewed here as the core reason behind CS. Although, this can be a relevant explanation for developing countries; risk of money returns caused by a volatile flexible exchange rate brought about by other causes rather than differential inflation rates, may account for the presence of CS in developed countries [see Miles and Steward (1980)]. In the case of centrally planned economies, CS may deserve other explanations.

[2] See articles by Guillermo Calvo and Carlos Rodriguez (1977), Russell Boyer (1978), David King, B. Putnam, and D.S. Wilford (1978), Marc Miles (1981), Miles and Marion Stewart (1980), Roland Vaubel (1977, 1978, 1980), Arturo Brillembourg and Susan Schadler (1979), Lance Girton and Don Roper (1980, 1981), Bruce Brittain (1981), Michael Melvin (1982), Ronald McKinnon (1982a), and Douglas Joines (1985). Miles (1978) presented the first empirical evidence of CS between the U.S. and Canada. His results were criticized by Michael Bordo and Ehsan Choudhri (1982). See also Steven Husted's (1980) Ph.D. dissertation. John Bilson (1979) presented different exchange rate determination approaches, including the effect of CS. Federico Rubli (1981) studied CS under a small-country assumption and Guillermo Ortiz (1983) presented an empirical analysis of CS for Mexico, and Victor A. Canto (1985) for the Dominican Republic.

[3] See Robert Mundell (1968), Alexander Swoboda (1976), Rüdiger Dornbusch (1980), Stephen Turnovsky (1979), William H. Day (1979), for a further clarification on monetary policy under fixed and flexible exchange rates.

[4] Miles (1978), Boyer (1978), Brittain (1981), and McKinnon (1982a) have emphasized the lack of monetary policy independence once CS holds. This view was criticized by Vaubel (1980). He suggested that it is important to make a difference between monetary policy independence and monetary policy autonomy. Flexible exchange rates supporters advocate monetary autonomy defined as national self-determination over the national money supply and thus the freedom to use a national policy instrument for domestic ends while monetary independence is defined as independence of both supply of, and demand for, the national currency on foreign developments.

[5] Krueger (1983) and Bilson (1979) presented surveys of the theoretical and empirical literature on exchange rate determination.

[6] Kenneth Chan (1982, p. 2) pointed out that: "If currencies are risky, households would minimize risk by choosing a balanced portfolio. Consequently the equilibrium exchange rate is determinate even though currencies are perfect substitutes."

[7] Studies done by Mario Blejer (1978), Jose Viñals and Fritz van Beek (1979), and Vicente Galbis (1979), included the expected rate of devaluation as an argument in the demand for local currency to estimate that function for many Latin-American countries (Argentina, Bolivia, Brazil, Colombia, Mexico, Peru, and Uruguay). However, none of them specifically analyzed CS.

[8] A weak or a strong currency can be labeled as such with respect to its value <u>and</u> its acceptability in international transactions: e.g. the higher its value and acceptability the stronger the currency under consideration relative to others. Both characteristics are relevant because a currency can have a high value but if at the same time it is not internationally accepted, it cannot be considered a strong currency.

3 The exchange rate policy and the demand for money in Argentina, 1959-76

3.1. INTRODUCTION

The exchange rate is not only an important price but also a crucial instrument in economic policy. It is used to (partially) solve balance of payments problems by altering the relative price of tradeable and non-tradeable goods as well as the return of domestic monetary assets relative to foreign ones. Therefore, it has a direct effect on the real sector (e.g., economic activity and the distribution of output), and also an indirect effect through the monetary sector.

The important link, most of the time neglected by policy-makers in developing countries, between the exchange rate and the interest rate was already emphasized in the previous chapter. It is our purpose here to relate in the analysis both rates, the demand for local and foreign currency, and their impact on the balance of payments. This will help us to gain a historical perspective of why CS turned out to be an important phenomenon in Argentina. Note that the existing CS literature has been developed within a framework of flexible exchange rates and no restrictions to capital and money flows. The Argentine experience becomes a relevant case to test CS within a different institutional framework (fixed rates or passive crawling-peg, interest rate ceilings, capital movement control). In the last section, the CS effect is incorporated in estimations of money demand functions for Argentina in the period 1960-76. This effect will be captured by the expected rate of devaluation. Its coefficient must be negative and statistically significant in order to conclude that there is strong evidence of CS. The stability of these functions is also tested because it is generally argued that the demand for money becomes unstable in the presence of such an effect.

3.2. EXCHANGE RATE POLICIES

Different exchange rate policies were implemented in Argentina from 1959 to 1976:

(1) dirty floating exchange rate, January 1959/April 1962
(2) flexible exchange rate, April 1962/March 1964
(3) crawling-peg (21 devaluations), April 1964/February 1967
(4) fixed exchange rate (there were only two devaluations in March 1967 and June 1970), March 1967/March 1971
(5) timid crawling-peg, April 1971/August 1971

(6) fixed dual exchange rates (a commercial and a financial rate. The last one was fixed in September 1972), disguised devaluations, September 1971/February 1975

(7) crawling-peg, March 1975/March 1976

Table 3.1 below summarizes the institutional framework as well as the (average) value of the most important macroeconomic indicators considered in the description of events and in the analysis that follows (also see Table 1).

3.2.1. January 1959 to March 1964

During this period the authorities were basically committed to a flexible exchange rate regime but they reserved the option to intervene in the foreign exchange market and they did it during the first three years. Under this circumstance, there was no difference between the value of the official and the black market exchange rate[1]. There were no exchange and capital flow controls or restrictions, it was legal to hold foreign currency balances, and commercial banks were allowed to accept foreign currency deposits owned by local residents.

In January 1959, the Argentine authorities introduced a single fluctuating exchange rate that replaced the earlier multiple rate structure. However, the central bank periodically intervened in the foreign exchange market from January 1959 until March 1962 to support the parity within a certain margin. From January to December 1958, the exchange rate was devalued by 84 percent when domestic inflation was 31.5 percent[2]. After this important real devaluation, the nominal exchange rate remained quite constant, until the first quarter of 1962 (from January 1959 until March 1962, it was devalued by 26 percent, when inflation was equal to 225 percent during the same period).

The government refused to withdraw its support to sustain the exchange rate, in spite of the real appreciation, that was taking place since 1959 because it considered the exchange rate as one of the cornerstones of its development program to decelerate inflation and to attract foreign capital. This stubborn exchange rate policy stagnated exports (measured in constant dollar amounts) while imports increased by 7.8 percent a year as Figure 3.1 shows. There was a small trade balance surplus in 1959, but 1960 and 1961 experienced deficits, reaching US$ 496 million in the last year, while the net outflow of short-term non-compensatory private capital was equal to US$ 329.3 million in the same year. Exports were subject to retention taxes that ranged between 10-20 percent which coupled with the real appreciation, discouraged even further export growth. On the other hand imports were also subject to a high surcharge as well as advance deposits; but the government abolished the advance deposits requirements and reduced nominal tariffs (from a range of 20-30 percent to a maximum level of 150 percent) at the end of 1959[3]. Therefore, it was not surprising that a trade deficit appeared. After the recession of 1959, the recovery in the next two years was led by the industrial and service sectors (real wages increased by an average of 13 percent each year) while the agricultural sector showed no growth. Again, the interaction of real wages and the real appreciation brought about a temporary demand-pull recovery as explained in chapter one.

TABLE 3.1

ARGENTINA – CAPITAL FLOW RESTRICTIONS, AND PRINCIPAL ECONOMIC INDICATORS DURING DIFFERENT EXCHANGE RATE POLICIES; 1959-76

Exchange Rate Policy	Capital-Flow and Exchange Controls Policy:	Annual Average Growth Rate of Principal Economic Indicators (in percent):[a]
Dirty-Floating January 1959 - March 1964	No exchange and capital-flow controls or restrictions were in effect. Residents were allowed to hold foreign currency deposits at commercial banks.	1960-1963: deposit interest rate (i_d) : 5-15[b] inflation rate(WPI-gen.)^d : 23.2 real GDP (1960 prices) : 2.4 official exchange rate devaluation (x_o) : 15.0 black market exchange rate depreciation (x_{bm}) : 14.7[c] US inflation : 0.0
Crawling-Peg: April 1964 - February 1967	Capital movement Restrictions were in effect. Foreign currency deposits owned by residents were not allowed.	1964-1966: i_d : 8-15 WPI : 27.0 real GDP : 7.0 x_o : 14.5 x_{bm} : 20.9 US infl. : 2.0
Fixed Exchange Rate: March 1967 - March 1971	No exchange and capital-flow controls or restrictions were in effect. Residents were allowed to hold foreign currency deposits at commercial banks	1967-1970: i_d : 8-15 WPI : 13.6 real GDP : 7.0 x_o : 16.3[d] x_{bm} : 12.4 US infl. : 2.5
Crawling-Peg: April 1971 August 1971	Exchange rate controls imposed during the last quarter of 1970	1971: i_d : 8-15 WPI : 39.0 real GDP : 5.9 x_o : 54.1 x_{bm} : 63.2 US infl. : 3.5
Crawling-Peg: Disguised devaluations: September 1971 - February 1975 April 1976 - November 1976	Capital movement Restrictions were in effect. Residents were not allowed to hold foreign currency deposits.	1972-1974: i_d : 18-24 WPI : 47.2 real GDP : 4.9 x_o : 19.6[e] x_{bm} : 38.9 US infl. : 6.9
Crawling-Peg: March 1975 - March 1976	Foreign exchange controls and capital movement restrictions	1975-1976: i_d : 40-freely determined WPI : 319.0 real GDP : - 1.3 x_o : 232.4[e] x_{bm} : 490.6 US infl. : 6.9

[a] annual average growth rates were calculated as: $((1 + v)_t \cdot (1 + v)_{t+1} \ldots)^{1/n.y}$, where v: variable and n.y.: number of years in the period. - [b] range of deposit interest rates at commercial banks in the period. - [c] wholesale price index (general) as published by I.F.S. (the IMF). - [d] a maxi-devaluation took place in March 1967. - [e] a two-tier or dual exchange rate system was introduced in September 1971. Devaluation rate reported here corresponds to the financial exchange rate market. The unification of the market did not occur until the end of 1976 . In March 1976 two exchange rates existed: an official and a fluctuating free one. Therefore, the black market exchange rate was practically abolished with the implementation of this fluctuating rate. From April 1976 and until November of the same year, the policy-makers implemented a disguised crawling-peg by moving the proportions or percentages at which commodities were traded between the official and the fluctuating rates. During the disguised devaluations of the September 1971 - February 1975 period, the commercial and financial exchange rates were used, both rates under government control.

Source: Banco Central de la Republica Argentina Memorias Anuales and Boletin Estadistico Mensual, and Pick's Currency Yearbook.

FIGURE 3.1

ARGENTINA - EXPORTS AND IMPORTS IN REAL TERMS, 1951-81

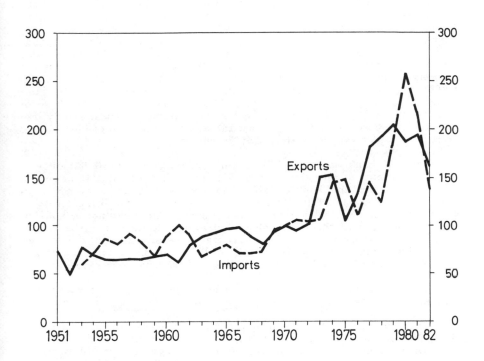

Source: Own calculations based on Table 1

Note that while the average yearly inflation rate was 43.7 percent from 1959-1961, the nominal interest rate on time and savings deposits at commercial banks averaged between 5-12 percent a year. However, as soon as domestic inflation went down from 133.7 percent annual rate in 1959 to 10 percent in 1961, the demand for real balances increased an average of 8 percent a year while real quasi-money (time and savings deposits) experienced an annual increase of 10 percent in 1960-61. The fact that the exchange rate was fixed, the relatively higher real return of domestic money, and the rise in wage-earners real income may explain the increase in the local money demand. In 1961, there was a net short-term private capital inflow of US$ 125.5 million. This was another indication that people were holding higher local currency balances. Also recall that commercial banks were allowed to accept deposits denominated in foreign currency owned by local residents since the banking reform of 1957. Nevertheless, these deposits were never under the official guarantee of the central bank in case of a bank default as was the case of deposits in local currency (in 1961 foreign currency deposits only represented 10 percent of the total amount of time and savings deposits at commercial banks; approximately US$ 70 million).

The central bank was a net buyer of foreign currency (US$ 120 million) in 1960 and during the first four months of 1961. But it became a net seller during the rest of 1961 and the first quarter of 1962. In 1961, it sold US$ 100 million to support the parity at the official rate of m$n (pesos moneda nacional) 82.9 per dollar. The growing balance of payments deficit and the suspension of drawing rights under the stand-by arrangements with the IMF in 1961, made the situation in the foreign sector unsustainable at the beginning of 1962. In March, a military government took power and signed a new stand-by arrangement.

On March 19, 1962, the exchange market operations were suspended until April 4. The central bank stopped supporting the peso and it depreciated by 78 percent from March to November 1962. Inflation accelerated and economic activity went down mainly because of the decline in the industrial and service sectors, since agriculture output showed signs of recovery. Exports increased of the average by 20 percent, while imports decreased by 17.4 percent from 1962 to 1963. The gain in real income of wage-earners of the past two years evaporated since it declined by an average annual rate of 12 percent in 1962-1963.

Nominal interest rates were slightly increased after 1961, they ranged between 8-15 percent while inflation almost reached 43 percent in 1963. The trade balance showed a surplus of almost US$ 500 million (total amount in 1962-1963), but the net outflow of short-term private capital was almost US$ 600 million. Foreign currency deposits at commercial banks declined (they represented 6.7 percent of total time and savings deposits by 1963). This does not suggest that people were not shifting into foreign currency (actually, there was an outflow of short-term private capital in 1963), but that foreign currency was not coming back into the financial system. The substitution was also implicitly pointed out in the 1962 Annual Report of the central bank. In a letter from the president of the central bank (Dr. Mendez Delfino) to the Minister of Economics (Dr. Coll Benegas), the former stressed that while businessmen claimed that there existed illiquidity in the financial system, and therefore economic activity lacked the means of payments to properly function, in only four days at the beginning of January 1962, the central bank had to sell US$ 34.4 million in the "free" exchange market, equivalent to almost m$n 2,900 million which were provided by an apparently illiquid domestic financial market. Note that while a significant disequilibrium in the exchange rate market was obvious since April 1961; only a year after, intervention was stopped and the parity allowed to find its own equilibrium.

The Argentine experience indicates that a foreign sector crisis may still take place even in the presence of an important trade balance surplus. With respect to this, Brodersohn (1977, p. 121) has said that:

> In spite of a surplus in the current account during 1962, there was a serious crisis in the foreign exchange market. The reason for this weak position of the external sector must be found in the outflow of capital ... The pressure on the international reserves was so high that the central bank had to give up support of the peso at the given parity (the net sales of foreign currency by the central bank during the first four months of 1962 was equal to US$ 170 million). In April 1962, there was a devaluation but in June the new parity had to face again new pressures. [4]

Also Simone (1972, p. 65) suggested that "the fact that the real interest rates were negative can be considered responsible for the severe balance of payments crisis and for capital outflows." In sum, by mid-1961, after two years of a stable exchange rate, the perception that the exchange rate was overvalued increased the demand for foreign exchange and the central bank became a net seller. In 1962, after the significant devaluation in the first quarter, the real exchange rate was at the same level as in 1959. Inflation increased and the economy experienced two recessionary years. In spite of the devaluation, the trade balance experienced a surplus only in 1963, but the net outflow of private capital reached record amounts, bringing about a balance of payments deficit. The real interest rate became extremely negative and the restrictive monetary policy implemented was not enough to change expectations and to reduce the demand for foreign currency. In October 1963, a constitutional government took office. The exchange rate continued to pursue an unstable path: it reached a maximum of m$n 148 per US dollar and then started to appreciate until February 1964, when it reached the minimum value of m$n 132.08 per dollar (the last time that the exchange rate was below that value was in October 1962).

3.2.2   April 1964 - February 1967

In the second quarter of 1964 the authorities implemented a stabilization program. Its core objective was to reactivate the economy through an increase in the purchasing power of urban groups. A crawling-peg was established within this program, but before the central bank intervened in the foreign exchange market to sustain the parity a m$n 137 per US dollar until August 1964. Restrictions were also introduced to prevent unauthorized capital movements. These measures made the functioning of the exchange market quite different from the last period.

Import payments required the specific approval of the central bank. Exports were still free of direct controls, but now exporters were required to repatriate and sell in the exchange market the foreign exchange proceeds of their exports within 5 working days after shipment (it was extended to 10 days in May 1964). Other restrictions implemented were: the banks and institutions authorized to deal in foreign exchange were permitted to sell exchange for many categories of invisibles up to established limits, subject to the submission of documentary evidence or sworn declarations of the bona fide nature of the transaction. Capital outflows by residents were restricted (purchases of foreign currency in excess of US$ 50.0 a person a month required a sworn declaration attesting the bona fide nature of the transaction); financial institutions were forbidden to accept deposits in foreign currency on behalf of residents, and existing deposits had to be liquidated; and the operations of authorized exchange houses were restricted and closely supervised by the central bank.

The exchange rate was devalued from April 1964 to February 1967 by 86 percent, while inflation was 105 percent during the same period. Exports grew at a stable rate of 3.3 percent a year, measured in real terms, and imports grew by 3.1 percent a year also in real terms. The trade balance experienced a continuous surplus over the whole period, averaging US$ 365 million a year, which helped to avoid a balance of payments bottleneck due to an interrupted net outflow of short-term private capital of US$ 130 million a year. Nominal interest rates on bank deposits remained unchanged at a range between 8-15 percent per year (the average annual inflation rate was 27.1). Thus, there existed a high negative interest rate in these years which may explain why the difference between the official and the black market exchange rate was so wide: e.g., in 1965 the black market rate was 45 percent higher than the official one, with a continuous outflow of short-term private capital. Therefore, the situation in the foreign sector remained "weak" since during the whole period the international reserves held by the central bank represented no more than two months of imports during the year. At the same time, the excessive expansionary monetary policy followed by the government created a further pressure in the exchange market that precipitated a balance of payments crisis at the end of the period.

During 1964-1965, the economy grew by 7.1 percent a year in real terms, led by the growth of the industrial sector. This was expected since wages increased faster than inflation. Thus, real consumption also grew by an average of 6.4 percent a year in this period. In 1966, after two years of more than average growth rate, real GDP increased only by 0.8 percent. A more restrictive monetary policy had to be implemented since mid-1965 to protect the balance of payments (that experienced a lower trade surplus and a higher capital account deficit in 1965).

As expressed before the exchange rate was kept quite in line with the rise in domestic prices by implementing periodic devaluations: twenty-one from April 1964 to February 1967, approximately one every month-and-a-half. This policy sustained a trade balance surplus in spite of higher than average GDP growth and did not accelerate inflation. Nevertheless, the significant negative real interest rates, encouraged a higher demand for foreign currency that kept the difference between the official and the black market exchange rate at record levels (it remained approximately 24 percent higher). While the indexation of the nominal exchange rate showed the important positive impact on the trade balance as well as a lack of direct link in accelerating inflation of this policy; the authorities once again disregarded the role of the interest rate in avoiding a balance of payments crisis and in sustaining economic growth. Also the crawling-peg system was successful in avoiding a drastic real appreciation without the need for a simultaneous reduction in real wages[5].

3.2.3. March 1967 - March 1971

In March 1967, a new stabilization program was introduced. The program started with a massive devaluation of the exchange rate which went from m$n 225 to m$n 350 per dollar. That is, it was devalued by 37.3 percent, and was then fixed for 39 months, until June 1970. In order to reduce the inflationary impact of the devaluation, import duties were reduced, export taxes increased, and a "voluntary" agreement between the government, the labor unions and the private firms was reached to limit further increases in wages and prices.

The real interest rate on bank deposits was positive in 1968 and 1969, not because the government increased the nominal rates which remained at a range of 8-13 percent, but because of a drastic reduction in inflation to a single-digit rate. This positive real rate of return on local currency, the expectation that the exchange rate was not going to be devalued in the near future, and the fact that the government implemented monetary and fiscal restraints on public finances, reduced inflationary expectations. These were all elements that discouraged CS. For instance, in the 1967 Annual Report of the central bank (p. 59) it was stated that "the main source of net private capital inflow (US$ 232.1 million) was believed to have been the private sector dishoarding of foreign currency". As expected, an important increase in the demand for local currency took place in these years.

There were no limitations on inward or outward capital transfers by residents or nonresidents. In 1968 (circular B612, February 5, 1968) the authorities again allowed foreign currency demand and time deposits at local commercial banks. Foreign demand deposits could not receive interest payments, and foreign currency deposits were not subject to any government guarantee as stated by article 11 (Bank Law of 1967) where it was established that only the deposits made in local currency were guaranteed in case of a bank default. Foreign currency deposits only averaged 1.5 percent of the total savings and time deposits in the period.

During 1967-70, real GDP grew at 5 percent average per year. The source of growth must be found in the increase of gross domestic investment which experienced an average annual increase of 11 percent, with construction (public and private) growing by as much as 14 percent a year. No former period surpassed this rate. The high rate of investment was necessary in order to increase the productive capacity of the economy, since by 1965 it had already reached a full-employment level and growth could only be sustained by increasing investment. The measures used to encourage investment were mainly tax-incentives and less restrictive facilities to import capital goods.

Real exports grew at almost 6 percent a year, although imports grew faster (8.7 percent) due to the incentives to import capital goods. Despite this, the trade balance was always in surplus during the period, but with a declining trend. The short-term net private capital account also experienced a continuous inflow with the exception of 1969. In March of that year, political events (el Cordobazo) had created uncertainty. This was translated into pressure in the foreign exchange market and in an outflow of capital. The 1970 Annual Report of the central bank (p. 2) stated that "the monetary authorities feared that part of the loans obtained by the private sector were going to be used to buy foreign currency". In 1970, the foreign exchange market was closed twice (June 9-7 and October 15-16). On June 18 the peso was devalued from $ 3.50 to $ 4.00 per dollar (14.3 percent devaluation). This devaluation was also partially compensated by increasing export taxes and reducing import surcharges as in 1967. The political crisis in October 1970 again forced the closing of the exchange market for two days. In Pick's currency yearbook (1971, p. 55), we can read that "the crisis sparked a run on monetary reserves, which dropped over US$ 300 million in a matter of hours and forced a closing of the exchange markets. The black market immediately leaped to life with the quotation dropping to as low as $ 4.40 per dollar." This black market rate was 40 percent higher than the official rate. Officially a rate of $ 4.40 per dollar was not reached until eight months later (June 1971). By the end of 1970, exchange rate controls were reimposed and the June-parity was kept until March 1971.

3.2.4. 1971 - 1976

During this period there were nine Ministers of Economics and four presidents. No stand-by agreements were signed with the IMF but the country used twice the compensatory financing facility (in 1972 and in 1975). Although three different exchange rate policies were implemented in these years, they were all within the context of a crawling-peg system, differing in the frequency and the way (disguised or open) devaluations took place[6].

Martirena-Mantel (1981) distinguished three periods in the exchange rate policies implemented from 1971 to 1978:

(1)   timid crawling-peg, between April and August 1971,

(2)   mixed period of disguised and open crawling-peg, between the fourth quarter of 1971 and first quarter of 1976,

(3)   open crawling-peg, between November 1976 and December 1978. A unified exchange rate market was reintroduced during this period.

In February 1971, some important modifications were introduced to the law of 1969 that regulated the financial system. These were: the market of acceptances (or commercial papers) became regulated. This market was an important source of funds to firms since the mid-1960s. People were also willing to deposit funds in such a market because the interest rate was not subject to government control. However, despite the new regulations the interest rate still remained freely determined. Commercial banks were also permitted to offer various kinds of time deposits, characterized by different maturities and interest rates. In April of 1971, the government initiated the policy of monthly adjustment of the exchange rate: starting with a parity of $ 4.00 per dollar in March 1971, it reached $ 5 on August 24 (a 25 percent devaluation)[7].

Two new policies were introduced at the beginning of this period to increase the demand for local currency and to reduce the unproductive hoarding of foreign currency: (1) a continuous revision of interest rate ceilings, (2) and the introduction of a domestic bearer bond issue, denominated in US dollars, tax free and freely transferable, yielding at least 8 percent per annum. The interest rate was to be linked to the six-month Eurodollar rate and the principal was to be repaid within five years. The purpose of this bond was to "lure back some US$ 8 billion in flight capital" [Pick's currency yearbook (1971), p. 56]. However, the public's response was not as expected.

1971 ended with a trade deficit of US$ 128 million (1962 was the last time there had been such a deficit), a short-term net private capital outflow of almost US$ 400 million and a decline of international reserves (they were US$ 724.7 at the beginning of 1971 and US$ 316.7 million by the end of the year). It should be noted that exchange rate controls reimposed during the last quarter of 1970, reduced foreign currency deposits to only 2.0 percent of total deposits. A $ 0.50 tax was placed upon foreign exchange bought by residents for travel purposes in July 1971, thus creating a de facto resident travel rate.

By September 1971 net international reserves had shrunk to US$ 110 million. At the end of the month a two tier foreign exchange market was established, composed of a financial exchange market for capital movements, travel and foreign remittances which was freely determined, and a commercial exchange market for all foreign trade transactions to be conducted at the fixed official rate of $ 5.00 per dollar. The financial rate was 30 percent higher than the commercial rate in September; by December it was 70 percent higher. At the same time a mixed exchange rate was created de facto, resulting from the negotiation of a certain percentage of foreign trade transactions in the commercial market and the rest in the financial market. The percentage negotiated within the two different rates changed several times. This represented disguised devaluations because generally a higher percentage was negotiated in the financial exchange rate market which was higher than the commercial rate. In September 1972, the commercial rate was still equal to $ 5.00 per dollar while the financial rate had reached $ 9.98 per dollar, a difference of almost 100 percent. The aforementioned parities remained unchanged until March 1975.

The period between September 1972 and the first maxi-devaluation in March 1973 can be labeled as one of fixed exchange rates but characterized by disguised devaluations as suggested by Martirena-Mantel since the mixed rate was never constant. For instance, in September 1971, 90 percent of trade transactions covering imports and nontraditional exports were to be settled in the commercial market and 10 percent in the financial market. By March 1973, it was 36 percent in the commercial market and 64 percent in the financial market; in July 1973 it was changed again to 30 and 70 percent respectively. Recall that the commercial rate remained fixed from September 1971 and the financial rate from September 1972, until March 1975. Meanwhile the domestic inflation rate was equal to 145 percent from September 1972 to March 1975 or 335.1 percent from September 1971 and until March 1975.

Martirena-Mantel pointed out that the disguised crawling-peg succeeded in reducing inflationary expectations, as well as private short-term capital outflows. This is surprising due to increasing real negative interest rates which had been slightly positive in 1974. For instance, in 1972, deposit interest rates at commercial banks varied according to the type of transaction and maturity from 18 percent to 24 percent nominal annual rate. In the acceptance market it reached almost 30 percent per year for six-month deposits; while the inflation rate was 76 percent from December 1971 to December 1972; and the purchase of different types of index-linked assets were not available until 1973 when it was experienced a net inflow of private short-term capital. There was an outflow in 1974 and again an inflow in 1975. Looking at uses and sources of international reserves, 1972-73 were years of net purchases of foreign currency by the central bank, while 1974-75 were years of net sales, that reached a maximum of US$ 1741 million in 1975. Martirena-Mantel suggests that 1975 did not show massive capital outflows due to the availability of indexed financial assets.

From 1972-1974 the trade balance showed a surplus due to excellent crops related to favorable weather conditions and the higher international price of traditional exports. However, in 1974 the exchange rate was considered to be drastically overvalued. It had lost 72 percent of its value in real terms since 1970. Nevertheless, the trade balance was in surplus but 60 percent lower than in 1973. The black market rate was 70.3 percent higher than the official one and while the offical rate was not openly devalued until March 1975, the black market exchange rate depreciated by 50 percent in 1974 (the inflation rate was 19.9 percent in that year).

As expected the industrial and services sectors were the most important sources of growth during these years while agriculture output only experienced a significant increase in 1973 (16.8 percent). Holdings of quasi-money continued to increase due to higher real income and return on the variety of financial assets that became available after 1973. But, on the other hand, velocity of a narrow definition of money experienced an increase (this is common when inflation shows an upward tendency) as Figure 3.2 below shows.

On March 3, 1975, the first open devaluation took place after almost three years of disguised ones. The commercial rate was devalued by a 100 percent and the financial rate by 51 percent. On August 14, a special financial rate was created to channel receipts and payments of freight, insurance, tourism, and other services. At the end of 1975, the commercial, financial, and special financial rates were devalued by 688, 509, and 37 percent respectively. In spite of all these devaluations, the black market rate remained 135 percent higher than the financial rate, real exports decline by 31 percent while imports remained constant. In 1975, real quasi-money went down by almost 90 percent, inflation reached a three-digit rate, the economy experienced the first recession in many years, and the decline in international reserves brought about a balance of payments crisis.

There is no doubt that Argentina has tried a variety of exchange rate policies. What are the lessons that can be drawn from this experience? Taking into account the performance of five variables (the trade balance, short-term private capital flows, the domestic inflation rate as measured by WPI, real GDP growth rate, and the real exchange rate) in each one of the four periods considered above (1959-1963, 1964-1966,

FIGURE 3.2

ARGENTINA – INCOME VELOCITIES, 1960–81

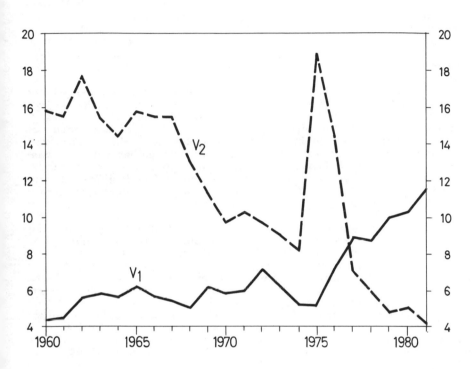

Source: Table 5

1967-1970, and 1971-1975), only in 1964-1966 (crawling-peg) and 1967-1970 (fixed exchange rate policy) did all the aforementioned variables experience an acceptable performance. For instance, the trade balance was always in surplus (annual average of US$ 365.0 million and US$ 173.4 million in 1964-1966 and 1967-1970 respectively), the annual average inflation rate was below 30 percent in 1964-1966 and 13.8 percent in 1967-1970, and real GDP experienced record growth rates in both periods. However, there was a relevant performance difference: in 1964-1966, a continuous outflow of short-term private capital occurred (annual average net outflow of US$ 130.8 million), while in 1967-1970 there was an annual average inflow of US$ 128.4 million (net) with the exception of 1969, when there was an outflow due to political events.

Such a difference is not surprising if we recall that in 1964-1966 the domestic real interest rate was negative and the official exchange rate showed signs of appreciation (the black market exchange rate was 45 percent higher than the official one in 1965). This, as mentioned before, encouraged CS. But in 1967-1970, the decline in the inflation rate brought about positive real interest rates which together with the massive devaluation of March 1967 reduced the expectations of a sudden exchange rate change (the first one occurred in March 1971), discouraging CS. Inflation was reduced but not at the expense of growth during 1967-70.

The choice between a fixed exchange rate and crawling-peg or mini-devaluations will therefore depend on the ability of the authorities to achieve and keep the domestic inflation rate similar to the international one. If domestic inflation remains quite above the foreign inflation, a crawling-peg policy coupled with an interest-rate policy on domestic monetary assets which aims to keep the real return of these assets above the expected return of foreign currency, seems to be the best response to avoid a trade deficit and CS according to the Argentine experience. Therefore, the authorities should see the significance of coordinating the exchange rate and the interest rate policy to reduce the chances of a balance of payments crisis and a recession and to facilitate the road towards lower inflation.

It is our purpose now to present a study of the money demand function for Argentina that specifically incorporates the effect of the expected rate of devaluation. This will give a further empirical evidence of CS in this Latin American country. At this point it must be stressed that it is relevant for policy-makers to verify the existence of CS because, in its presence, a tight monetary policy will generally be insufficient to reduce the inflation rate. It is also necessary that the authorities simultaneously implement a credible exchange rate policy as well as a consistent interest rate policy.

3.3. STUDIES OF THE DEMAND FOR MONEY FOR ARGENTINA

One of the first studies was done by Diz (1970). It covered the period 1935-1962. He estimated the demand for per capita real money balances as a function of the cost of holding money (proxy by the expected rate of inflation), real per capita (permanent) income, and inflation uncertainty (proxy by the variance of inflation). The result of his estimations showed that the three independent variables explained a very high fraction of the observed variation in per capita real money holdings, and this conclusion was held even if savings and time deposits were included in the definition of money. The values of the estimated coefficients revealed that savings and time deposits holdings were more responsive to changes in the inflation rate and less responsive to income variations, while for a narrow definition of money (currency plus demand deposits) the opposite was true. Finally he also found that an increase in uncertainty tended to increase desired money holdings, although this variable was statistically significant only when time and savings deposits were included in the definition of money.

Salama (1978) presented estimations of the demand for narrow money from the second quarter of 1968 to the first quarter of 1977, where the independent variables were the expected rate of inflation and real income (proxy by GDP at market prices). He used a partial adjustment mechanism and concluded that both variables were important and the adaptive expectations approach performed well as a proxy for the expected rate of inflation. Khan (1980) was also interested in determining the role of the expected rate of inflation in explaining the demand for money in highly inflationary countries (Argentina, Brazil, and Chile). The dependent variable was defined in real per capita terms and he used two definitions of money: narrow and broad money (currency plus demand and time deposits). The arguments in the money demand function were: the expected rate of inflation, and the expected real per capita income. Both variables were generated by adaptive expectations. However, while in a Cagan-type adaptive expectation approach the coefficient of expectation is assumed to remain constant over the period of analysis, he assumed that the coefficient varies positively with the rate of inflation. His estimation covered the period from the second quarter of 1960 to the fourth quarter of 1970 and the results showed that all estimated coefficients had the correct signs and were statistically significant. The values of the estimated coefficients, as found by Diz, suggested that money broadly defined is more responsive to inflation and less responsive to income variations than money narrowly defined. Finally, the fact of allowing the coefficient of inflationary expectation to vary proved to be relevant to better the results since it was verified a reduction of the time lag in the adjustment of expected inflation to current inflation of a little over three quarters from seven quarters when that coefficient was assumed constant.

Baliño (1980) presented a study of the demand for money from 1935 to 1969. He used a partial adjustment approach and estimated a narrow and broad definition of money as well as their components. Besides including the cost of holding money and income as arguments, he also incorporated as independent variables the rate of interest on saving deposits and the share of wages in national income. Once again, income and inflation proved to be the most important arguments. The interest rate coefficient turned out to be statistically significant in the case of demand deposits and currency and nonsignificant for quasi-money which is quite a puzzling result. Finally, Mathieson (1981) presented empirical results using quarterly data from the second quarter of 1977 to the fourth quarter of 1979, which covered the financial liberalization period. He used a much more complete model because he was interested in analyzing the effect of the financial reform; thus a banking and non-banking sector were also introduced. He included the real (expected) return on government bonds as an extra argument in the demand for money as well. His econometric results (with respect to the importance of the different independent variables in explaining variations in the demand for money) did not introduce new insights. However, a striking point in all the aforementioned empirical and theoretical studies, is that the expected rate of devaluation was never entered as an argument in the demand for money in spite of the strong evidence suggesting the presence of CS in the Argentine economy, as pointed out in the previous section.

3.4. THE DEMAND FOR MONEY IN THE PRESENCE OF CS

In research undertaken by Viñals and van Beek (1979), where the demand for money in Latin-American countries was studied from 1964 to 1978, we found, for the first time, that the expected rate of devaluation is entered as an argument in the money demand function. Unfortunately, it was included only in the demand for quasi-money (savings and time deposits). In the specific case of Argentina, once they included the interest rate and the expected rate of devaluation as independent variables, there was a significant improvement in the results for quasi-money relative to a first alternative, where only real income and the expected rate of inflation were incorporated as arguments. The adjusted R^2 jumped from 0.299 in the last specification to 0.753 once the aforementioned variables were included. In contrast, the estimation of a broad definition of money was not significantly improved by introducing the expected rate of devaluation and interest rate variables. Their estimation of a narrow definition of money, where only real income and the expected rate of inflation were increased as arguments, performed poorly since only 55 percent of the variation in the dependent variable was explained. Besides, the income elasticity coefficient turned out to be insignificant and of the wrong sign. Finally, their proxy for the expected rate of devaluation assumed that "market participants expect exchange rates to reflect purchasing power parity in the long-run" (p. 5).

Viñals and van Beek's research represented an improvement over the other ones because they recognized for the first time the importance of the substitution between local and foreign currency in an empirical study for Latin-American countries and specifically for Argentina, the results can only be considered as a timid step in analyzing the presence of CS in the demand for money. Our purpose here is therefore twofold: to study the effects of expectations about future exchange-rate adjustments on different definitions of money demand for Argentina in 1960-76 and to determine whether or not CS makes the money demand function unstable.

The specifications of the money demand function studies, as expressed above, have generally included real income (defined as permanent or actual) and the expected rate of inflation as the major determinants. The expected yields on alternative assets, like government bonds, has only been included recently in the work done by Mathieson. The interest rate was generally not seen as an important explanatary variable because in the organized financial sector it was controlled and typically set at a rate below the domestic inflation rate. The portfolio choice was thus considered to be composed of domestic money and real assets while foreign currency was generally an alternative left out in previous studies.

We hypothesized that the demand for money, defined either as currency, demand deposits, currency plus demand deposits, and quasi-money (time and savings deposits), responded primarily to the level of real income, the inflation rate, and the expected rate of devaluation:

$$M/P = f\ (y, \pi, x) \qquad (3.1)$$

equation 3.1 can be rewritten in Ln form as:

$$Ln\ (M/P)_t = a_o + a_1 ln\ y_t + a_2 \pi_t + a_3 x_t + u_t \qquad (3.2)$$

where:

M = nominal demand for money
P = the price level measured by the wholesale price index (general)
y = actual real income measured by GDP at factor costs at 1960 constant pesos,
π = inflation rate calculated as: $ln\ (P_t/P_{t-1})$,
u = stochastic error term.

We estimate quasi-money (QM), currency (CC), demand deposits (DD) and a narrow definition of money (M_1 = CC + DD) according to equation 3.2, where the income elasticity coefficient was expected to be positive (a_1), the price elasticity coefficient negative (a_2), and the expected rate of devaluation coefficient (a_3) was hypothesized to have a negative sign, that is, an increase in the expected rate of devaluation will reduce the demand for local monetary assets. Our period of estimation was from 1960 to 1976, using annual data and OLS estimation procedure. We do not include the real domestic interest rate as an argument in spite of the fact that it was positive in 1968-70 and 1974, because for the most part of the period the nominal interest rate was kept fixed and, given the relative high rate of domestic inflation experienced by Argentina, this exclusion did not seem inappropriate.

Since during much of the period, the institutional framework corresponded to one of interest rate ceilings, exchange controls, and fixed rate or passive crawling-peg, the black market exchange rate was the relevant variable to be linked to the expected rate of devaluation. Therefore, the following relationship was used:

$$x_t = LnP_t - LnP_t^* - Ln\ e_t^b \qquad (3.3)$$

where:

P_t^* = U.S. wholesale price index as a proxy for world prices

e_t^b = black market exchange rate (from Pick's Currency Yearbook).

The above relationship implied that changes in the domestic price index (asuming for simplicity a zero rate of inflation abroad) were fully reflected in the value of the black market exchange rate (if the government did not intervene). This approach was empirically supported by the data of the black market exchange rate depreciation presented in Table 3.1. As Vinals and von Fristz assumed, we observed that the rate of depreciation has quite closely followed the difference in inflation rates according to purchasing power parity[8].

3.5. THE ECONOMETRIC RESULTS

The results were presented in Table 3.2. We found that substitution occured chiefly between local currency/demand deposits and foreign currency, as the CS literature has generally suggested. The expected rate of devaluation coefficient was negative and statistically significant for all definitions of money used except for quasi-money where it came out with the wrong sign and was statistically insignificant after using the Cochrane-Orcutt method. But, once the estimation of M_1, CC, and DD were also corrected for autocorrelation, the expected rate of devaluation turned out to be a more significant variable than the actual rate of inflation to explain variations in the money demand functions. Therefore, there was a strong evidence that CS was an important empirical phenomenon in the period of analysis.

Our results have shown that currency holdings were a more elastic asset with respect to a change in the rate of inflation than demand deposits and quasi-money. On the other hand, DD were more elastic than CC holdings to changes in the expected rate of devaluation. However, this coefficient was statistically less significant for DD. The estimated income and inflation elasticity coefficients had the expected sign and were statistically significant for money narrowly defined, currency, and quasi-money. In the case of demand deposits the inflation rate coefficient turned out to be statistically insignificant. This finding is not surprising if it is assumed that the local currency is mainly held by households while demand deposits by firms. Since transactions among firms may be carried out mostly in foreign currency, they only need to keep their demand deposits balances at a minimum level to pay their bills to the public sector. If the government does not index this debt, demand deposits will be quite insensitive to changes in the inflation rate but much more elastic to changes in the expected rate of devaluation.

The lack of substitution between quasi-money and foreign currency can be rationalized by the fact that the real interest rate on time and savings deposits was generally negative, as a result quasi-money never represented more than 7 percent over GDP in the whole period, with the exception of the years when the real interest rate was positive. Currency holdings and DD were the most important monetary assets held in the economy until the mid-1970s. For instance, CC plus DD represented 75 percent of a broad definition of money in 1960, in 1975 they represented 69 percent. That is, wealth-holders did not consider quasi-money an important way to hold wealth. This is obviously not true after the financial reform took place in 1977, when the interest rate on deposits at financial intermediaries were freely determined. We expect that from 1977 to 1981, there must have been support for the substitution to occur between quasi-money and foreign currency.

Another important issue raised by the presence of CS is whether or not the estimated demand for money functions are stable over time. We have divided the overall period in two sub-samples: (1) 1960-65/1971-76, (2) 1966-1970. Although these may be considered to be arbitrary sub-samples, the first one showed a higher and more unstable domestic inflation rate (average inflation rate was 46.6 percent with a standard deviation(s) of 51.9) while the contrary happened in the second one (average inflation rate equals 15.9 percent and s = 7.9). Therefore, the CS effect is expected to be more relevant in the first subperiod than in the second one.

TABLE 3.2

ARGENTINA - ESTIMATIONS OF THE DEMAND FOR MONEY FUNCTIONS, 1960-76

dependent variable	constant term	income elasticity	inflation elasticity	expected[a] rate of dev. elasticity	adjusted R^2	sum of squared residuals	Durbin-Watson	estimated coefficient of autocor.	standard error of estimate
$\ln(M_1/P)_t$	-1.6823 (-1.2769)	0.9913 (5.3143)	-0.2771 (-3.4100)	-0.3060 (-3.1363)	0.8260	0.18148	1.1926	-	0.1182
$\ln(M_1/P)_t$	-0.0997 (-0.6302)	0.7857 (17.3075)	-0.2529 (-3.1799)	-0.2565 (-3.4819)	0.9523	0.15500	1.7051	0.548	0.10919
$\ln(CC/P)_t$	0.8455 (0.6671)	0.5527 (3.0798)	0.3377 (-4.3199)	-0.3324 (-3.5406)	0.7286	0.16796	1.2619	-	0.11367
$\ln(CC/P)_t$ [b]	-0.2038 (-1.0412)	0.7231 (15.2950)	-0.3499 (-4.9281)	-0.2645 (-3.8267)	0.9436	0.12103	1.8667	0.449	0.10039
$\ln(DD/P)_t$	-6.1706 (-3.9664)	1.5082 (6.8472)	-0.2269 (-2.3647)	-0.2789 (-2.4209)	0.8687	0.2531	1.1807	-	0.13950
$\ln(DD/P)_t$ [b]	-0.0215 (-0.0777)	0.6455 (8.9858)	-0.1211 (-1.0423)	-0.2975 (-2.6843)	0.8437	0.3425	1.2438	0.492	0.16230
$\ln(QM/P)_t$	-10.2320 (-8.8087)	2.0905 (12.8419)	-0.2254 (-3.1789)	-0.0380 (-0.4460)	0.9421	0.13823	1.2380	-	0.10312
$\ln(QM/P)_t$ [b]	-6.1728 (-6.2953)	2.2650 (8.8670)	-0.2401 (-3.3789)	0.0341 (0.4845)	0.8526	0.1059	1.6288	0.462	0.09393

[a] t-statistic between paranthesis. - [b] the Cochrane-Orcutt method was applied to correct the autocorrelation in the disturbances. The period corresponds to 1961-76.

To test for instability, we calculated the F-statistics:

$$F_{k,N-K} = (SSR - \sum_{i=1}^{2} SSR_i)/k/ \sum_{i=1}^{2} SSR_i/N-K \qquad (3.4)$$

where:

SSR = the sum of the squared residuals of the pooled regression (1960-1976),

SSR_i = is the sum of the squared residuals corresponding to each sub-sample.

N = is total observations, equal to 17,

k = is the rank or number of constraint parameters, equal to 4,

K = total number of parameters to be estimated, equal to 8.

The null hypothesis to test for stability is that the coefficients (including the constant term) are the same in each subperiod. If the calculated F-value according to 3.4 is higher than the critical F-value at $\alpha = 0.05$, then we reject the null hypothesis, implying that the function was unstable. We also tested the hypothesis that the variance was constant between the different subsamples. The results are shown in Table 3.3.

The F-test supports the hypothesis of a stable demand for money function as well as of equal variances. However, a look at the absolute values of the estimated coefficients in Table 3.4 where the econometric results were presented for the different subperiods and definitions of money, shows that in fact they are not equal. This suggests that due to the few degrees of freedom, the power of the test, that is the availability of the test to recognize correctly that the null hypothesis is false and hence, that it should be rejected, is very low and no definite conclusion can be drawn. Nevertheless, it can be pointed out that given the fact that the demand for money was proved to depend on the expected change in the (black market) exchange rate, then it becomes necessarily unstable when one studies it without this important variable. However, even its inclusion cannot solve the instability issue. Friedman (1956, p. 16) has said that "there is indeed little if any difference between asserting that the demand for money is highly unstable and asserting that is a perfectly stable function of an indefinitely large number of variables." CS is adding a new argument that can make even more difficult to forecast the demand for money. Also note that in Table 3.4 the expected rate of devaluation coefficient was no longer important in the period 1966-70 characterized by low inflation, slightly positive real interest rates, a fixed exchange rate, and higher than average GDP growth.

TABLE 3.3

ARGENTINA - TEST OF STRUCTURAL CHANGE FOR MONEY DEMAND FUNCTIONS

definition of money	F test for structural changes in the coefficients 1/ (1)	F test for homoscedasticity 2/ (2)	Critical values for:			
			(1)			(2)
			F0.05	F0.01	F0.05	F0.01
M_1	$\dfrac{(0.18148 - 0.15401)/4}{0.15401/(17 - 8)} = 0.4013$	$\dfrac{0.017757}{0.011910} = 1.49$	3.63	6.42	239	5,982
Currency	$\dfrac{(0.16796 - 0.13615)/4}{0.13615/(17 - 8)} = 0.5257$	$\dfrac{0.01659}{0.00341} = 4.86$	3.63	6.42	239	5,982
Demand Deposits	$\dfrac{(0.2531 - 0.21656)/4}{0.21656/(17 - 8)} = 0.3796$	$\dfrac{0.03033}{0.02328} = 1.30$	3.63	6.42	5.32	11.3
Quasi-Money	$\dfrac{(0.13823 - 0.09892)/4}{0.09892/(17 - 8)} = 0.3940$	$0.01763 = 1.73$	3.63	6.42	5.32	11.3

1/ The general test for structural changes between two subperiods is the F test calculated as follows:

$$F_{k,N-2k} = \frac{(SSR - \sum_{i=1}^{2} SSR_i)/k}{\sum_{i=1}^{2} SSR_i / N-2k}$$

where: SSR is the sum of squared residuals of the pooled regression (in our case for the period 1960-76; SSR_1 is the sum of squared residuals corresponding to the subperiod 1960-65 and 1971-76; SSR_2 is the sum of the squared residuals corresponding to the subperiod 1966-70; N is the total number of observations and k is the number of constraint parameters (including the constant term) or the rank. The number of degrees of freedom in the numerator is 4 (four constraint parameters) and in the denominator is 9 (N = 17). The null hypothesis tested here is:

$$H_o : \beta_o = \beta_1 \qquad H_a : \beta_o \neq \beta_1$$

where β is a vector of coefficients (including the constant term). Since the calculated F values ((1)) were all below the critical values either at F0.05 or F0.01, we rejected the H_a.

2/ The null hypothesis in testing two population variances is: $H_o: S_1 = S_2$ and $H_a : S_1 \neq S_2$. The degrees of freedom in the numerator for H_o and currency is 8 and in the denominator is 1; for demand deposits and quasi-money is 1 in the numerator and 8 in the denominator.

TABLE 3.4

ARGENTINA - ESTIMATIONS OF THE DEMAND FOR MONEY IN DIFFERENT PERIODS[a]

Period (years)	dependent variable[b]	constant term	income elasticity	inflation elasticity	expected rate of dev. elasticity	adjusted R^2	sum of squared residuals	Durbin-Watson	standard error of estimate
1966-1970	$Ln(M_1/P)_t$	-6.2199 (-1.0684)	1.6414 (2.0062)	-10.642 (-0.8619)	-0.1833 (-0.2151)	0.6434	0.01191	1.8412	0.1091
1960-65 – 1971-76	$Ln(M_1/P)_t$	-1.0342 (-0.6391)	0.8957 (3.8790)	-0.2357 (-2.3358)	-0.3267 (-2.8177)	0.8286	0.1421	1.1864	0.1333
1966-1970	$Ln(QM/P)_t$	-15.2890 (- 2.1588)	2.8092 (2.8227)	-1.1062 (-0.7365)	-0.1519 (-0.1465)	0.7676	0.01763	1.8412	0.1328
1960-65 – 1971-76	$Ln(QM/P)_t$	-10.0620 (- 8.2199)	2.0680 (11.8392)	-0.2190 (-2.8691)	-0.0209 (-0.2378)	0.9576	0.08129	1.9457	0.1008
1966-1970	$Ln(CC/P)_t$	-2.5782 (-0.8275)	1.0478 (2.3930)	-1.0317 (-1.5613)	-0.1765 (-0.3868)	0.8091	0.00341	1.8412	0.0584
1960-65 – 1971-76	$Ln(CC/P)_t$	1.6299 (1.0421)	0.4357 (1.9521)	-0.2841 (-2.9128)	-0.3663 (-3.2689)	0.7226	0.13274	1.3129	0.1288
1966-70	$Ln(DD/P)_t$	-12.3780 (- 1.3325)	2.3919 (1.8322)	-1.1508 (-0.5841)	-0.1733 (-0.1274)	0.5203	0.03033	2.8412	0.1742
1960-65 – 1970-76	$Ln(DD/P)_t$	-5.6032 (-3.0243)	1.4258 (5.3931)	-0.1948 (-1.6862)	-0.2879 (-2.1693)	0.8791	0.18623	1.2938	0.1526

[a] t-statistic between paranthesis. – [b] QM: quasi-money, CC: currency, DD: demand deposits the number of observations for the period 1966-70 is 5 with 1 degree of freedom; and the number of observations for the period 1960-65 – 1971-76 is 12 with 8 degrees of freedom.

APPENDIX FOR CHAPTER 3

ARGENTINA - PRESIDENTS AND ECONOMIC MINISTERS, 1958-1980

President	Economic Minister	lasted	took office on
A. Frondizi	E. Donato del Carril	13 months	May 1, 1958
	A. Alsogaray	22 months	June 25, 1959
	R. Alemann	8 months	April 26, 1962
J.M. Guido*	J. Wehbe	10 days	March 26, 1962
	F. Pinedo	24 days	April 6, 1962
	A. Alsogaray	8 months	April 30, 1962
	E. Mendez Delfino	5 months	December 10, 1962
	J.A. Martinez de Hoz	5 months	May 21, 1963
A. Illia	E. Blanco	10 months	October 12, 1963
	J. Pugliese	22 months	August 19, 1964
J. Ongania*	J. Salimei	5 months	June 29, 1966
	A. Krieger-Vasena	30 months	January 4, 1967
	J. Dagnino Pastore	12 months	June 12, 1969
M. Levingston*	C. Moyano Llerena	4 months	June 18, 1970
	A. Ferrer	7 months	October 26, 1970
A. Lanusse*	J. Quillici	5 months	May, 1971
	C. Licciardo	12 months	October, 1971
	J. Wehbe	7 months	October, 1972
H. Campora	J. Gelbard	17 months	May, 1973
R. Lastiri (protem)	J. Gelbard		
J.D. Perón	J. Gelbard		
M.E. Martinez de Perón	J. Gelbard		
	A. Gomez Morales	8 months	October, 1974
	C. Rodrigo	1 month	June, 1975
	P. Bonani	1 month	July, 1973
	A. Cafiero	7 months	August, 1975
	E. Mondelli	1 month	February, 1976
R. Videla*	J.A. Martinez de Hoz	60 months	March, 1976

*military government

NOTES

[1] It is important to keep in mind the policital instability that con-
strained much of the economic policies implemented. In the appendix
to this chapter the Argentine presidents and economics minister that
held office in the period 1959-1980 are listed. On average each minister lasted approximately 10 months in office (Wehbe, Pinedo and
M. de Hoz were excluded).

[2] The inflation rate used as a reference, is measured by the general
wholesale price index according to INDEC. The figures or tables
referred in this chapter can be found in the Statistical Appendix I
and II.

[3] Although this represented the first attempt to reduce nominal tariffs
in Argentina, it cannot be considered a reduction in protection,
since it mainly affected products not domestically produced or of
relatively low demand.

[4] Translation from the original Spanish version was made by the
author of this book.

[5] It is a well-known result of open macroeconomic theory that the cost
of a successful devaluation is a reduction in real wages. This seems
to be true only in the moment of achieving the new real level but
not afterwards. The Brazilian experience with crawling-peg since
the mid-1960s showed that the authorities managed to keep the real
exchange rate relatively constant at the same time that real wages
were increasing.

[6] For an account for the Argentina experience with IMF conditionality, see Marshall, Madones, and I. Marshall (1983). Fischer, Hiemenz, and Trapp (1984) presented an analysis of the economic policies and performance of the Argentine economy in the period 1970-
83.

[7] A currency reform took place in 1970. The peso moneda nacional
(m$n) was renamed Argentine peso ($) and two zeros from the old
denomination were chopped off.

[8] Viñals and van Beek (1979) calculated the expected rate of
devaluation as follows:

$$(\Delta X) = (1 - \hat{X}^e/X)$$
$$\hat{X}^e = (1/\alpha) \, (P_d / P_i)$$

where

(ΔX) = the expected percentage change in the exchange rate,

$\hat{X}^e$ = expected long-run exchange rate,

P_i = foreign price level,

P_d = domestic price level,

α = scale coefficient that reflects the point in time when PPP was
last believed to prevail.

Blejer (1978) presents a similar approach to the one used here.

4 The orthodox and unorthodox policies of Martinez de Hoz's economic program

4.1. INTRODUCTION

Crockett (1981, p. 54) defined economic stabilization as "an improvement in the balance between supply and demand in an economy, aimed at moderating inflationary pressures and strengthening the balance of payments." Therefore, a stabilization program is generally designed to achieve internal and external goals. After the goals have been decided upon, the policy-makers have to answer two questions: (1) how to achieve them: through a gradualistic or shock treatment approach, and (2) which instruments should be used. A problem that may arise due to the implementation of such a program is that its scope is generally short-run (e.g. 1 to 3 years), but the authorities may have placed it within a framework of an economic development plan that has a longer-run perspective. A trade-off may appear between the objectives of both plans. It is also important to consider that any stabilization program will hurt some groups harder than others in the society and, depending on the power of every group affected, it may become politically unacceptable and/or short-lived.

Prior to the stabilization program implemented from April 1976 to March 1981, and analyzed in this chapter, several other programs were implemented in Argentina which usually had to solve: an exchange rate crisis, a high rate of domestic inflation and a recession. For instance, after the government of president Frondizi embarked in 1958 on a program of large general wage increases, expansionist monetary and fiscal policies; it was faced, a year later, with an unsustainable foreign sector position. The authorities decided to carry out an stabilization program based on a reduction of aggregate demand (i.e. monetary and fiscal restraints, nominal wages increases below inflation, and a massive devaluation of the exchange rate) using a shock-treatment approach in order to solve the balance of payments crisis. This program represented the first Argentine experience with an IMF-type approach[1]. The result was a sharp decline of economic activity and an acceleration of the rate of inflation. The exchange rate remained fixed for almost three years; the government refused to adjust it because it was considered one of the cornerstones of its development program (i.e. the encouragement of foreign investment). The domestic recession improved the balance of payments as expected.

When the 1964 plan was put into effect, the main problems were once again: a balance of payments deficit caused by an outflow of short-term capital, accelerating inflation, and a recession which started in 1962. The core objective of the authorities was to reactivate the economy, mainly through an increase in the purchasing power of urban groups. Contrary to previous plans, the government decided to implement expansionary fiscal and monetary policies and to grant nominal wage increases above inflation. The results were positive on the level of economic activity and reduction of inflation. However, the situation in the foreign sector, remained weak due to a very low level of international reserves (equivalent to only two months of imports)[2].

In 1966 inflation started to accelerate and economic activity to decline. The balance of payments was still weak, but did not pose a serious threat. In 1967, the new authorities decided to carry out a program that would increase the productive capacity of the economy and reduce inflation. The latter was achieved by a policy under which business firms entered into "voluntary" agreements with the government to limit price increases, by adjusting wages according to productivity increases, and by a tariff reduction. The last measure attempted to subject the industrial sector to increased competition from abroad, and thereby to achieve both greater price stability and improved allocation of resources[3]. This program had several similarities with the one implemented since 1976: the government not only had short-term objectives but also wanted to make the economy more efficient.

Several other plans were implemented since 1967. For instance, in June 1975, the government attempted to reduce inflation and to improve the balance of payments through a shock-type approach consisting of a massive devaluation, adjustment in public sector tariffs, and wage restraints. By the end of 1975, inflation reached a three digit level, the economy was in a recession and the balance of trade, for the first time since 1963, experienced a deficit[4].

The lessons that arose from these previous stabilization efforts were:

(1) a shock treatment approach (1959, June 1975) had resulted in severe contractions in real output and sharp accelerations of price increases (recall the characteristics of the Argentine explained in chapter one). The effect on the balance of payments was apriori uncertain due to the possible opposite effect on the trade balance (i.e. generally a surplus is expected) and on the capital account (i.e. there could be substantial capital outflow due to expectations of further devaluations);

(2) any stabilization policy based on a reduction of real output to reduce inflation was short-lived since conflicts over maintaining income shares were intensified in the recession. The oligopolistic structure of the industrial sector favored an increase in prices to compensate for a decline of output;

(3) price controls had only a temporary effect in holding-down inflation, and it was generally followed by an acceleration of inflation;

(4) balance of payments crises did generally originate in the capital account rather than in the trade balance, emphasizing the importance of implementing an "adequate" exchange policy with a consistent interest rate policy.

In March 1976, there was a military coup d'etat. At that time, the Argentine economy was confronting three major economic problems: (1) a three-digit inflation rate (e.g. between March 1975 and March 1976, the wholesale price index increased by 738 percent), (2) a domestic recession that started in the third quarter of 1975, (3) external payments default, (4) international reserves loss of US$ 1.0 billion in 1975, and (5) the government budget deficit represented 13.5 percent of GDP (current Treasury income did not even reach 20 percent of total expenditure in the same period) which was mainly financed through monetary issues. These were typical problems before the implementation of former stabilization program.

The new government attributed the origin of such problems "to the political and economic policies pursued in the last thirty years," (Argentine Economic Development Report - AED - 1980) that is:
(1) growing state intervention in the economy reflected in the ownership of many public enterprises formerly owned by the private sector and which brought about huge government deficits;
(2) closed-economy system: the search for self-sufficiency resulted in domestic economic stagnation since "growth in any sector could only be achieved at the expense of another, and this gave rise to intersectoral pendular swings," (AED, p. 6).

Given the above view of the origin of the Argentine economic crisis, it became obvious why the government based its economic program on: (1) a subsidiary role to be played by the state, and (2) a free and open economy. The short-run objectives of the stabilization program were to strengthen the balance of payments and to prevent hyper-inflation. The long-run ones were to reduce domestic inflation to the international level and to force the economy, particularly the industrial sector which benefited for many years from high tariff protection, to become more efficient. The latter would bring about an improvement in the allocation of resources and only the most efficient and competitive industries would remain, creating the basis for rapid and stable growth.

4.2   THE MARTINEZ DE HOZ'S ECONOMIC PROGRAM AND ITS PHASES

The program implemented in Argentina since April 1976 had the twofold purpose of stabilization and restructuring the economy. That is why, it was labeled "economic program" and not just stabilization program. The restructuring of the economy was aimed at creating a basis for sustainable growth avoiding the stop-go pattern. It is important to keep in mind the distinction between the short-run or stabilization objectives, and the long-run, or restructuring goals, in order to judge its outcome.

The program can be separated into two distinctive phases. The first one was characterized by the use of orthodox policies (e.g. reduction of the public sector deficit, decline in real wages, minidevaluations, price controls, etc.) and the liberalization of the domestic financial sector to curb inflation and to raise the level of international reserves. The major structural change during this first phase took place in the financial sector: domestic interest rates after being always set by the government, were allowed to be freely determined. Thus, real interest rates could become positive and improve the allocation of resources. This first period lasted from April 1976 until December 1978.

During the second phase (from January 1979 until March 1981) a further decline in inflation and restructuring of the economy was sought. The improvement of economic activity remained a paramount objective to avoid widespread unemployment and consequently social unrest. In this period characterized by "a global-monetarist approach", the same instruments (a preannounced schedule of exchange rate devaluations and a five-year tariff reduction program) were used to achieve stabilization and restructuring goals. The authorities implemented a new and an unorthodox exchange rate policy: a schedule of the devaluation rate covering several months was preannounced in December 1978. Note that in both phases the authorities decided to follow a gradualistic approach.

It was difficult to assess which changes described and analyzed below can be labeled "structural" or "temporary" because the economic program only lasted five years (1976-1981). Furthermore, it was also difficult to specifically associate structural changes either with trade liberalization, with high real interest rates, or with an overvalued domestic currency. Our main hypothesis was therefore that people considered high real interest rates and an overvalued currency as temporary phenomena which would be eventually reversed. Thus, these prices were only used to make short-run decisions. On the other hand, tariff-reduction and the financial reform were viewed as a change in "policy-regime" which affect economic decisions on a permanent basis. That is, relative price changes brought about by trade liberalization must be considered sufficiently binding and relatively permanent to cause structural changes, otherwise they have to be viewed as temporary.

As a methodology, it was considered that there was an indication of a structural change whenever the trend of a specific variable (e.g. share of the textil industry output in total industrial production, exports over GNP, etc.) was different from the previous years. It was used the period 1971-75 for a comparison with the first phase of the program. The period 1971-78 and/or 1976-78 were also considered in order to determine if a change in the tendency of a variable took place during the 2nd phase (1979-80). Some comparisons were made between the pre-liberalization years (1971-75) with the total duration of the program (1976-80) as well. After a break in the trend was found, the next task was to determine what actually caused it. Once the source(s) was identified, it followed the tentative classification as structural or as temporary.

4.3 THE FIRST PHASE: APRIL 1976 - DECEMBER 1978

4.3.1 Objectives and Instruments

When the military government came to power at the end of March 1976, the economic team had to improve the balance of payments, restructure the external debt, and prevent hyperinflation. To resolve the external crisis, a stand-by agreement was signed with the IMF, but it was only partially used (60 percent of it). A second agreement was signed in 1977 which was finally not needed.

Since the main cause of hyperinflation was thought to be one of excess demand brought about by an overall public sector deficit of 13.5 percent of GDP (in the first quarter of 1976) entirely financed by issuing money, the most important task was to cut such a deficit[5]. At the end of 1976, the deficit was reduced to 9.5 percent of GDP. This was achieved by a reduction of government expenditures (from 39.5 percent of GDP in 1975 to 36.5 percent in 1976) and an increase in tax revenue, mostly as a result of measures to increase tax collections, indexation of unpaid-tax debt by individuals and/or firms, increase in public enterprises tariffs, reduction of real wages, and in the number of public employees (this last measure was quite insignificant when the public sector as a whole is considered). At the same time, the new authorities financed most of the deficit by selling government bonds. In 1978, the central bank did not participate in the financing of the deficit which was mostly covered by internal and foreign credit; thus eliminating a <u>direct</u> inflationary impact. The consolidated public sector deficit as a percentage of GDP was reduced to 3 percent in 1977 and increased to 3.6 percent in 1978. An important measure undertaken to reduce the deficit was the decrease in national treasury transfers to the provinces (93 percent decline in real terms over the period 1975-1978) and to State Enterprises (73 percent in real terms over the period 1975-1978). At the end of 1978, current revenue covered 72 percent of current expenditures [see Tables 26 and 27].

Additional contraction in demand was pursued by reducing the rate of expansion of the money supply: real M_1 declined by 12 percent from December 1975 to December 1976 [see Table A-4]. Real wages experienced a slight decline by the end of 1976 taking the second quarter of 1976 as a base, but if the base is 1975, they declined by 30 percent [see Tables 11 and 12]. Since most of the industrial production is consumed domestically, this contraction in public and private demand made the recession in this sector even deeper (it started in the third quarter of 1975, after the shock-treatment program of Minister Rodrigo under the Perionist government), and did not show signs of a significant recovery until the second quarter of 1977 [see Table 10]. However, such a recovery was quite uneven. Due to the continuing decline in real wages, industries like food, beverages, and tobacco, textiles, clothing, and shoes, whose level of activity is closely related to domestic consumption, either experienced negative growth or a growth below the average of the whole industrial sector [Table 23]. In contrast to the deep recession in the industrial sector for almost two years, the agricultural sector and gross domestic investment showed an improvement since the first quarter of 1976, that is, before the new government took over. The recovery in these two areas was the cause behind a 2 percent increase in real GDP in the third quarter of 1976 with respect to the same period in 1975. The rise in gross domestic investment was due to an increase in public construction (e.g., the 2nd and 3rd quarters of 1976 experienced a growth of 107.6 percent and 99.1 percent in real terms with respect to the same period in 1975, respectively), with private construction actually declining since the 2nd quarter of 1976 [see Table 20].

In 1977 all the sectors of the economy experienced economic growth (with the exception of some industries as mentioned before). However by 1978 there was a widespread recession except in the agricultural sector. This positive growth in the primary sector since 1976 may be explained by: (1) favorable international prices, particularly for cereals and soyabeans; (2) elimination of export taxes, and of quantitative restrictions on exports; and (3) a significant increase in productivity. This performance owed much to the incentives established by the government, in particular the correction of relative prices in favor of the agricultural sector through the exchange rate policy, as well as the adoption of a policy of allowing domestic farm prices to rise to international levels. Note that this correction started at the end of the Peronist regime when the exchange rate system was simplified.

4.3.2 The Exchange Rate Policy

In 1975, a multiple exchange rate regime was in effect. There were official, commercial, financial, special financial, mixed, and travel exchange rates. However, by the end of the same year, the regime was simplified and only three were in effect (the financial, the special financial and the travel rates). As mentioned in Chapter 3, the Peronist government, after keeping the exchange rate fixed since 1973, devalued the financial rate 20 times from March 1975 until March 4, 1976, approximately once every 18 days. However, since December 1975, the devaluations interval was shortened to one every 14 days and by February 1976, there was on average a devaluation once every 7 days. These devaluations were successful in increasing the real exchange rate by 18 percent with respect to 1970, which was probably the core reason behind the significant increase in agricultural exports during 1976.

A fluctuating free rate was established on January 7th, 1976, and on the same day the travel rate was abolished. Then, on March 6th, the financial and the special financial rates were merged into an official rate established at $ 140.3 per US dollar; which represented an average devaluation of approximately 50 percent. Thus, before the new government took over at the end of March, a dual regime existed (an official and a fluctuating free rate). This simplification of the market initiated by the Peronist administration, reduced the difference between the official and the black (or free) market exchange rate from 135.2 percent in 1975 to less than 50 percent in March 1976.

From April 1976 and until the final unification of the exchange market on November 22, 1976, the crawling-peg implemented since March 1975 under the Peronist government was interrupted but the structure of the market was kept the same. During these eight months the policymakers followed a policy of disguised crawling-peg, as was the case during 1973-74. That is, the effective rate at which commodities were traded was the result of moving the proportions allowed to be negotiated at the two prevailing rates. With the establishment of a single exchange rate, and until the first quarter of 1978, the authorities were committed to a daily adjustment of the foreign exchange that took into account the evolution of internal and external prices. Table A-2, column (5), presents the evolution of the real exchange rate, defined as the nominal exchange rate (Argentine pesos per one US dollar) and deflated by WPI the wholesale price index (general). It is important to note that although the real exchange rate was above 1976 levels in 1977, the devaluations were not enough to avoid a declining tendency: the index went down from 118 in the first quarter of 1977 to 103 in the same quarter of 1978 [6]. This real appreciating tendency was not avoided by the government due to the significant surplus in the current as well as in the capital account during 1976-1978. At the same time, such a surplus was creating difficulties in controling the money supply. Table

15 (in Appendix I) shows that by the end of 1978 the external sector contributed 51 percent to the increase in the monetary base which may have encouraged the authorities to change their exchange rate policy for the third time.

In April 1978, the government announced that they would implement a flexible exchange rate policy but the central bank would reserve the right to intervene in the market to avoid disrupting fluctuations. By the end of 1978, the peso had appreciated 25 percent with respect to the 1976 level. This policy was interrupted in January 1979. Although, there may be little doubt about the influence of the exchange rate policy on exports and its significant growth during 1976-1978 (e.g. agricultural exports in real terms, grew on average by 29 percent a year, while industrial exports, also in real terms, grew on average by 30.7 percent a year), note that on the contrary imports declined in real terms on average by 3.3 percent a year from 1976 to 1978. This suggests, once again, the importance of the real exchange rate in affecting mainly the level of exports, while imports are principally affected by the level of industrial activity: e.g., in 1978 industrial output declined 11 percent, the real average exchange rate appreciated 12 percent with respect to 1976, real exports grew only by 5.1 percent, quite below the average of the last two previous years, and real imports declined by 14.1 percent.

4.3.3   The Financial Reform

From September 1973 until May 1977 a system of nationalized deposits was in effect in Argentina. In such a system, deposits in financial intermediaries are accepted on the account of the central bank. The central bank pays interest and the intermediaries receive a commission. The objective of this system is to maximize monetary control and to distribute financial resources to specific industries and geographical regions. Levels and direction of credit are determined through the rediscount policy which is established by the central bank. Resources are thus assigned according to this policy. While this centralized system was in effect, the nominal interest rate was controlled and set by the government, generally at a rate below domestic inflation, a tradition in the Argentine economy which resulted in negative (ex-post) real interest rates. The presence of negative rates implies that the credit must be rationed because of the subsidy that the lucky borrower is receiving, encouraging an excess demand for credit. This brings about the development of a curb market where interest rates are freely determined; it is not controlled by the government and therefore it has zero-percent reserve requirement. This curb market is not necessarily illegal. In the case of Argentina, the "acceptance" market is a good example of a financial market of non-centralized deposits with no reserve requirements and it has existed since the mid-1960s. The Peronist regime started to relax this centralized system in 1975 by allowing financial intermediaries to issue credit in relation to the amount of specific term deposits that they captured and to set free the interest rate on these loans and deposits.

The coexistence of the non-centralized financial system, operating parallel to the official financial market, made monetary control very difficult. The new government decided to officialize the curb market. Therefore, the interest rate was now freely determined and deposits were decentralized. One of the purposes of this reform was to allow the interest rate to become positive because negative rates were seen as a cause of misallocation of resources which in turn causes inefficiency and higher costs. However, since no reliable data exist about how much credit was channelled through the curb market before the financial reform, and how much through the official credit market, it is not possible to assess how "inefficient" the economy was, particularly the private sector, due to the possibility of borrowing at negative real interest rates.

The reorganization of the financial system was achieved through the adoption of the law on the decentralization of banking deposits (Law No. 21,495 passed on January 17, 1977) and the Law on Financial Institutions (Law No. 21,526 passed on February 14, 1977). Both laws became effective on June 1, 1977. This shows that the authorities were following a gradualistic approach since the sector was liberalized more than one year after they took office.

The new system established a non-centralized deposits regime with a fractional reserve requirement. Financial entities recovered the full-intermediation role. The central bank had only a supervisory role and the determination of monetary policy through the application of a minimum reserve requirement and through open market operations. The reform also established competition as the means to obtain an efficient financial market by allowing easy entry into the market. At the same time, it continued with the policy of guaranteeing deposits in national currency in all financial entities. The most important feature of the reform, as mentioned before, was to permit interest rates on loans and deposits to be freely determined. It was thought that this would always result in positive real interest rates, thus eliminating the subsidy that for decades some firms, either public or private, received. State enterprises were directly hurt by the liberalization because they were now compelled to finance their deficit by obtaining credit from the financial market rather than through transfer from the Treasury.

The deregulation of interest rates did not always result in positive real interest rates. The ex-post deposit rate was positive in the IV quarter of 1977 and the I quarter of 1978 during 1976-1978 (see Table A-2). On the other hand, the borrowing real interest rate was positive from the IV quarter of 1977 until the III quarter of 1978 (see Table A-1.1). Note the high spread between deposit and borrowing interest rates and the extreme real rates reached: from the IV quarter of 1977 until the III quarter of 1978, the average deposit real interest rate was 4.0 percent in annual terms, an acceptable rate. However, the borrowing rate reached an average of 30.0 percent a quarter in annual real terms. The spread was mainly caused by a high reserve requirement which was established at 45 percent in 1977[7]. This brought about a high cost of intermediation, resulting in higher borrowing rates and lower deposit rates. The central bank was aware of this situation and established an account of "monetary regulation". Through this account, the central bank would pay an interest rate on the amount of the legal reserves made on time deposits while the financial entities would pay an interest rate for the use of sight deposits as credit. Since the structure of deposits of the financial system was approximately 60 percent time deposits and the rest sight deposits, the account always showed a deficit. The central bank had to pay financial institutions more than it actually received as interest payments from them. At the end of 1978, this account contributed almost 24 percent to the increase of the monetary base (see Table 15), hampering the implementation of a stable monetary policy.

The financial reform dramatically pushed up financial costs: e.g., Table 24 (in Appendix I) shows that these costs increased by only 9.0 percent for firms that produce non-traded goods and up to 363.3 percent for medium size firms as a percentage of total sales from 1976 to 1978. For Argentine savers, the reform was expected to protect their savings against inflation. There was a considerable increase (time and savings deposits): from March 1977 to March 1981, the average annual increase (in real terms) in quasi-money was 48.0 percent. However, the most important increase of almost 205.0 percent in real terms occurred from March 1976 to March 1977, that is, before the financial reform took place. How could this increase in time and savings deposits be explained in just one year when at the same time, real income was negative in 1975 and 1976 and the nominal average deposit interest rate was officially set at 4.02 percent a month (the average monthly inflation rate as measured by CPI from March 1976 to March 1977 was above 10.0 percent)? The 1976 Annual Report of the central bank gave the answer. According to official statistics the black market exchange rate reached a maximum of $ 400.0 per US dollar in the third week of March 1976 and thereafter it declined to $ 230.0 toward the last quarter of the same year. Pick Currency Yearbook (1979) also reported that the peso reached $ 300.0 per US dollar in February 1976 and in October of the same year, the rate was equal to $ 245.0. Both sources showed a relevant appreciation, this meant that wealth denominated in US dollars was declining. The appreciation of the black market exchange rate was expected after the new authorities took office since it previously depreciated by more than the difference between domestic and international inflation (the annual average black market exchange rate depreciated by 342.4 percent in 1975 while inflation was 192.5 percent in the same year). "This encouraged a dishoarding of foreign currency which was estimated at almost US$ 500.0 million" by the central bank (Annual Report, 1976, p. 21). At the same time, there was a change in the structure of deposits at commercial banks. Time deposits represented 44.5 percent of total quasi-money by the end of 1976, against 9.9 percent in 1975.

The deregulation of domestic interest rate was also regarded as a necessary measure to eliminate monetary imbalance. That is, the money supply was being restricted and people were encouraged to increase their holdings of domestic monetary assets by increasing their rate of return. The increase in the demand for quasi-money generally avoids the implementation of a very restrictive monetary policy and reduces inflation because the government can rely on the financial sector to finance its deficit instead of printing money. At the end of 1978, domestic savings represented 26.5 percent of GDP against an average of 23.5 percent a year in the period 1970-75. At the same time, the government stated that this "financial reform has secured profitable investment opportunities for local savers and thus avoided their diversion towards the foreign currency market," (AED, p. 34). This is another acknowledgement by the authorities of the significance of CS in the Argentine economy and the importance in reducing it.

What were the consequences of the financial reform? It was successful in stimulating savings in domestic currency and expanding banking credit [e.g., commercial bank loans to the private sector were 18.0 percent higher in real terms in June 1977 with respect to December 1975; at the end of 1978, they were 84.0 percent higher (see Table A-6)]; but it also brought about a change in the velocity coefficients. Looking at Table 5, the velocity coefficient of quasi-money (V_2) declined from 18.7 percent in 1975 to 5.8 at the end of 1978, while the velocity coefficient of a narrow definition of money (V_1) went up from 5.2 to 8.7 percent over the same period. The latter represented an increase of 67 percent while V_2 declined by 69 percent. If inflation is believed to be mainly affected by a narrow definition of money, the significant increase in its velocity coefficient may partially explain why domestic inflation remained so high. Also, an expected by-product of the reform was to promote the monetization of the Argentine economy. Was this achieved during 1976-1978? The answer is affirmative if we look at the real increase experienced by quasi-money (see Table A-5), while it is negative if we look at currency plus demand deposits (a narrow definition of money) since it declined in real terms. As mentioned before, it is important to recall that the most dramatic increase in real quasi-money occurred before the financial reform took place, despite the negative real deposit interest rates. It was suggested that this occurred because the holding of foreign currency was not considered a profitable alternative asset any more, due to the appreciation that it was taking place during the most part of 1976. This suggests that CS can be dampened, at least temporarily, when there are expectations of a future appreciation, despite the fact that the country is experiencing a domestic inflation rate much higher than the rest of the world.

The reform did not increase very much the number of financial institutions: in June 1977 there were 681 while by the end of 1978, there were 686 (see Table 16). However, there was a significant change in the structure of the sector. The 1977 legislation favored the establishment of all-purpose commercial banks and made entry of new financial institutions easy. Therefore, many savings and loans associations (Sociedades de Crédito), as well as specialized credit institutions for private consumption (Sociedades de Crédito para Consumo) became either financial companies (Financieras) or commercial banks. These last two types of institutions increased by 75 percent and 43 percent respectively from June 1977 to December 1978. At the same time, the sector achieved a relatively significant increase in productivity and growth.

As the financial reorganization took place in an inflationary environment, it developed serious problems: (1) volatile and high real interest rate which increased financial costs and eroded profits rapidly; (2) a very short-term structure of deposits (banks generally operated on a 7-day or 30-day basis on time deposits); (3) the financing of long-term loans (e.g., one year loans) with short-term funds made the system potentially unstable (there was a financial crisis in 1980), and the portfolio structure of most financial entities was therefore very "weak"; (4) due to a high inflation rate, there was a lack of incentives to offer long-term deposits; (5) the freeing of the interest rate plus the free access to foreign currency in an inflationary environment, increased the link between the changes in the domestic nominal interest rate and the expected rate of devaluation, in spite of the fact that the domestic financial market was still relatively closed to the international capital market[8].

A final relevant point has to do with the implementation of a financial reform when domestic inflation still remains at a much higher rate than the international one, and the public has free access to buy and sell foreign currency. Microeconomics tells us that a monopolistic firm will charge a higher price than a pure competitive one. However, if the government allows foreign firms which produce a close-substitute at a lower price to compete with the domestic monopolistic firm, we will now be dealing with a monopolistic competitive market. The domestic firm may now have to charge a lower price, other things being equal, to retain a share of the market. The same idea can be used to explain the issuing of domestic money by the central bank which acts as a monopolistic firm within a country.

The central bank has the power to affect the rate of inflation: if it wants the public to hold (buy) more domestic currency, it has to increase its value (i.e., to reduce prices). As long as asset-holders have no access to foreign currency, the central bank can manipulate the value of the money without any constraint. But, if it is now assumed that the people have the option to hold foreign currency, the domestic central bank may lose customers because the value of that money can be higher than the local one. This substitution can be avoided if the local money now offers a higher value. If prices cannot be reduced, then an interest payment can be granted to those who hold domestic monetary assets (e.g., demand and time deposits). However, the central bank still keeps some power and the analysis can continue within a monopolistic competitive market framework assuming that foreign currency is still not used for transactions purposes. But, if it is also used for transactions purposes, the domestic and the foreign currency can become an standardized product. The analysis should now be carried out within a perfect competitive market framework. This has important implications: the local central bank will completely lose all its customers if the local currency offers a lower value than the foreign one since demand is now perfectly elastic. Having this analogy in mind, the Argentine authorities made a terrible mistake in liberalizing the financial and exchange markets, at a time when domestic inflation was still high. They started to reduce inflation 18 months later (2nd phase of the program). Meanwhile, since the increase in prices could not be lowered, the authorities attempted to encourage the public to hold more domestic monetary assets only by offering a higher real rate of return with its negative impact on the level of economic activity.

4.3.4 The Role of the Government

The new government specified that the functions of the state were (AED, p. 17): (1) administering justice, (2) providing for defense and security, (3) issuing regulations governing coexistence and securing compliance with such regulations, (4) providing for health services, education, social security, and essential public services. Therefore, the authorities were committed to decrease the importance of the state as an economic agent by reducing public expenditures, its role as a producer of goods and services, and as a development agent. As can be seen from Table 26, fiscal expenditures as a proportion of GDP increased from 39.5 percent in 1975 to 41.4 percent in 1978 after declining almost 14.0 percent from 1975 to 1977. The government related this increase of fiscal expenditures to the military budget which was considered to be necessary, given the border conflict with Chile in the southern part of the country. It also blamed higher real wages paid to government employees. However, real public investment as a percentage of GDP averaged 11.1 percent a year in the period 1976-1978 against an average of 7.4 percent a year in 1970-1975. This represented an increase of 50 percent. In particular, there was an important rise in the share of public construction in gross domestic investment (from 33.6 percent in 1975 to 49.5 in 1978).

Two state banks: Banco de la Nación Argentina (Argentine National Bank, ANB) and Banco Nacional de Desarrollo (National Development Bank, NDB) increased their importance in the financial system. For instance, the NDB showed a significant expansion in the period 1977-1980, it ranked 33rd in the banking system according to deposits in June 1977. It climbed to 4th place by the end of 1980, with deposits amounting to US$ 1.500 million, and a loan portfolio over US$ 3.500 million. The ANB expanded mainly in the international capital market; whereas in 1976 it did not figure among the first 500 institutions in the international capital market it moved into 136th position with approximately 595 branches, of which 20 were overseas operational branches and 10 were agencies in 1980. The experience of these two banks can hardly be viewed as one of a decreasing participation of the state as an economic agent. At the same time no relevant privatization of state-owned firms took place.

4.3.5   The External Sector

The total external debt increased by 59 percent in current U.S. dollars from 1975 to 1978. It was particularimportantthat the increase in the public sector debt of a 108 percent, while for the private sector it only rose 7.4 percent (see Table 18). This implied that the share of the public sector debt went up from 51.1 percent in 1975 to 66.9 percent of total debt in 1978.

The importance of total industrial exports with respect to agricultural exports was not altered. Although within each major category some changes were significant: e.g., vegetables and animal oils increased their share from 3 percent to 7 percent in the period 1975-1978, the same change was experienced by leather goods while cereals and other vegetable products declined from 43 percent to 35 percent of total exports over the same period (i.e., agricultural, food, beverage, tobacco, and leather goods). Primary and traditional-manufactured commodities accounted for 73 percent of total exports in 1975. The share was practically the same in 1978 (74 percent)[see Table 14]. Exports as a percentage of GNP rose from 7.0 percent in 1975 to 15.7 percent at the end of the first phase. This did not mean that the country was becoming more open. Recall that most of the rise in exports corresponded to agricultural products. Besides, much of the increase of manufactured exports could be easily accounted for the decline in domestic consumption. As explained in chapter one, Argentine exports were generally the left overs of domestic consumption.

4.3.6   The Industrial Sector

The structure of GDP by sectoral origin shows that some changes were taking place (see Table 19):

(1) the agricultural sector was increasing its importance (over the period 1971-1975, its average share was 11.6 percent while in 1976-1978 it increased to 12.2 percent);

(2) total construction accounted for 5.6 percent in 1976-1978 (the average share was 4.7 percent in 1971-1975). The share of the two categories of real gross domestic investment (durable equipment and construction) showed insignificant changes from 1975 to 1978. However, there were relevant changes in the subcategories (see Table 17). For instance, public construction increased its share in total construction by 47 percent (another indication that the role of the state was not declining). Also, imported total durable equipment increased its share by 31 percent with respect to national durable equipment over the same period;

(3) the relative importance of the service sector remained practically unchanged. But banking's share rose from 3.4 in 1971 to 3.8 percent in 1978 and government services from 13.2 to 14.5 percent over the same period;

(4) the industrial sector accounted for 35.7 percent in the period 1976-1978, as against 37.7 percent during 1971-1975. Deindustrialization was taking place.

Table 21 displays the structure of the industrial sector divided into eight different industries. If it is compared the period 1976-1978 to 1971-1975, the following conclusions arise:

(1) the textile, clothing and shoes industries declined in importance. However, note that their share started to decrease at the beginning of the 1970s. It is likely that the policies implemented since 1976 speeded up this declining process;

(2) only two industries, wood and wood products, and paper, paper products, printing, and publishing, seemed to have started their decrease in 1976 because their share remained quite stable in the period 1971-1975 but it began to decline in 1976;

(3) metal products, machinery, equipment and transport vehicles increased their importance in the industrial sector. It should be noted again that this started at the beginning of the 1970s. The decline of industries that generally used more labor intensive technology (e.g., textiles) and the rise in the share of industries that use more capital intensive technology (e.g., vehicles) seems to be a usual outcome in the development process of developing economies;

(4) the food, beverage and tobacco industry almost recover the same relative importance that it had in 1970 in the period 1976-1978. Other industries did not show a specific trend.

If now we examine Table 23, where 25 different industries were considered, one notes some interesting trends:

(1) productivity increased over the period 1971-1975 but it was quite insignificant. However, in the break-down of the twenty-five industries, twelve experienced a decline while thirteen an increase from 1971 to 1975. But only 44 percent of the industries have productivity levels above the base year. The general productivity index increased from 102.5 in 1975 to 107.0 in 1978. Sixteen industries showed productivity levels higher than in 1975 and only eleven with respect to 1971. The increase in productivity was thus unevenly distributed, being concentrated in those industries that were increasing their share in the industrial sector;

(2) in 1975, only three industries had real output level below 1970, in 1978 the number increased to nine. With respect to employment, only four industries had level below the base year but it increased to twelve in 1978.

The above points indicate that the industrial sector was going through some significant changes, particularly there seems to have been a process of deindustrialization as the trend in output share in real GDP revealed. Did these changes start under the new government due to specific policies? As we mentioned above, some of these changes seemed to have started before 1976. It must be added that the changes undergone by the industrial sector not necessarily meant that it was becoming more efficient. The inefficiency of the industrial sector was blamed on negative real interest rates and high tariff protection before 1976. However, we are not aware of any study that actually proves this inefficiency. Under the new government, the extremely high real interest rates, inflation variability, and overvaluation of the exchange rate rather than helping the sector to become more efficient, may have contributed to distort the allocation of resources in the economy even more and to worsen allocative as well as technical efficiency.

4.3.7   The Outcome Of The First Phase

After reducing the rate of inflation, as measures by changes in the consumer price index, from a monthly average of 21.3 percent in the first quarter of 1976, it remained at 9.1 percent from the second quarter of 1976 to the fourth one of 1978 (with a standard deviation of 2.5). Despite of a reduction of real cash balances and of real wages, a four-month price "truce", and less reliance on monetary issue to finance the government, inflation was approximately 160 percent a year from 1976 to 1978. The persistence of high inflation was hard to explain. Total consumption was going down due to the decline of real wages and government expenditures, so that there was no evidence of excess demand. The government deficit was now financed through foreign loans and the issuing of bonds. It is a well known argument that one of the consequences of bond-financing is the crowding-out effect, through the increase of domestic interest rates, on the level of private investment. In the case of Argentina it is very important to determine the effect of bond-financing on domestic interest rates and its impact on the cost of financing working capital. If the government, by borrowing money in the domestic financial market, increases the real interest rate and therefore pushes economic activity down, particularly manufacturing, the result would be higher inflation. That is, in a relatively closed economy with oligopolistic markets, firms generally adjust their price rather than quantity, as explained in chapter one. Thus, total consumption was declining, the industrial sector experienced negative growth while the service sector was practically stagnant. Only the agricultural sector showed an average real growth of 2.9 percent over the period 1976-1978. Inflation was obviously not demand induced.

By the end of the first phase of the economic program, the external sector was not a problem any more. The central bank accumulated international reserves by almost US$ 6.0 billion. This was achieved by rapid (agricultural) export growth (an average of 22.5 percent a year in constant US dollars during 1976-1978), a substantial decline of imports (average annual decline in constant US dollar amount of 3.4 percent in 1976-1978), a decrease in aggregate demand due to a reduction of real wages which in turn increased the amount of domestic goods available to be exported; and by a significant inflow of short-term private capital. However, as the government was faced with stagflation, the objective in the second phase was to reduce inflation but not at the expense of a lower level of economic activity, given the fact that in the last three years real per capita income had gone down. Since inflation was not demand induced, then the alternatives were structural, expectational and/or cost induced. The Economic Minister, Dr. Martinez de Hoz considered the accumulation of foreign reserves as one of the most important sources of inflation until 1978 in his 1982 book. He pointed out that this accumulation increased monetary base which stimulated inflation. It was true that in 1977-78, the external sector explained around half of the increase in the monetary base. But, the real monetary base was actually declining and could not, therefore, explain the increase in prices.

The only stabilization goal achieved was the significant improvement in the balance of payments due to a decline of imports, high agricultural exports, and an inflow of short-term capital. Hyperinflation was avoided but price increases still remained at a very high rate. The financial reform pushed domestic savings up but at the expense of economic activity by achieving extremely high real borrowing interest rates[9].

4.4 THE SECOND PHASE: JANUARY 1979 - MARCH 1981

4.4.1 Why a New Approach?

The reduction of the inflation rate continued to be the main objective in this new phase but not at the expense of economic activity. Since the former orthodox policies were not successful, the authorities modified their anti-inflationary strategy. The program implemented between January 1979 - March 1981 was aimed at stabilization without causing unemployment and the long-run objective of making the economy more efficient. This time, however, the same instruments were used to achieve both objectives. As mentioned before, the inflation was believed to be caused by expectational and/or cost factors, the program was thus built around preannounced schedules for monthly adjustments at declining rates of: 1) the exchange rate, 2) prices of fuel and other public sector services, 3) minimum wages, 4) monetary resources of internal origin. Stabilization took place within a framework of a five-year tariff reduction program and free capital movement in order to increase the link between the domestic and the international capital market. The expected outcome of the program was that during 1979 the domestic rate of inflation would converge toward the sum of the rate of devaluation plus the international inflation. As long as there was a divergence between the rates of domestic inflation and exchange depreciation, there would be a real appreciation of the peso. This appreciation plus the liberalization of trade, were expected to encourage imports, especially of those goods whose price increases were exceptionally large. Consequently, there would be a discouragement of a rise in domestic prices. This amounted to a price control policy without the stigma of being implemented directly by the government.

The government also wanted to accelerate the long-run objective of making the economy more efficient. In this phase, therefore, the stabilization and the restructuring programs became one through the implementation of a liberalization program within the framework of the "Global Monetarist Approach".

Martinez de Hoz stressed that in the new strategy to curb inflation, the rate of devaluation will not accommodate the rise in domestic prices. He wrote (1982, p. 239) that:

> The indexation of the exchange rate to the evolution of the domestic price index only serves to recycle inflation. It administers a temporary drug ... Yet, in a short-time, there is a rebirth, may be even stronger, of the cost-price spiral. Therefore what is asked as a way to improve the possibilities of export, does not turn out to be the most appropriate method. Since through this process, the increase in domestic costs withdraws once again the competitiveness of exportable goods in the international market. The most stable and effective solution consists of reducing costs ... The policy implemented in 1979-1980, implied the decision within the framework of the anti-inflationary program, of not increasing the exchange rate because of a rise in prices, on the contrary, it demanded a serious effort of reduction of costs by the producers through the mechanism of competition ... Competition replaces the direct control of prices by the government[10].

The substantial net inflow of capital and the current account surplus over the period 1976-1978, were thought to be the main cause behind the increase of prices and undermining of monetary policy. Therefore, the authorities implemented controls over external capital movements (e.g. minimum maturity, deposit requirements for foreign loans in local currency and without receiving interest) in order to increase the cost of foreign borrowing. In October 1977, the authorities established a one-year minimum maturity on foreign borrowing, and this was increased to a two-year minimum maturity in December 1977. An additional capital control measure was introduced in May 1978: a 20 percent deposit on foreign borrowing was required to be made in domestic currency in zero interest deposits.

In this second phase of the program, the authorities had to increase the link between domestic and international capital markets because the exchange rate policy was set independently from the situation in the balance of payments. Thus, high domestic interest rates would attract foreign capital and this would increase the supply of external financial resources. If this represented a net capital inflow, the exchange rate would tend to appreciate in a flexible exchange rate regime or the authorities would not completely follow purchasing power parity under a managed floating or passive crawling-peg, other things equal. The appreciation would lower the cost of borrowing abroad even further and force domestic interest rates down. Therefore, the open-up of the capital account would directly affect domestic interest rates. Although, the above mechanism was a possible outcome, another point that should be taken into account is that the appreciation of the domestic currency enhanced the probability of a sudden devaluation, adding a significant risk premium. Thus, the interest rate instead of going down, may rise. The inflow of more capital rather than pushing the interest down, will push it even further up. An outflow of capital may follow and the nominal interest rate will rise further.

Why did the government implement such a liberal approach to capital movements? Arriazu, an advisor to the Econmic Minister, pointed out (1983b, pp. 179-180):

> Should we control capital movements? And if the answer is affirmative can we really control capital movements? ... But do the authorities control capital movements or does the public? My own experience in Argentina makes me very doubtful of the possibilities of controlling capital flows. In 1975, for example, Argentina introduced one of the more severe and extensive sets of capital controls in force in the international economy; during that year the current account registered a deficit exceeding US$ 1 billion, at the same time that Argentines accumulated foreign assets abroad also exceeding US$ 1 billion. How could this accumulation take place with so many controls? Basically, through overinvoicing and underinvoicing ... The experience of 1978 also tends to confirm this fact ... In order to stop these flows, the government decided to introduce an interest equalization tax, ... with this measure, capital flows disappeared as such, but capital continued flowing in, now in the form of export prepayments. As a deposit was also required for these flows, capital then began to flow in the form of export prefinancing, and when these flows were also restricted, the movements took the form of overinvoicing and underinvoicing. Exchange sales by tourists also increased durign the period, even though these "tourists" were obviously Argentines.

Obviously, the government did not believe that it could control capital movements and therefore decided to completely open-up the capital account. Arriazu also explained that the preannouncement of the exchange rate was not primarily aimed at changing expectations in such a way as to help reduce inflation. He claimed that the government wanted to have the advantages of a fixed exchange rate regime, but since it confronted a large fiscal deficit, the question was how much an inflationary tax was needed to finance it. With respect to this, he explained (p. 181):

> Start by estimating how large the fiscal deficit is going to be and how much monetary base will be created as a consequence of this and other factors. This allows an estimate of how large a flow demand for monetary base is required to be able to maintain balance of payments equilibrium, given the fiscal deficit. Once this disequilibrium is estimated ... a devaluation increases the prices of tradeables ... This increase in prices will normally be accompanied by an increase in the nominal demand for money, which, in turn, determines an increase in the flow demand for base money. The problem is, therefore, how to estimate the size of a devaluation needed to generate the required flow demand for base money to compensate for the effects of the fiscal deficit.

Although the authorities were awared of CS, this did not seem the case in the above statement by Arriazu. In the presence of CS, the

increase in prices will normally be accompanied by a decrease in the
nominal demand for pesos which in turn brings about a decrease in the
flow demand for base money. He finally pointed out that since the objective of the government was to reduce the fiscal deficit, a declining
adjustment of the exchange rate did follow, indirectly dampening inflationary expectations.

In 1979, the exchange rate moved in accordance with the preannounced schedule. However, this schedule was not announced for the
full-year at the beginning of the program in December 1978: the schedule through August 31, 1979 was announced on December 21st and the
schedule for the rest of the year was announced on April 9th, 1979.
These schedules involved a nominal depreciation of the peso of 61.5
percent for the whole year, with the monthly rate of depreciation declining from 5.2 percent in January to 3 percent in December. The
schedule for 1980, was announced on October 1st, 1979. The peso would
be devalued in January 1980 by 2.8 percent and thereafter, there would
be successively smaller adjustments (0.2 percent point less each
month). The total devaluation was going to be 24 percent in 1980 and a
zero depreciation would be reached by March 1981.

However, on September 16th, 1980, the first change in the preannounced schedule occurred: it was established that the devaluation
would be one percent a month during the last quarter of 1980 instead of
the previously announced devaluation rate and nothing was said about
the first quarter of 1981. Again, on December 10th, 1980, it was announced that during the first quarter of 1981 the preannounced schedule would not hold and the monthly rate of devaluation was changed to
2 percent. This was not the last change; on February 2 an out-of-schedule devaluation occurred, equal to 10 percent and on the same day a
new schedule was announced until August 31, 1981. This last schedule
proposed a monthly devaluation of 3 percent. The declining rate approach was thus abandoned.

The new government that took office in April 1981 kept the above
schedule but with several out-of-schedule devaluations. The whole exchange rate policy was finally abandoned in June of the same year when
a dual-exchange rate regime was implemented.

4.4.2 The Global Monetarism Approach: Key Assumptions

The Argentine program of December 1978, was framework within the
"Global-Monetarism Model". A brief description of this model's key assumptions may be useful to understand the rationale of the economic
policies implemented[11]:

(1) the neutrality assumption:

$$M^d = L(P,Y) \tag{4.1}$$

where:

M^d = desired nominal money balances,
P = money price of goods and services in terms of domestic currency,
Y = real output (exogeneously determined and assumed to be at the
     full-employment level).

Equation (4.1) is the standard money demand equation (LP, L_p 0, L_y 0). Assuming that all prices are flexible, there is a one-to-one relationship between money and the aggregate price level that implies an absence of money illusion and the long-run neutrality of money vis-à-vis real variables. It is also generally assumed that the demand for money is interest-inelastic and a stable function. Graphically, in an IS-LM framework, the LM curve is a vertical line (or a very steep one) that makes fiscal policy ineffective to alter real income.

(2) The law of one price:
The law of one price or the perfect commodity arbitrage assumption holds if the domestic and the world commodity markets are integrated (e.g. no tariff, quotas or any other restriction to trade exist), and if local and foreign goods are perfect substitutes. This implies that domestic prices (P) are equal to foreign prices (P*) times the exchange rate (E, defined as domestic currency price of foreign exchange):

$$P = P^* . E \qquad (4.2)$$

Equation (4.2) can also be expressed in rate of change form:

$$\dot{p} = \dot{p}^* + \dot{e} \qquad (4.3)$$

If we also assume that there exists a bond market then the Fisher hypothesis may also hold. This hypothesis states that nominal interest rate differentials between international tradeable assets (e.g. bond) that are identical in all aspect except for the currency of denomination, can be explained by the expected rate of change of the exchange rate of those two currencies over the holding period; that is,

$$i = i^* + \dot{x}^e \qquad (4.4)$$

where:

i = domestic interest rate,
i* = foreign interest rate,
$\dot{x}^e$ = expected rate of devaluation.

In order for this assumption to hold, there must be perfect integration between the domestic and the international capital market (i.e. no restriction to capital movements). The law of one price and the Fisher hypothesis imply that the domestic price level and interest rate are exogenously determined, under a fixed exchange rate regime, by the foreign price level and interest rate respectively. This is also equivalent to the "small country assumption". Note that if (4.3) and (4.4) hold and given the definition of real interest rate (r) as:

$$r = i - \dot{p} \qquad (4.5)$$

we can write the following relationship:

$$i - \dot{p} = i^* - \dot{p}^* + (\dot{x}^e - \dot{e}) \qquad (4.6)$$

(4.6) shows that only if $\dot{x}^e = \dot{e}$, will the domestic real interest rate be equal to the foreign real one. With the implementation of a credible active crawling-peg, it is possible that the preannounced schedule influence expectations enough, otherwise the real domestic interest rate will differ from the international one.

(3) The monetary approach to the balance of payments:
The monetary approach stresses that the balance of payments is essentially a monetary phenomenon. That is, balance of payments disequilibria must be viewed as a stock disequilibrium between demand for and supply of money. This implies that the demand for money is a stock demand and, the notion of equilibrium must also be of stock equilibrium. However, since this equilibrium is not achieved instantaneously, a flow demand for money arises due to the gradual adjustment of actual money balances toward the desired stock.

The monetary approach also assumes that under a fixed exchange rate regime, international reserves flows cannot be sterilized. Therefore, the money supply ceases to be a policy instrument because it cannot be controlled by the authorities, which only control the domestic component. Let us define:

$$M^S = a \ (R + D) \tag{4.7}$$

the money supply (M^S) equals the money multiplier (a) times the supply of high powered money, defined as international reserves (R) plus domestic monetary base (D). Assume that the demand for and supply of money are equal (equation 4.8), one then finds the expression for R by equating equation (4.1) (the demand for money) and (4.7) (the supply of money), and taking first differentiation (Δ) one gets equation (4.9), that is:

$$M^S = M^d \tag{4.8}$$

$$\Delta R = (1/a) \ [\Delta \ L \ (P,Y)] - \Delta D \tag{4.9}$$

Equation (4.9) shows that an increase in D, ceteris paribus, leads to an equivalent decrease in R, which leaves the money supply unchanged. Thus, the money supply becomes an endogenous variable that is mainly demand determined. This equation also helps to understand why global-monetarists advocate a fixed exchange rate regime: starting from equilibrium in the money market, a devaluation increases the stock demand for money because the law of one price (equation 4.3) implies that a rise in "$\dot{e}$" pushes domestic prices up ($\dot{p}$), and a higher level of prices will therefore increase M^d. Given the supply of money, an excess demand for money will appear in the market. Equation (4.9) shows that this disequilibrium will be closed by an inflow of foreign reserves (R) that progressively satisfies that higher demand.

However, when the stock equilibrium between the supply of and the demand for money is reached once again, the balance of payments will also return to its initial equilibrium position. A devaluation, therefore, has only a transitory effect on the balance of payments and has no real effects because it will not permanently alter the relative prices of domestic and foreign goods (due to the law of one price); there is a long-run neutrality on any real variable. The only permanent effect is the once-and-for-all jump in the domestic price level by the full amount of the devaluation. Even if a devaluation can speed up the adjustment toward equilibrium in the balance of payments, proponents of this approach point out that this would happen anyway because of the automatic mechanism embodied in all the key assumptions, although in the case of excess demand for money this may imply a deflationary process (e.g. higher domestic interest rates needed to attract an inflow of foreign capital).

An important policy-implication of the global-monetarist approach is that fiscal, monetary and exchange rate policies cannot permanently affect the level of real income and therefore, they are not appropriate instruments for stabilization purposes. For instance, fiscal policy is not effective to increase real income because the increase in government expenditures can be offset by a trade balance deficit, other things equal. Monetary policy is ineffective to increase income because any change in the domestic component of the monetary base will be offset by a similar change in the international component, as shown in equation (4.9). Finally, a devaluation only brings about a temporary improvement in the balance of payments but has no real effect.

4.4.2.1 The monetarist approach to the balance of payments in the presence of currency substitution:

According to the monetary theory presented in the previous section, a devaluation reduces the supply of real balances by raising the price level. Given that people want to restore their initial holding of real balances, and the authorities keep constant the domestic component of the money supply, this rise in prices increases the nominal demand for money, restoring real balances but, at the same time, reducing absorption. This last effect, generally labeled "positive liquidity effect", improves the balance of payments. However, in the presence of CS, asset-holders may not want to restore their initial holding of real balances in domestic currency, but may want to reduce it, and increase their demand for foreign currency. Thus, instead of an excess demand for local currency, a reduction of absorption, and the resulting positive effect on the balance of payment, the opposite may occur, which is in sharp contrast to the expected outcome expressed by the monetary approach to the balance of payments. This approach postulates a direct relationship between the balance of payments and the money supply: a sustained reduction of the domestic component of the money supply is the advised policy to increase international reserves. In the presence of CS, the demand for money has a relationship as relevant as the supply of money with the balance of payments. It is thus possible that a tight credit policy (reduction of D) may actually not improve or not be sufficient to encourage an increase in international reserves[12].

Going back to the demand for money equation, a new argument must be introduced that captures the CS effect. This argument is the expected rate of devaluation as suggested in chapter three. Since the exchange rate is the price of two monies, their expected rate of return is reflected through the expected rate of devaluation. Now, equation (4.1) can be rewritten as:

$$M^d = L\ (P,Y,x) \tag{4.10}$$

where "x" is the expected rate of devaluation and M^d is the desired demand for local currency. A negative relationship is expected between these two variables ($L_x < 0$). The monetary approach has never included the expected rate of devaluation as an independent variable in the demand for money unless capital movements are allowed. But even if this is the case, the expected rate of devaluation would only indirectly affect the demand for money through the effect on the domestic interest rate. Note, however, that we are stressing that the expected rate of devaluation must be included as a very important argument even if the authorities implement strict exchange rate controls and prohibit the holdings of foreign currency. Also, recall that the CS concept includes interest-bearing as well as non-interest bearing assets. The expected rate of devaluation can also affect a narrow definition of money. We should include "x" in equation (4.9) as well; it thus becomes:

$$\Delta R = (1/a) \ (\Delta L \ (P,Y,x)) - \Delta D \qquad\qquad (4.11)$$

Equation (4.11) has important policy implications. It reflects a monetary approach to the balance of payments in the presence of CS (note that capital movements are not considered). Although, the authorities are implementing a tight credit policy (D is going down), the simultaneous existence of higher expectations of a devaluation (x is rising) will cause a decline of international reserves because the demand for local currency is going down faster than "D". Therefore, the policy recommendation resulting from the monetary approach may not bring about the expected outcome. According to equation (4.11), any stabilization program enhances its chances of success if it starts by both undervaluing the local currency and reducing the fiscal deficit. The undervaluation of the local currency will reduce expectations of a devaluation for a certain period of time; it will also increase the demand for local currency and cause the dishoarding of foreign currency. This rise in the demand for local money (money defined as M_1) may reduce the velocity of circulation and therefore the inflation rate. Consequently, the success of the stabilization program is not only achieved in the foreign sector (a higher level of international reserves) but also in the internal sector (a lower rate of inflation). A practical example of this approach may be found in the program implemented by Krieger-Vasena during 1967-69.

Many economists will say that any change in "D" is generally associated with the fiscal deficit, which in turn, is related to the rate of inflation. However, a tight credit policy (meaning, a reduction of the government budget deficit and thus in the inflation rate) may still not immediately influence the expected rate of devaluation downward; this is particularly true if expectations are adaptive. So, again, any tight credit policy must be accompanied by an exchange rate policy that influences "x" downward or at least keep it fixed at a credible rate. Dornbusch (1982, p. 176) wrote that "any successful stabilization program must start by undervaluing the currency ... the worst thing to do is to liberalize the capital account to allow the public to get into dollars before the necessary real depreciation has been achieved". His statement also supports the approach presented here.

Let us now introduce another argument in the demand for money function: the interest rate on money (e.g. time deposit interest rate) rather than on bond, because in Argentina, people's portfolio is mainly composed of time and savings deposits. This extra argument implicitly assumes that we are now dealing with a much broader definition of money than before. Thus, the higher the interest rate the higher the demand for broad money, other things being equal. The government may use the interest rate as another instrument to influence the demand for money. If the interest rate is raised by the same amount as the expected rate of devaluation, since both affect the demand for money in opposite directions, they will offset each other, again leaving us with the original outcome proposed by the monetary approach. If this is the case, the Fisher condition holds and domestic and foreign assets will have the same return, the public will be thus indifferent about which one to hold (recall that assets must be perfect substitutes and riskless or equally risky). But if asset-holders are risk-adverse, the return on domestic assets must be much higher than the expected rate of devaluation. This situation could be unacceptable for a long period of time, given the negative effect of higher real interest rates on the level of economic activity, particularly on the industrial sector. Besides, as expressed by Dornbusch (1983, p. 176), "countries can maintain an overvalue currency only by financing the resulting deficit - in the balance of payments - by forcing up real interest rates; however, in the end, they cannot avoid an exchange crisis." Then, even if very high real domestic interest rates can stop a run toward foreign currency, they cannot avoid a recession which may be hard to accept. The Argentine experience, particularly during 1979-1980, showed that extremely high domestic real interest rates could not avoid an increase in the demand for foreign currency.

Finally, it is important to stress that in the presence of CS, within a framework of free access to foreign currency, may explain why domestic inflation was much higher in the period 1977-1980 than in 1967-74 for an almost similar government budget deficit as a percentage of GDP (3.7 percent and 3.2 percent respectively while the inflation rate was 16 percent and 120 percent average a year in every period). Frenkel (1983, p. 169) pointed out that:

> The liberalization of the capital account is likely to encourage the process of CS. This phenomenon results in an effective reduction of the tax base for inflationary finance. Unless the need for inflationary finance is reduced, the opening up to the capital account and the resultant shrinkage of the inflationary tax base may result in an accelerated rate of inflation as the government attempts to collect the needed revenue from the smaller tax base.

That is, given the above equations, the expansion of "D" to finance a fiscal deficit, increases the supply of money and this creates a disequilibrium in the monetary sector as well as in the balance of payments. In order to equilibrate the money market, the demand for nominal money will go up due to an increase in prices. However, if people now have the opportunity to hold foreign currency and also use it for transaction purposes, the same government budget deficit monetization must now require a higher level of prices to achieve equilibrium in the money market and therefore in the balance of payments.

4.4.3. The Results Of The 1979-1980 Program

4.4.3.1 Stabilization objectives: In the initial stage of the program the real interest rate went down due to the decrease in the nominal intereat rate (the expected rate of devaluation declined) while there was a lack of immediate response of the inflation rate to the plan. The negative ex-post real interest rates encouraged economic activity. In 1979, the industrial sector grew by 10.0 percent in real terms against a decline of 10.5 percent in 1978. At the same time, the higher level of economic activity plus low unemployment, increased real wages.

The inflation rate did not decline as fast as expected and this was attributed to the excess demand in the non-traded goods market. This sector was not being affected by the tariff-reduction program and could pass the higher demand or higher cost on to prices. However, either the consumer price index or the wholesale price index (general level) give a higher weight to traded goods. For instance, the CPI gives traded goods and services a weight of 73.8 percent, non-traded goods and services 10.4 percent, and government controlled goods and services 9.0 percent. The WPI gives a 26.5 percent weight to domestic agriculture, 68.7 percent to domestic non-agriculture, and 4.8 percent to imported non-agriculture. Therefore, a decline of inflation should have been expected, particularly as measured by CPI. Table 10 shows that the average monthly inflation rate as measured by the CPI remained fairly constant between the IV quarter of 1978 and the I quarter of 1979 (from 9.2 to 9.3 percent). Table 25 shows a break-down of the CPI. There, we can appreciate that while the average quarterly inflation rate of traded goods and services and government controlled traded goods and services went down from the fourth quarter of 1978 to the first quarter of 1979 (from 10.2 to 9.4 percent and from 9.4 to 8.9 percent respectively), the inflation rate of non-traded goods and services increased from 7.4 percent to 10.2 percent. Note that if the comparison is made with the first quarter of 1978 rather than with the fourth quarter, traded goods and services experienced higher inflation and non-traded goods and services a lower one.

The inflation rate of domestic non-agriculture products actually accelerated from a monthly average of 8.5 percent in the last quarter of 1978 to 9.5 percent in the first quarter of 1979. In this case the lack of immediate response to the program may be explained by the fact that not all the industries were affected by an immediate drastic reduction of tariffs; also the program was quite gradual. For instance, industries like tobacco, chemicals, oil products, rubber, non-metallic, minerals, metals; vehicles and machinery and electric machinery were still highly protected [see Table 28]. They represented approximately 40 percent of the total domestic non-agriculture index and within this index the most important single item is food and beverages with a weight of 28.2 percent, of which little is imported. Nevertheless towards the end of 1979, there was a deceleration of the inflation rate, but it was not fast enough to follow foreign prices adjusted by the rate of devaluation. In the third quarter of 1979 there was an acceleration of the inflation rate caused by a significant increase in the price of food (with a weight of 41.5 percent in the CPI). At the same time, although the intention of the authorities was to implement the trade-liberalization program in order to reduce the monopolistic or oligopolistic power in the goods market, it turned out that several leading local firms engaged in the distribution of foreign products that were supposed to compete with their production. Consequently a power was developed in the distributional channels and because of this, businessmen could still influence domestic prices[13].

Table 29 shows that the accumulated difference in the period 1977-78 between domestic inflation and foreign inflation adjusted for the rate of devaluation was equal to 39.4 percent. Such a difference continued during the first nine months of 1979 (29.4 percent) and a convergence, as required by the program, was achieved during the last quarter of that year. Martinez de Hoz expressed that the decline of the real exchange rate was not relevant because in 1976-1978 the peso was undervalued; that is why, the trade balance experienced a surplus during those three years (we have already explained the other significant variables to take into account to explain such a surplus). Table A-2 shows that the real exchange rate started to decline in the third quarter of 1977 although it was still above the 1976 level. In the second quarter of 1978, when the government implemented a managed floating regime, the real exchange rate tended to appreciate faster and by the end of the year, the peso was 25 percent overvalued with respect to 1976. Therefore, from the start of the 1979 program the peso was already overvalued.

The program implemented since December 1978 reduced inflation but the predicted "convergence" was only achieved in the last quarter of 1979 and January 1980. During this last year, domestic price increases adjusted by international inflation and the rate of devaluation (see Table 29) remained on average 1.73 percent higher a month. In spite of this, the program started with an annual inflation rate as measured by domestic non-agriculture index of 166.2 percent in the last quarter of 1978 and by the end of the program (the first quarter of 1981) the annual inflation was 69.6 percent. In January and March 1981, the convergence seemed to have been again achieved though out-of-schedule devaluations. But the real exchange rate was 57 percent below the 1976 level.

It was expected that after convergence was achieved, a period of domestic inflation below the foreign inflation adjusted by the rate of devaluation, would have followed in order to correct the overvaluation of the exchange rate. However, it was not explicitly pointed out which "forces" would push the domestic inflation rate below such a convergence. Probably, producers in the non-traded sector would be eventually encouraged to decrease prices because after the initial excess demand, supply would increase due to a favorable change in relative prices. This implies that the resources required to increase production might have come from the traded goods and services sector. But these resources are not easily exchangeable. Besides, the reduction of the production of traded-goods would negatively affect the trade balance. On the other hand, given the level of overvaluation of the exchange rate by the end of 1979 and the announcement of only a 23 percent devaluation during 1980, a period of deflation rather than relatively lower domestic inflation would have been necessary to increase the real exchange rate.

Therefore, why was the government so stubborn in keeping such a low rate of devaluation. The Economic Minister said that the peso was undervalued before the start of the program and the overvaluation was, therefore, returning the peso to its long-run equilibirum. He supported this argument by stressing the significant surplus in the current and capital accounts not only during 1976-1978 but also during 1979. During this last year, the trade balance experienced a US$ 1.0 billion surplus and an inflow of short-term capital of approximately US$ 5.0 billion. The resulting increase in international reserves (US$ 4,442.0 million) was thought as another reason to avoid any change in the predetermined schedule of devaluation.

Given the fact that initially the public believed the commitment of the government to the preannounced schedule, domestic assets gave a higher rate of return than the holding of US dollars. For instance, the devaluation rate started at 5.4 percent in January and declined to 3.0 percent by the end of the year, while the nominal short-term deposit interest rate at commercial banks was always above 6.0 percent average a month in every quarter (see Table A-2). This and the relative cost of borrowing abroad (e.g., in 1979, 62 percent of the private sector foreign debt corresponds to financial loans, see Table A-6) encouraged a dishoarding of dollars as well as an inflow of capital. Besides, 1979 may have been considered an excellent year for the government: real GDP grew by 7.1 percent, the average monthly inflation rate as measured by CPI was 4.6 percent, a significant reduction from a 9.2 percent in the last quarter of 1978, real wages were increasing, the central bank had accumulated foreign reserves for almost US$ 10.0 billion, exports increased by 8.4 percent in real terms but imports increased by 53.6 percent also in real terms, and unemployment was only 2.0 percent.

The decrease of the inflation rate as well as the increase in international reserves may have actually been caused by the overvaluation rather than by the anti-inflationary policy being implemented. It is a well-known result that many governments used an overvalued exchange rate to reduce domestic inflation through the reduction of the price of tradeable goods and to encourage a capital inflow as long as the exchange parity is credible. The increase in economic activity was mainly related to negative real interest rate. The tariff reform plus the decline of the real exchange rate dramatically increased imports during 1979-1980 and discourage exports (1980 experienced the first trade balance deficit since 1975). Due to the high level of international reserves, the government did not worry about financing this trade deficit.

By the end of 1979 there was a widespread belief that an out-of-schedule devaluation would occur. This kept nominal interest rate high at a time when the domestic inflation rate was goind down: e.g. real ex-post average short-term lending interest rate reached an annual rate of 51.7 while deposit rate reached 60.2 percent (see Tables A-1.1 and A-2). This significant increase in domestic real interest rate seemed to have been enough to discourage CS (real quasi-money went up by 20.0 percent from the 3rd to the 4th quarter of 1979) and to encourage a capital inflow (e.g. there was an inflow of US$ 1.4 billion of autonomous capital in the last quarter of 1979). Such an increase postponed a balance of payments crisis but pushed the economy into a recession in 1980.

The lack of confidence in the predetermiend schedule of devaluation after an immediate lack of convergence kept the nominal interest rate at high levels, despite the reduction of the inflation rate. As expressed before, a wide margin of uncertainty remained in the exchange market. Recall that the rate was preannounced in three occasions, nothing was said about the first quarter of 1981 until December 1980, and several changes in the rate of devaluation took place during the program.

During 1980, inflation started to accelerate and not even a high real interest rate could avoid a run toward the US dollar; the central bank had to sell US$ 4,124.2 million in the exchange market to defend the announced "schedule". In the first quarter of 1981, a real deposit interest rate of 34.4 percent in annual terms could not avoid a loss of almost US$ 4.0 billion. At the same time, industrial activity was declining (see Table 10). Therefore, not even extremely high real interest rates avoided an exchange crisis, it was just postponed at the expense of economic activity during 1980.

Another important event during 1980 was the financial crisis in March-May. The downfall of two important financial institutions (Promosur and B.I.R.) precipitated a run on private bank deposits and caused a consequent central bank intervention. Real quasi-money declined by almost 8.0 percent in real terms from the first to the second quarter of 1980 and the central bank had to sell US$ 2,120.6 million at the end of the second quarter of 1980 in order to support the exchange rate parity. As the central bank's deposits guarantee had been reduced in late 1979, the crisis led to speculation against the peso and a transfer of deposits from private banks to state and foreign banks. To restore confidence, the central bank increased the amount being guaranteed and introduced a special discount facility for banks affected by a reduction of deposits. The use of this facility carried an interest rate and relatively rapid repayment schedules. Disbursement under the special discount facility during April – May 1980 were approximately US$ 2.7 billion. Also the central bank moved to raise interest rates in the third quarter of 1980 by increasing the acceptance rate for bids on treasury bilds and thus reduce the loss of foreign reserves. In conjunction with the increase in interst rates, the central bank also raised minimum reserve requirement from 11 percent to 12 percent effective June 1, 1980, partially to absorb excess liquidity generated by the special discount facility. Because of this facility the monetary base increased by 7.0 percent in real terms during 1980 (see Table 15).

4.4.3.2 Structural changes: The government was also committed to restructuring the Argentine economy, particularly the industrial sector by forcing it to become more efficient. The open-up of the domestic market to international competition through a tariff-reduction program was thought the appropriate way to achieve such objective. The program was supposed to reduce nominal import tariffs from a range between 10 percent to 85 percent at the beginning of 1979 to a range 10-40 percent by January 1984. Thus, average tariff would fall from over 40 percent to less that 20 percent. The government stated that it would reduce tariffs even further and faster for goods whose domestic price increases exceeded international price increases plus the preannounced rate of devaluation. In March 1979, tariffs for capital goods were eliminated in order to facilitate the re-equipment and modernization of the Argentine industrial sector.

The tariff-reduction program was not immediately reflected in the domestic inflation rate. It takes time to convince customers to buy imported goods instead of the national ones because it is not clear if service and parts will be easily available. There are also organizational problems (e.g. building the distributional network of newly imported goods) and there may be a lack of confidence in the duration of the strategy. Given these considerations, the significant increase experienced by imports (from US$ 3.8 billion in 1978 to US$ 6.7 billion in 1979) must have been caused by the real appreciation of the exchange rate rather than by the lowering of tariffs. It is important to notice the change in the composition of imports: consumer goods which represented only 3.3 percent of total imports in 1975, increased their share to 17.6 percent in 1980 (see Table 4). Also, total imports as a percentage of real GDP increased from 8.7 percent to 12.6 percent over the same period. It is difficult to assess how much of the increase of imports and decrease of inflation was related to this tariff-program during 1980 while at the same time the peso was so overvalued. A decline of the real exchange rate always encourages higher imports and decreases prices of tradeable goods.

Did the tariff-program change the structure of the economy? Since the program was interrupted in 1981, two years may not be enough to draw any conclusion of its effects. It is likely that the high real interst rate that the financial reform brought about, as well as the decline of the real exchange rate since 1978 and which became more drastic under the preannouncement of the exchange rate policy, were the main causes behind any "structural" change, if they can be labeled as such.

From Table 19 which shows the structure of real GDP in 1971-1975 and 1976-1980, the following conclusions can be drawn:
(1) the agriculture and service sector were increasing their share while there was a clear process of deindustrialization (the share of industry declined by 6.4 percent);
(2) within the service sector, the subsectors: electricity, water, and natural gas, banking, and government services experienced a significant increase in their share;
(3) mining, construction, and banking were the only sectors that had a higher annual average growth rate above the 1971-1975 period, all the others were substantially below, especially the industrial sector which had averaged yearly negative growth rates in 1976-1980;
(4) the fact that the service sector was becoming more important may indicate that the economy was turning more service-oriented. This raises two important questions: can the service sector become "the engine of growth" as an alternative to import-substitution and/or export-promotion growth strategies?; and, if the answer is positive, can this sector absorb or create enough employment to avoid widespread unemployment[14]. The answer to these questions is not clear. For instance, the absorption of employment by the banking sector whose real output grew at a yearly average of 9.1 percent from 1976 to 1980, was practically insignificant. However, it is important to emphasize the need of a "balance growth" in any economic development strategy;
(5) the deindustrialization process mentioned above, was accompanied by internal changes within the industrial sector. Table 22 shows that four industries increased their share in the structure of the manufacturing sector from 1971-1975 to 1976-1980: food, beverage, and tobacco; chemicals and petroleum derivates, and plastics; basic metals, machinery, and transport vehicles. This is not surprising if we recall that the first one may have "comparative advantages" due to the characteristics of the Argentine economy; although at the same time it had one of the highest rates of effective protection (see Table 28). Petroleum and petroleum derivates, and basic metals (e.g. steel) were produced by two

powerful state enterprises. The last industry aforementioned had a relative high effective protection and its share was almost 30.0 percent of
the industrial sector GDP.

With respect to the declining industries: textiles, shoes, and clothing, experienced an acceleration in their downward trend within the
industrial sector. While others, like wood and wood products, paper,
printing, and publishing seemed to have started their decline since
1976. How much of these changes were caused by the specific policies
implemented during 1976-1980; and were they the necessary ones to
turn the economy more efficient? As suggested before, it seems that the
economic program carried out in 1976-1980 accelerated a re-structuring
process that was already under process in the Argentine economy. That
is, industries that were generally more labor-intensive reduced their
share and gave room to more capital and advanced technology intensive
industries.

Table 23 shows output, productivity, and employment in different
industries. This table supports the fact that most of the policies implemented during the Martinez de Hoz time had drastic depressing effects on the industrial sector: employment in 16 industries out of 25
was lower than in 1970, and all industries had employment level below
1975 (recall that 1975 was a recessionary year). But since the same
industries also experienced a significant increase in productivity, either
with respect to 1970 or 1975, this could mean an advance in (technical)
efficiency. However, if we now add to the analysis the figures for output, they show that only those industries that in 1980 had a lower employment level, higher productivity and output may now be considered
to be more efficient than in 1975. Not surprisingly, these were the industries that increased their share in the industrial sector by 1980:
petroleum derivatives, rubber, vehicles, plastics, beverages, iron,
among others. However, food and tobacco actually increased their share
in spite of having a lower level of production in 1980 with respect to
1975. Obviously, this intra-industry comparison between output, productivity, and employment levels is not very conclusive to determine
increases in efficiency. It is important to stress that with a 40 percent
overvaluation of the peso by October 1980, all the industries faced a
negative effective protection, while according to the tariff-reduction
program only two industries (leather and leather products; and petroleum and petroleum derivatives) were supposed to face a negative one.
It seems therefore that the industrial sector had to fear more from the
revaluation of the local currency than from the liberalization program.

Agricultural and traditional industrial exports represented 74 percent of total exports in 1980, the same as in 1975. However, due to the
increase in both exports and imports, the economy was becoming more
opened: e.g. exports as percentage of GDP increased from 11.6 in 1970
to 14.3 percent in 1980. The structure of the external debt (see Table
18) shows that 48.1 percent of the total debt (US$ 27.2 billion) was
considered to be short-term in 1980, that is, less than one year, while
it was 25.1 percent short-term in 1978. The public sector became an
important borrower in the international capital market. The structural
change in the financial sector succeeded in keeping the balance of pay-

ments in surplus for five years due to the inflow of short-term capital and to the increase in domestic savings. However, the inflow of capital was very short-term and sensitive to changes in expectations while the increase in savings was brought about by high real deposit interest rates which in turn negatively affected economic activity.

In sum, after five years, the objectives of the economic program were not reached. By all accounts, it failed: real GDP per capita grew an average of almost three percent per year during 1960-74 but it experienced zero growth during 1976-80; the annual rate of inflation in the first quarter of 1981 was 70.0 percent more than double the annual average inflation in 1960-74; during 1980 and the first quarter of 1981, the central bank lost almost US$ 6 billion in international reserves, giving room to a balance of payments crisis, and the real exchange rate was at a historical low level. The government did not reduce its participation in the economy and de-industrialization was another by-product of the program.

NOTES

[1] See Eshag and Thorp (1965), Maynard and van Rijckeghen (1966), Brodersohn (1967), Frenkel and O'Donnell (1978), Marshall, Madones, and I. Marshall (1983) for further analysis of orthodox-IMF type stabilization programs effects on the Argentine economy. Cardoso (1982) introduced a theoretical framework to interpret the results of orthodox programs in LDCs. Robichek (1967), in his unpublished lectures, presented the IMF stabilization-program approach. Dornbusch (1980) analyzed the lessons from stabilization policies in developing countries.

[2] See Brodersohn (1967) and Mallon (1968) for a further discussion on the early 1960s stabilization programs.

[3] de Pablo (1970) presented an analysis and description of this program.

[4] See de Pablo (1980) for further clarification on the economic-policy of the Peronist regime.

[5] The tables refer in this chapter can be found in the statistical Appendices I and II.

[6] The calculation of the real exchange rate based on a purchasing power parity concept is generally highly criticized. In particular, the choice of the base year (or quarter) can give a completely different picture. For instance, Nogués (1984) found that the real exchange rate depreciated by 18 percent in 1977 with respect to the previous year (the base was 1969 = 100). Our own calculations showed a depreciation of 13 percent. Nogués also calculated the real effective exchange rate for different categories of exports. In this case, there was a real appreciation of 18 for the category manufactures from 1976 to 1977 and of 23 percent for non-traditional manufactures. On the other hand, the effective real exchange rate for agriculture products experienced a real depreciation of 37 percent. Certainly, the exact value of the real appreciation (or depreciation) is always debatable.

[7] A high interest rate spread can be explained by the following:

$$1 = (1-k) \, d \tag{1}$$

$$\pi = [i_B (1-k) + i_R \, k \, q - i_d] - \bar{c} \tag{2}$$

$$i_B = i_B^* + \delta_1 (0.2 \, \dot{p}^e) + \dot{x}^e + p + s \, \phi \left[\frac{M}{R}\right] \tag{3}$$

where:

1 = nominal demand for loans
d = nominal supply of loans (or total deposits),
k = legal reserve requirement on deposits,
π = total profits on loans,
i_B = nominal borrowing interest rate,
i_d = nominal deposit interest rate,
i_R = nominal interest rate paid by the central bank on legal time-deposits reserves,

q = time deposits over demand deposits ratio,

$\bar{c}$ = administrative costs and other costs,

i_B^* = foreign nominal borrowing interest rate,

$\dot{p}^e$ = expected rate of inflation,

$\dot{x}^e$ = expected rate of devaluation,

ϕ = coefficient of risk-aversion

s = exchange rate variance,

$\dfrac{M}{R}$ = ratio of imports over foreign international reserves at the central bank

δ_1 = is equal to 1 from December 1977 - May 1978 and 0 otherwise due to the implementation of a 20% required deposits on all foreign loan, made in local currency and without receiving an interest rate.

p = is a variable that will push the interest rate up whenever there is an increase in the legal maturity of loans borrowed abroad: e.g. in October 1977 minimum maturity was set at one year; in December 1977, it was set at two-years; and in July 1980 it was abolished any maturity limit.

$\phi s \dfrac{M}{R}$ = risk

Equation (1) represents the equilibrium condition in the credit market. From (1) and (2), i_B can be expressed as (assuming = 0):

$$i_B = \frac{1}{1-k}(i_d - i_R \, k \, q + \bar{c}) \tag{4}$$

if we now subtract i_B from both sides of (4), it is obtained:

$$i_B - i_d = \frac{k}{1-k}(i_d - i_R \, q) + \frac{c}{1-k} \tag{3}$$

and given (3) and (4), i_d can be rewritten as:

$$i_d = i_B^* + \delta_1 (0.2 \, \dot{p}^e) + \dot{x}^e + p + s\phi(\frac{M}{R})(1-k) + i_R k \, q - \bar{c} \tag{6}$$

These last two expressions emphasize that the interest spread can be affected by: 1) any variable that influence the borrowing interest rate (the spread changes by a proportion 'k'); 2) the legal reserve requirement policy; 3) costs (c); 4) the interest rate paid by the central bank, and 5) the ratio between time and demand deposits. For instance, the significance increase in the spread in the last quarter of 1977 can be explained also by the implementation of a 20 percent deposit on foreign loans in local currency at no interest rate, the increase in the minimum maturity of foreign loans. See Mathieson (1981) for further explanation on interest rate spread.

[8] Baliño (1982) showed in an econometric work that the nominal interest rates were mainly determined by the foreign interest rate but particularly by the expected rate of devaluation. The weekly interest rate on 30-day deposits was used and covered the period June 1977 - September 1980.

[9] It may not be correct to assess an increase in total private domestic savings after the financial reform. It is quite possible that such a reform induced a change in the composition of the private sector portfolio. That is, from holding monetary assets available in the curb financial market and foreign currency (holdings not covered by the official statistics) into time and savings deposits in the offical financial sector after the reform.

[10] The translation from the original Spanish version was done by the author of this book.

[11] This section was based on Whitman (1975). For a further theoretical support for the program see Rodriguez (1979).

[12] See Guitian (1977) for a discussion of the use of credit as an instrument of control and improvement in the balance of payments.

[13] See de Melo and Urata (1983) for some empirical evidence of this point in the case of Chile.

[14] See Baer and Samuelson (1981) for an analysis of a service-oriented growth strategy.

5 Why did the stabilization-liberalization program fail?

5.1. INTRODUCTION

Several reasons have been given to explain the failure of the program, in particular during the second phase. They ranged from implementation errors or internal inconsistencies to sharp criticism to the free-market approach itself [1]. The consequences of a traditional stabilization approach have been extensively studied [2]. Therefore, the first phase of the plan did not receive too much attention here. It was in the second period that we were interested in because the stabilization experiment was framework within a further push in capital and trade liberalization as well as in the use of unorthodox policies, such as the preannouncement of key macroeconomic variables.

In view of the fact that the inflation rate remained around 150 percent a year from 1976 to 1978, the government, by the end of 1978, decided to fight inflation by implementing a strategy based upon exchange rate and tariff policies which did not depend on the conventional tool of reducing aggregate demand and on prolonged periods of recession and high unemployment. In December 1978, a predetermined schedule of decreasing monthly exchange rate devaluations was announced, together with a 5-year program of tariff reductions. The preannouncement of the exchange rate, the rate of increase in government controlled goods and services prices, minimum wages, and the domestic component of the monetary base, were expected to generate anti-inflationary effects by reducing inflationary expectations. The increased foreign competition in the domestic market that would come from lowering tariffs was perceived as a means of inhibiting domestic-price increases in traded goods.

Under the 1979-strategy, the devaluation rate was not linked to the rate of growth of domestic prices. This was supposed to require the private sector to make a "serious" effort to reduce its costs of production. Thus, replacing the traditional policy of former governments of directly imposing price controls. Besides, since the exchange rate was not used to solve balance of payments disequilibria, the government had to open-up the capital account; thus, capital flows now financing disequilibrium. Furthermore, this policy was thought to reinforce the objective of the financial sector reform, that is to say, to reduce the real cost of credit to the private sector by allowing a closer link between the domestic and the international capital markets.

Calvo and Fernandez (1982) explained that there was an "inconsistency" between the fiscal deficit and the preannounced rate of devaluation. They presented a simple formulation that related the budget deficit to the inflationary tax needed to finance it. Through this, they concluded that a fiscal deficit of 4 percent of national income in 1980 was compatible with an inflationary tax between 37 percent and 44 percent depending on the value assigned to the monetary base as percentage of national income. However, "la tablita" announced a rate of devaluation of only 24 percent for 1980 [3]. As a result, the peso continued to be even more overvalued. Arriazu (1983) disagreed with stressing the failure of the program due to that inconsistency. He stressed (p. 184) that "abandoning wage indexation would have allowed the real exchange rate to recuperate, at the expense of real wages. The fact that the government was pushing real wages upward made the system inconsistent". Rodrigues (1982) also stressed this kind of inconsistency in the program in a later paper, although in his 1979-article where the program received theoretical support, nothing was said about the behavior of real wages. On the other hand, Sjaastad (1983, pp. 20-21) concluded that:

> The fiscal deficit eroded the credibility of the plan not only because permanent reliance on foreign finance of the deficit was regarded as implausible, if not impossible, but also because the low rate of inflation indicated by a stable exchange rate (the objective of the plan for February 1981) could not generate enough inflationary tax to finance the fiscal deficit ... This inconsistency between exchange-rate and fiscal policy strengthened the conviction that the exchange-rate "table" would ultimately be violated, a conviction clearly revealed in the interest rate.

Sjaastad pointed out as well that the failure of the program cannot be interpreted as evidence of the failure of economic liberalism - trade liberalisation, financial sector reform -. The failure must be found in the internal inconsistency of the stabilization program; he (p. 22) added that "it is tragic that the central bank of Argentina spent two years and more than US$ 10.0 billion defending an exchange rate policy that, in retrospect, was clearly doomed in its first six months". This is quite an statement from someone who was a strong supporter of the program. His position was quite contradictory; for instance, Sjaastad and Rodriguez (1982) found no support, through their empirical results, to the claim that the peso was highly overvalued in 1979-80 (only by 10 percent).

McKinnon (1982b) deduced that the failure of the exchange rate policy happened because complete removal of exchange controls on foreign capital movements should come last in the liberalization process, whereas domestic financial liberalization should accompany a move toward free trade. That is, the government should first free the real sector and then the domestic financial one. Argentina did just the opposite. However, Chile followed the rule pointed out by McKinnon and it also turned out to be a failure. Sjaastad (1983) said that this happened because the Chilean financial sector was subject a complex set of rules at the

same time that domestic inflation was going down due to the trade liberalization program: the result was very high real interest rates that
brought about a recession. That is, the delaying in fully liberalizing
capital flows was a terrible mistake in the Chilean case.

Canitrot (1979, 1980) focused on the political aspect of the program.
He said that stabilization programs generally harm unevenly each sector
of the economy; and they rarely survive the complaints of those who
have to bear the costs of correction. In this particular strategy, every
sector seemed to have something to lose, this made it possible to fore-
see the collapse of the plan since the very beginning. Diaz-Alejandro
(1981, p. 129) pointed out that:

> Reliance on a preannounced and declining rate of exchange rate
> devaluation as the key instrument to lower inflation also ap-
> pears as excessively risky. Stubborn inflation in the prices of
> nontraded goods can lead to overvaluation ... Preannounced
> exchange rates reduce the uncertainty of financial speculators
> while increasing that of exporters, a peculiar trade-off ... Yet
> if the preannounced and slower devaluation pace fails to reduce
> inflation fairly quickly, expectations will grow that sharper
> devaluations lie ahead. The government will be faced with the
> 1950s dilemma of giving in to such expectations, rekindling
> after all the inflationary spiral and losing any remaining cre-
> dibility, or adopting very contractionary policies to validate the
> overvalued exchange rate.

Martinez de Hoz, the Economic Minister, wrote the following about the
results of his economic program (1982, p. 211): "during 1976-1980, Argentina could reduce the rate of inflation without sacrificing growth and
achieving deep structural changes. This represents, undoubtly, a success." According to the analysis and description of events presented
above, his statement was very far from reality; particularly if we recall
that the authorities were committed to achieve permanent and not temporary changes (e.g. inflation was "artificially" reduced in 1979-1980 because of the overvaluation of the exchange rate).

Figure 5.1 depicts four key-macroeconomic variables in the period
1977-81: real wages (w), annual average real ex-post lending interest
rate (r), the real exchange rate (e_r), and real manufactured output
growth (Q). It is interesting to note that real wages changed from a
downward trend in the first phase to an upward one during the second
phase. The real interest rate continued with its volatile swings but, in
particular during the second period, it ranged between very high positive levels. The real exchange rate kept up its appreciation. Therefore,
a traditional outcome of the Argentine economy was once again obvious
since 1979 (as explained in chapter one): a period of economic recovery
and lower inflation rate was brought about by a real appreciation and
higher real wages [4]. This demand-pull recovery had a negative impact on the balance of payments with a foreign exchange crisis around
the corner, in particular, due to CS and capital flight. Consequently,
there was nothing new and surprising in the failure of the program.
Nevertheless, there were new institutional aspects that were not present
before in the Argentine economy. These new institutional aspects were:
the open-up trade and capital accounts, the complete liberalization of
the domestic financial market, and the free access to buy and sell foreign currency in the presence of high and persistent inflation rate.

FIGURE 5.1

ARGENTINA – KEY MACROECONOMIC VARIABLES, 1977–81

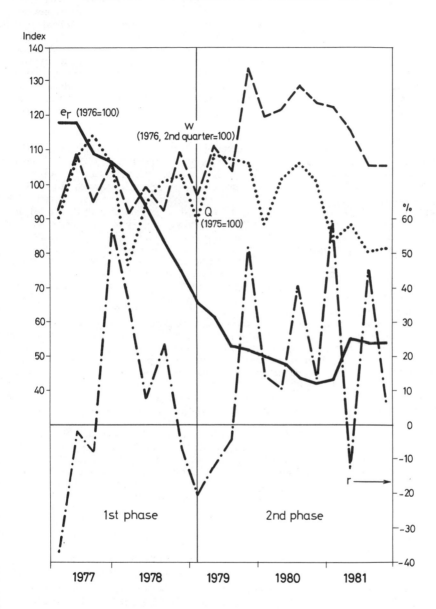

Sources: w : Table 11 (third column, 1976, 2nd quarter = 100)
       r : Table A-1.1 (1st column)
       Q : Table A-1 (1st column, 1975 = 100)
       e_r: Table A-2 (5th column, 1976 = 100)

It is not clear, ex-ante, how a real appreciation and higher real wages would affect the balance of payments and the economy within the new institutional framework. For instance, the real appreciation encourages expectations of a future devaluation pushing up the interest rate. This reduces economic activity which in turn reduces import. At the same time, a higher interest rate brings about a capital inflow and higher domestic savings. This positive impact on the balance of payments of interest rate liberalization can be, however, offset by trade liberalization and CS. Higher real wages encourage a higher demand for imported (consumer) goods and more travelling abroad. The free access to foreign currency now allows firms as well as households to openly engage in CS.

As expressed above, the real exchange rate and real wages worked in opposite directions to generate a period of temporary growth and lower inflation. However, after the liberalization of the financial sector (in 1977), this relationship was not so obvious. For instance, in 1980 a significant real appreciation and higher real wages were associated with negative real GDP growth per capita and an increase in the rate of inflation. After the financial reform, periods of growth were mainly caused by a decline in the real interest rate. But why did real appreciation not bring about higher growth? The economic program (1977-81) was inherently unstable because real appreciation caused expectations of a future devaluation, this pushed interest rates up which depressed economic activity. At the same, high domestic interest rates bought time to avoid a balance of payments crisis by encouraging capital inflows but, once again, at the expense of growth and higher inflation. Therefore, the relationship between exchange rate and interest rate was completely neglected during the whole program. On the other hand, an upward trend in real wages was not associated this time with higher economic activity because the real appreciation plus the decline in tariffs meant that such increase spilled over towards the foreign sector by raising the demand for final consumer goods from abroad (e.g., as a percentage of total imports consumer goods rose from 2.2 percent in 1976 to 17.6 in 1980) rather than by raising primarily domestic demand.

Therefore, the failure of the program was not related to the open-up of the trade and the capital accounts; although, this may have speeded up its collapse. The causes of such a collapse were the traditional combination of high real wages and real appreciation. Certainly, the complete liberalization of the domestic financial market and the free access to buy and sell foreign exchange in the presence of high and persistent inflation made the program inherently unstable. Now, under the new institutional framework, expectations of a (higher) devaluation:

(1) did not allow the nominal interest rate to go down as fast as inflation, therefore, pushing real interest rate up and initiating a recession, particularly in the industrial sector; and

(2) encouraged CS even more. The sharp decline of international reserves during 1980 and the first quarter of 1981 showed how weak the external position of the country was since the accumulation was based on short-term capital. The balance of payments crisis that was evolving during 1980, was thought to be solved not by the orthodox policy of reducing absorption through fiscal and monetary restraints (as was the case before financial liberalization) but by higher real interest rates which the adjustment mechanism of the program would bring about.

That is, higher real interest rate would cause a capital inflow and reduce economic activity.

In order to support the above point of view, it was important to determine to which extent CS was still a significant phenomenon in Argentina even after the financial liberalization took place as well as the relationship between real interest rates and economic activity. For such a purpose, a two-sector (real and monetary) disequilibrium macro model was introduced and applied to quarterly Argentine data from 1977 to 1981. An analysis on the order of economic liberalization was also necessary to carry out in order to detect some policy-inconsistencies in the program. With respect to this, it is certainly obvious that in the face of high and persistent inflation, a government has to impose exchange controls in order to retain a certain seignorage on its currency. Although, it is a well-known lesson from empirical evidence that government control of speculative exchange or capital flows undertaken by the non-bank sector is very ineffective; the complete removal of such controls was a terrible mistake but not necessarily inconsistent given the other measures. Also, to believe that inflation could be reduced just by open-up the economy, did not recognize that a government that runs large and persistent deficits and that monetizes a large fraction of them will still experience high inflation but now coupled with more severe balance of payments disequilibria.

5.2. THE MODEL

This is a two-sector macroeconomic model where the real sector is being represented by a supply and a demand function for industrial goods produced domestically and the monetary sector is composed of a demand for local currency (defined narrowly and broadly) according to a partial adjustment hypothesis. It is presented also a demand for foreign currency as proxied by the central bank net purchase of foreign currency from authorized agencies or banks which deal with foreign exchange. The CS effect on the demand for local currency was again captured by the expected rate of devaluation but this time proxied by the difference between the nominal borrowing domestic interest rate and the international one given the new institutional framework. This proxy for CS implied that the Fisher hypothesis holds. That is, the interest rate differential in 1977-80 was explained by the expected exchange rate change. A study undertaken by Blejer (1982) showed that the Fisher condition did hold in Argentina from June 1977 to August 1981. This was surprising because a risk premium was always a relevant component of the interest rate differential after the Financial Reform (June 1977). Blejer (1982, p. 287) concluded that:

> Since it would not be realistic to rule out the existence of a risk premium and postulate perfect substitutability, a possible rationalization for the results is that the Argentine market is indeed informationally efficient and that the risk premium appears to be time varying and serially uncorrelated. An implication is that interest rates have responded quickly to news, that is, new information that appears randomly in the market."

The model was specified as follows:

The Real Sector:

$$Q_t^s/Q_{t-1}^s = \beta_o \left[(1+i_{b,t})/(1+i_{b,t-1})\right]^{\beta_1} \cdot (M_t^d/M_{t-1}^d)^{\beta_2} \cdot \tag{5.1}$$

$$\left[(1+i_{b,t-1})/(1+\pi'_{t-1})\right]^{\beta_3} \cdot E_{t-1}^{\beta_4} \cdot e^{\beta_5 D_1} \cdot e^{u_{1t}}$$

$$Q_t^d/Q_{t-1}^d = \alpha_o \, (M_t^d/M_{t-1}^d)^{\alpha_1} \cdot \left[(1+i_{d,t-1})/(1+\pi_{t-1})\right]^{\alpha_2} \cdot \tag{5.2}$$

$$(Y_t/Y_{t-1})^{\alpha_3} \cdot E_{t-1}^{\alpha_4} \cdot e^{\alpha_5 D_1} \cdot e^{u_{2t}}$$

$$\pi'_t = (Q_t^d/Q_t^s)^h - 1 \tag{5.3}$$

where:

E = proxy variable for inflation uncertainty created as the standard errors of moving first order autoregressive regressions of the inflation rate as measured by wholesale price index (general),

t = time, quarter

Q^s = industrial domestic output in constant 1970 prices,

Q^d = demand for industrial domestic goods,

i_b = doemstic borrowing interest rate from commercial banks, average in the quarter,

M^d = demand for local currency,

M^s = money supply (broadly defined) in constant 1970 prices, at the end of the quarter,

π' = inflation rate of industrial domestic goods, average in the quarter,

π = wholesale inflation rate (general), average in the quarter,

i_d = average domestic deposit interest rate at commercial banks,

Y = income as proxied by GDP at factor cost and in constant 1970 prices,

D_1 = dummy variable that takes into account the influence of foreign competition which equal to 1 from the first quarter of 1979 up to the first quarter of 1981, and 0 otherwise,

u_{it} = disturbance terms, i = 1,2

Equation (5.1), the supply of industrial goods domestically produced, specifically includes the real borrowing domestic interest rate as an argument lagged one period because the purchase of variable inputs was assumed to take place at time t-1 prior to product sale. Therefore, producers need to borrow money to finance such a purchase. The expected negative sign of the coefficient shows that the higher the financial cost the lower the level of production, for a given price. At the beginning of 1979, after the new exchange rate policy was announced, expectations of any sudden devaluation were reduced as well as the risk premium; thus, nominal interest rates went down. At the same time, domestic inflation did not decline as fast. This brought about negative real interest rate for most of 1979. Industrial production grew 10 percent during that year. A positive relationship between inflation uncertainty and the level of industrial production was postulated. This may indicate that businessmen pile up inventories in times of price uncertainty. The difference between nominal borrowing interest rate (i_b) at time t and t-1 was also included to stress the impact of higher nominal financial costs. At the beginning of time t, producers already know i_b and π_{t-1}, since the inflation of time t will not be known until t+1; they may also look at nominal rates to ascertain if financial costs will go up or down, given the inflation rate. The coefficient is expected to be negative.

Demand equation (5.2) indicates that there may be a positive wealth effect through a higher deposit real interest rate of the last period on today's consumption. That is, higher interest revenues in t-1 may encourage a higher level of consumption in period t. A positive relationship between inflation uncertainty and demand is expected, that is, the higher the price uncertainty the higher the demand. Households, as businessmen, are uncertain about next period inflation rate but certain that prices will not decline at least in Argentina. As usual, a positive income coefficient is hypothesized which reflects that the higher the growth rate of income, the higher the demand. The money market disequilibrium $(M^d_t/M^d_{t-1})_d$ is incorporated in equations (5.1) and (5.2), measured by $[Ln\ M^d_t - L\ Ln\ M^s]$, where L is a lag operator ($Lx_t = x_{t-1}$). Given the fact that we cannot measure the demand for money separately from the supply, the sign of the coefficient is unknown apriori. Only if the coefficient turned out to be negative, then we can say that our approach was correct. This implies that a higher demand for domestic money, given supply, will make the demand for industrial goods decline and therefore a reduction of industrial activity will occur. Also note the presence of a dummy variable in both equations. The expected negative relationship indicates that the presence of foreign goods reduce domestic production and demand due to a substitution effect. However, this dummy variable also captures the period when the peso became very overvalued. Thus, it can be interpreted as an evidence of the negative effect of overvaluation on domestic production as well.

Equation (5.3) shows that if the demand for industrial domestic goods is equal to its supply, then there is no inflation. We are assuming that a discrepancy between supply and demand may appear which seems to be a reasonable assumption given the use of quarterly data. Therefore, the equality between the two variables is not necessarily achieved in the quarter. Equation (5.3) can be also expressed as:

$$1 + \pi'_t = (Q^d_t/Q^s_t)^h \tag{5.4}$$

if we lag (5.4) one period, it becomes:

$$1 + \pi'_{t-1} = (Q^d_{t-1}/Q^s_{t-1})^h \tag{5.5}$$

Since demand is not observable and given the structure of the model, the two equations estimated were:

$$Ln \ (Q^s_t/Q^s_{t-1}) = \ \beta_0 + \beta_1 \ [Ln \ (1+i_{b,t}) - Ln \ (1+i_{b,t-1}) +$$

$$+ \ \beta_2 \ [Ln \ M^d - L \ LnM^s] +$$

$$+ \ \beta_3 \ [Ln \ (1+i_{b,t-1}) - Ln \ (1+\pi'_{t-1})] + \beta_4 \ Ln \ E_{t-1} +$$

$$+ \ \beta_5 \ D_1 + u_{1t} \qquad\qquad\qquad (5.6)$$

which resulted from taking the natural logarithms of equation (5.1) and represents the supply-side of the market. Equation (5.7):

$$Ln \ [\ (1 +\pi'_t)/(1 + \pi'_{t-1})] = h \ [Ln(Q^d_t/Q^d_{t-1}) - Ln \ (Q^s_t/Q^s_{t-1})] \qquad (5.7)$$

was obtained by dividing equation (5.4) by (5.5) and substituting Q^d_t/Q^d_{t-1}, by the natural logarithms of equation (5.2). Equation (5.7) is expressed in differential growth rate and is identified with the demand-side of the market.

The Monetary Sector:

Since the desired demand for local currency is not directly observable, the partial adjustment hypothesis was used, namely:

$$M_t/M_{t-1} = (M^*_t/M^*_{t-1})^\delta \qquad\qquad 0 < \delta \leqslant 1 \qquad\qquad (5.8)$$

where:

M^* = desired demand for domestic money in real terms;
M = actual demand for domestic money in real terms. Two definitions of money were used, a narrow (currency plus sight deposits) and a broad one (currency plus sight deposits plus time and savings deposits).

The following demand for money is postulated:

$$Ln \ M^*_t = \ Ln \ \varepsilon_0 +\varepsilon_1 \ Ln \ X^e_t +\varepsilon_2 \ \left[Ln \ (1+i_d)/(1+\pi)\right]_t + \varepsilon_3 \ Ln \ Y_t +u_t \qquad (5.9)$$

where:

X^e = expected·rate of devaluation.

Now, substituting $Ln \ M^*$ from (5.9) into equation (5.8) expressed in Ln form and rearranging, one obtains:

$$Ln \ M_{2t} = \delta \ Ln \ \xi_0 + \ \delta\xi_1 \ Ln \ X^e_t + \ \xi_2 \delta \left[Ln \ (1+i_d)/(1+\pi)\right]_t + \qquad (5.10)$$

$$\xi_3 \delta \ Ln \ Y_t + \ (1-\delta) \ Ln \ M_{2t-1} + \delta \ u_t$$

(5.10) is the equation finally estimated for a broad definition of money. For a narrow definition of money, the following equation is estimated:

$$Ln \ M_{1t} = \delta' \ Ln \ \gamma_0 + \gamma_1 \delta' \ Ln \ X^e_t + \gamma_2 \delta' \ Ln \ (P_t/P_{t-1}) + \qquad (5.11)$$

$$(1-\delta') \ Ln \ M_{1t-1} + \delta' \ v_t$$

The interest rate was not introduced in the estimation of a narrow definition of money because, under the period of analysis, the inflation rate remained at a three digit-level, with the exception of 1980. Therefore, local currency holdings were kept at the minimum possible level to avoid a significant loss of purchasing power. Besides, since the banking sector was offering time deposits at a 7-day minimum maturity, it was easy and fast to transfer money to demand deposits when needed.

Changes in foreign exchange as a proxy for the demand for foreign exchange, is postulated as a function of:

$$M_{ft}^{d} = \beta_0 + \beta_1 (Ln \ Y_t - Ln \ Y_{t-1}) + \beta_2 \ Ln \ E_{t-1} + \qquad (5.12)$$

$$+ \ \beta_3 \ (Ln \ M_t^d - L \ Ln \ M^s) + u_t$$

where:

M_f^d = demand for foreign currency expressed in constant local currency in 1970 prices (the average quarterly exchange rate as quoted by Banco de la Nacion – selling rate – was used in the calsulation), proxied by the net purchase of foreign currency by the central bank from exchange agencies.

The objective was to find a proxy for foreign exchange movements caused by CS. Although, the figures cannot be clearly identified with CS per se, they do certainly indicate the trend in the substitution from local currency into foreign money and viceversa. This is so, because during 1977-1981, people could go to exchange agencies and legally purchase foreign money up to an amount equal to US\$ 20,000 in cach transaction, without giving any specific reason for the purchase. Furthermore, there were no restrictions on how many times this transaction could take place.

We would have preferred to measure M_f^d in Ln but the data available were either net purchase or net sales (the latter enters with a negative sign). The inclusion of the money market disequilibrium as an argument in (5.12) captures the fact that whenever the demand for local currency declines, meaning that there is an excess supply of domestic money, the net purchases of foreign currency by the central bank also declines. In other words, the demand for foreign currency is going up. Note that the relationship proposed between the growth rate of income and the net purchase of foreign currency by the central bank is positive when traditionally, a negative relationship is expected. That is, the higher the level of economic activity, the higher the demand for foreign currency to buy foreign goods. However, the opposite sign is possible as well. This relationship can be rationalized as follows: the higher the level of economic activity, the more people will dishoard foreign currency due to a greater need for money for transactions purposes, and this dishoarding outweights the higher demand for foreign currency due to a higher level of imports. Apriori, the sign is therefore undetermined.

The following identity is introduced:

$$i_t = i_t^* + x_t^e + q \qquad (5.13)$$

where:

i^* = international borrowing interest rate,
q = expenses from borrowing abroad (e.g. taxes) [5].

Implicitly we are also considering three extra identities represented by the money supply, the government budget constraint, and changes in international reserve holdings of the Argentine central bank. The money supply is composed by a domestic and an international component. The domestic component reflects the way the government deficit is financed, that is, by selling bonds or by printing money. The international component reflects the situation in the trade balance, capital flows caused by interest rate differentials, public firms borrowing abroad and the adjustment in the private sector portfolio between assets denominated in local and foreign currency.

5.3 THE ECONOMETRIC RESULTS

The recursive model introduced above was estimated by the OLS method since it was assumed that the same period disturbances in the different equations were uncorrelated. It should be stressed that the results must be interpreted with care due to the fact that we were dealing with a very small sample. Seventeen observations were used (quarterly date, from the second quarter of 1977 to the second quarter of 1981).

The Real Sector Results:

The real sector results are shown in Table 5.1. The Cochrane-Orcutt iterative method was applied to equation (5.1) in order to resolve auto-correlation in the disturbances. Signs came out all correctly. The real borrowing interest rate and the nominal change in the interest rate were relevant in explaining the variation in the growth rate of industrial goods produced domestically. Also, note the negative sign on the dummy variable which reflected the fact that the increasing presence of foreign goods due to the liberalization program reduced domestic production. On the demand equation, the negative sign of the coefficient of the D_1 may indicate that the presence of foreign goods set a "price ceiling" on domestic industrial goods. There seems to be a weak evidence of a positive wealth effect that comes from last period interest revenues on today's consumption. The higher the inflation uncertainty, the higher the demand and the supply of goods. The results support the findings of Cavallo (1977) as well: a tight monetary policy is associated with a recession and with inflation since the coefficient of the disequilibrium in the monetary sector came out negative in both equations.

The Monetary Sector Results:

The results of the estimations are shown in Table 5.2. The proxy for the expected rate of devaluation that measures CS came out in all the equations with the right sign and statistically significant, supporting the hypothesis that there was substitution not only from local currency and demand deposits into foreign local currency but also from broad-money into foreign money. Note the important role of the real deposit interest rate as an instrument to encourage people to hold assets denominated in local currency according to the econometric results.

TABLE 5.1

ARGENTINA - ESTIMATIONS OF THE REAL SECTOR FUNCTIONS, II-1977/II-1981

(1) Supply Function

DEPENDENT VARIABLE	CONSTANT TERM B_0	$\ln(1+i_{b,t}) - \ln(1+i_{b,t-1})$	$\ln(1+i_{b,t-1}) - \ln(1+\pi_{t-1})$	$\ln M_t^d - \ln LLM_t^s$	$\ln E_{t-1}$	D_1	R^2	D.W.
$\ln(Q_t^s/Q_{t-1}^s)$ a/	0.1797 (1.9896)	-4.0658 (-1.8996)	-5.5054 (-2.6138)	-0.8277 (-1.5264)	0.0661 (1.4653)	-0.115 (-1.43)	0.427	2.298

a/ The Cochrane-Orcutt method was applied to correct for autocorrelation in the disturbances. The estimated coefficient of autocorrelation was equal to: -0.28114

(2) Demand Function

DEPENDENT VARIABLE	CONSTANT TERM	$\ln M_t^d - LLM_t^s$	$\ln(1+i_{d,t-1}) - \ln(1+\pi_{t-1})$	$\ln Y_t - \ln Y_{t-1}$	$\ln E_{t-1}$	D_1	$\ln Q_t^s - \ln Q_{t-1}^s$	R^2	D.W.
$\ln(1+\pi) - \ln(1+\pi)$	0.0199 (2.3158)	-0.2376 (-3.2194)	0.4541 (1.3680)	0.4052 (1.3860)	0.0013 (0.1887)	-0.016 (-1.462)	-0.0828 (-1.117)	0.66	1.635

TABLE 5.2

ARGENTINA— ESTIMATIONS OF THE DEMAND FOR MONEY FUNCTIONS, II—1977/II—1981

dependent variable	constant term	dependent variable lagged one period	expected rate of devaluation	Inflation uncertainty	real deposit interest rate (ex-post)	Inflation rate	Real Income	$\bar{R}^2$	D.W.	Durbin-h a/	b/
$\ln M_{1t}$	4.6689 (1.3490)	0.3652 (3.1744)	-0.1146 (-3.0939)	0.0109 (0.7418)	-	-0.8501 (-4.3759)	0.1179 (0.3666)	0.902	2.340	-0.796	0.58
	4.3583 (1.2931)	0.4077 (4.1669)	-0.1171 (-3.2397)	-	-	-0.8586 (-4.5082)	0.1125 (0.3567)	0.906	2.219	-0.493	0.69
	5.5280 (7.3520)	0.4236 (5.0357)	-0.1205 (-3.5712)	-	-	-0.8619 (-4.6917)	-	0.912	2.265	-0.583	0.74
$\ln M_{2t}$	1.1025 (0.2717)	0.7338 (16.3852)	-0.1164 (-3.7279)	0.0178 (1.2618)	1.8701 (3.5014)	-	0.1556 (0.4278)	0.971	2.126	-0.265	2.76
	-0.0238 (-0.0059)	0.7476 (16.8034)	-0.1247 (-3.7451)	-	1.7200 (3.3248)	-	0.2414	0.970	2.279	-0.585	2.96
	2.6384 (6.8239)	0.7623 (20.2893)	-0.1247 (-4.1370)	-	1.7930 (3.5122)	-	-	0.970	2.041	-0.085	3.21
LONG-RUN VALUES											
$\ln M_{1t}$	7.3549	-	-0.1805	0.0172	-	-1.3392	0.1857				
	7.3583	-	-0.1977	-	-	-1.4496	0.1899				
	9.5906	-	-0.2091	-	-	-1.4953	-				
$\ln M_{2t}$	4.1416	-	-0.4373	0.0669	7.0252	-	0.5845				
	-0.0943	-	-0.4941	-	6.8146	-	0.9564				
	11.0997	-	-0.5246	-	7.5431	-	-				

a/ Durbin-h was calculated as follows: $(1 - DW/2)\sqrt{N/(1 - N (\text{var} (\alpha)))}$ where DW is the calculated Durbin-Watson reported in column ten, N is the total number of observations (17 in this case), and var (α) is the squarred of the standard error of the coefficient of the dependent variable lagged one period.

b/ The average adjustment period was calculated as follows: $(1 - \delta)/\delta$, where δ is the adjustment coefficient obtained from the coefficient of the dependent variable lagged one period.

In the case of M_1, the findings indicate that: (1) the expected rate of devaluation turned out to be significant but actual inflation was more important in explaining its variations, and (2) the income elasticity coefficient came out with the expected sign, but surprisingly, statistically insignificant. It was also estimated the demand for M_1, including inflation uncertainty as an argument. The results show that the higher the inflation uncertainty, the higher the demand for local currency [Diz (1970) has obtained the same result], but this independent variable turned out to be statistically insignificant. As expected, the average adjustment period of the discrepancy between desired and actual real money balance, is faster the more liquid the monetary asset is. For instance, M_1 adjusts to its desired level within the quarter but it takes more than two quarters for broad-money. The adjustment time for broad-money seems too long given the fact that time and savings deposits remained an average of 30-day in deposit. However, recall that there were continuous roll-over of those deposits.

The results for a broad definition of money, M_2, is also quite satisfactory. Including inflation uncertainty as an extra argument, shows that the higher the inflation uncertainty, the higher the demand for broad-money. But it was, as for M_1, statistically insignificant. The expected rate of devaluation was more important in explaining its variations than the actual ex-post real deposit interest rate. However, the demand for broad money is much more inelastic to changes to the expected rate of devaluation than to changes to the ex-post real deposit interest rate. Note that the income elasticity coefficient came out of the expected sign in both definitions of money but statistically insignificant. The latter is a surprising result. However, this can be another indication that foreign currency was used for transaction purposes [6].

The econometric results for equation (5.12) suggests that:

$$M^d_{ft} = -0.5103 + 72.4700 \ (Ln \ Y_t - Ln \ Y_{t-1}) + 2.7549 \ Ln \ E_{t-1} +$$
$$\phantom{M^d_{ft} = } (-0.555) \quad (2.8904) (2.7549)$$

$$34.6640 \ (Ln \ M^d_t - LLn \ M^s)$$
$$(3.0465)$$

$$R^2 = 0.4720 \qquad dw = 2.1420$$

the higher the inflation uncertainty, the higher the net purchases of foreign money by the central bank, therefore the lower the demand for foreign currency by the public. Although, the opposite sign was expected to be more logical, this outcome can be rationalized by the fact that when inflation uncertainty went up, like in 1979, a year when asset-holders believed that the government was committed to the preannouncement of the exchange rate schedule; then, foreign currency was not a very attractive asset relative to assets denominated in local currency due to the interest rate perceived. The results also reveal that the lower the demand for local currency (e.g., due to an increase in the expected rate of devaluation) the lower the net purchases of foreign currency by the central bank; that is, the higher the demand for foreign currency by the private sector, according to the sign of the coefficient of the disequilibrium in the money market independent variable. In sum, the econometric results support the fact the CS was still a significant phenomenon in Argentina even after financial liberalization.

The interest rate played an important role in encouraging higher domestic savings (or a portfolio shift towards domestic monetary assets) and in originating severe volatility in economic activity.

Recall that as economic activity was declining in 1978, the government may not have wanted the same to happen in 1979. The new exchange rate policy pushed down nominal interest rates by reducing expectations of exchange rate changes. The domestic lending real interest rate became negative during 1979. Small and medium size firms saw a decline in their financial costs. This, coupled with the fact that there was a negative (ex-post) return on domestic assets and the belief that the government was committed to the preannounced schedule of the exchange rate devaluation, encouraged present consumption and thus a higher level of economic activity. A significant inflow of capital occurred in 1979 due to the exchange rate stability and the central bank was a net purchaser of foreign currency.

As mentioned before, according to the 1979-exchange rate policy, the peso was being devalued at a lower rate than the change in the ration of domestic to international price increases. CS was temporarily discouraged during the first nine-month of 1979 because the public believed that the government was committed to defend this strategy and that, no sudden exchange rate devaluation would occur. In 1979 industrial production grew by more than 10 percent.

By the end of 1979, the public realized that this exchange rate strategy was letting the peso to become dangerously overvalued since domestic inflation did not go down as fast as the program required it. Consequently a devaluation or a change in plans was expected at any time. The net purchases of foreign currency by the central bank reached a maximum of US$ 438.0 million during the second quarter of 1979, while it was only US$ 67.5 million in the last quarter of the same year [See Table A-3].

The real interest rate became positive in 1980. Industrial production went down. Net sales to authorized agencies to deal with foreign exchange by the central bank were equal to US$ 4,124.2 million. The traditional effect of real appreciation and higher real wages was still valid in Argentina during the Martinez de Hoz period. Nevertheless, the new institutional framework did alter the usual path towards a foreign exchange crisis and a recession. Therefore, at least in the case of Argentina, the failure cannot be related to the trade and capital liberalization per se. This also emphasizes that since the same traditional variables were behind the balance of payments crisis at the end of program, no fundamental structural changes took place in 1976-81.

5.4. THE ORDER OF ECONOMIC LIBERALIZATION.

There are three core controversial points that have emerged in studies of the liberalization attempt as emphasized by Edwards (1984): 1) the speed of liberalization: gradualism or shock treatment?, 2) the order of liberalization: how the order of liberalizing the current and capital account should be tackled in the path from a repressed economy into a liberalized one; and 3) the order of liberalization and stabilization: e.g., should the economy be first stabilized and then liberalized? A forth point is generally considered: the net welfare effects of liberalization. The first one aforementioned has a similar controversy in the stabilization literature. With respect to the last one, theory has stressed the positive net benefits of trade as well as financial liberalization.

Our concern here was with the second and third issues referred above: Further insights could be reached if both issues were interrelated by analyzing the (potential) disequilibrium that may have appeared in the trade account, government finances, and between savings and investment, during a liberalization process. The analysis here can help us to determine the presence of inconsistencies in the Argentine economic program.

5.4.1 An Overview

In studies done by McKinnon and Mathieson (1981) and McKinnon (1982b), it was argued that: 1) before starting any open-up of the economy, a process of stabilization must take place coupled with a liberalization of the domestic financial market: since in developing countries, the government generally relies on the inflationary tax to finance the public sector deficit; an increase in the interest rate together with keeping (non-interest-bearing) reserves requirements (high), provides additional net revenues to the government. That is, the inflationary tax falls heavily on demand deposits, on the official banking reserves, as well as on time deposits reserves[7]; and 2) the trade account has to be opened before the capital account.

The aforementioned authors also pointed out that due to the fact that transactions and holdings of the domestic currency are being taxed, exchange controls and capital movements restrictions must be imposed[8]. Under these circumstances, a freely floating exchange rate cannot be implemented. During the transition period, until government finances become under control, they propose the use of a passive crawling-peg. Only after the government reduces its need of an inflationary tax a further liberalization of the financial market can take place (e.g., reduction of reserves requirements) and the current account can be opened. While the trade liberalization takes place, it must be avoided a real appreciation of the exchange rate and/or a significant accumulation of foreign reserves which can undermine the anti-inflationary plan. This requires once again, the control of capital flows. Once trade and domestic financial liberalization are completed (together with a reduction of the government deficit), the exchange rate policy must change from a passive crawling-peg to an active one (accompanied by the elimination of indexation rules) in order to reduce inflation to an international rate. At this stage, the government loosens exchange and capital movements controls to also bring about a decline in the domestic interest rate.

In the above argument, there is a strong reason against opening the capital account before the current account <u>and</u> before the stabilization of the economy is reached: since liberalization attempts have taken place in high inflationary countries, no exchange and capital movements restrictions can be lifted until the stabilization of the purchasing power of the domestic currency has been achieved. Otherwise, due to currency substitution (CS) in those countries, it will be even harder to reduce the inflation rate and, as pointed out by Tanzi and Blejer (1982) the required interest rate to discourage CS can be much higher than the required one to promote (real) investments. Furthermore, although a decline in the rate of domestic inflation is not guaranteed by trade liberalization itself, it is through this policy that an improvement in the allocation of resources can be achieved, thus lower costs and less inflation. Consequently, trade liberalization can help to stabilize the value of the domestic currency while the open-up of the capital account cannot as pointed out before, particularly due to the net (potential) inflow of capital which exasperates the anti-inflationary plan.

Frenkel (1982) supported McKinnon-Mathieson's argument [9]. He emphasized that the speed of adjustment is faster in the asset market than in the goods market. Given the uncertainty involved during the transition towards equilibrium, he argued (p. 200), "it is easier to reverse wrong portfolio decisions than to reverse wrong real investment decisions", therefore the capital account must be opened after the trade account. Note, that if businessmen believe the capital account will be opened in the very near future, they may use the international interest rate (adjusted by difference in the expected foreign and domestic inflation rate) as the discount rate to determine the rate of return on a specific real investment. On the other hand, it is plausible that it may take longer for the domestic relative price structure to reflect the international
one;
thus, meanwhile investment decisions are based on distorted prices. At this stage, Frenkel's argument becomes relevant to propose opening first the current account. On the other hand, Edwards (1984), in spite of a well-done theoretical framework developed to answer the second controversy, has to conclude that no definitive theorem can be advanced. It seems to be more "prudent", as he wrote, to liberalize the current account first due to the effects of capital flows on the real exchange rate.

Summing up, stabilization (i.e. a substantial reduction of the fiscal deficit and of the inflation rate) coupled with domestic financial liberalization should take place before opening the capital account and this can only occur after the current account was completely opened. Therefore, according to this argument, the Argentine government made a terrible mistake in allowing a de facto free capital and currency movement when the trade liberalization was not still completed. In particular, the timing of the implementation of the active crawling-peg (preannouncement of the exchange rate) was miscalculated.

5.4.2 A Further Insight

Some of the points presented in the previous section can be generally supported if it is taking into account that three main imbalances can appear or worsen in the process of liberalization: in the trade account, between savings and investment, and the government deficit.

A (potential) trade deficit may show up because importers (in developing countries), use to trade restrictions and balance of payments crises, will take advantage of the trade liberalization. Inventories of imported capital goods and raw materials (essential inputs in the production process) will be built up. Higher imports can be financed by

credits from exporters who are eager to grant them in an expanding
market for their products; by taking a loan in the domestic financial
market and then buying the foreign currency from the central bank, by
taking a loan in the international market if no restrictions apply, or by
using the firm's own financial capital to get the required foreign exchange. Higher imports of consumer goods can also take place because
local consumers may want to adquire the latest consumer durable goods
available, generally at a price cheaper than the domestic (old-techno-
logy) ones. On the export side, agricultural exports will take some time
to respond to export incentives due to a natural cycle; while manufactured exports can be difficult to raise immediately since potential customers must be convinced of a steady supply, quality control, and services and spare parts promptly available.

The role of multinationals become important in this transition period
because it is much easier to convince customers to buy a world-wide
well-known brand than a domestic (international unknown) one. This
effect of the liberalization policy can be interpreted by local politicians
as helping only the multinationals rather than the domestic firms, thus
restrictions on foreign investment or policy-bias against multinationals'
exports may arise, hindering export growth. Besides, developing countries hardly grant export credits which can handicap an increase in exports even further. Therefore, it is quite plausible to expect a trade
deficit at the beginning of (trade) liberalization. Under these circumstances, the exchange rate policy becomes crucial, particularly, if an
increase in (short-term) foreign indebtedness wants to be avoided. In
order to increase export competitiveness and to smooth away the impact
of tariff reductions, a real depreciation is called upon during the transition towards full-liberalization. The Argentine policy-makers made a
terrible mistake for not recognizing this and for directing the exchange
rate policy towards lowering the inflation rate rather than in promoting
exports. The authorities can also start with a partial-trade liberalization
program on the export side. Once a target export level has been
achieved to finance the expected increase in imports, only then, can
trade liberalization be completed by dismantling all remaining trade barriers. However, this policy can prove to have some inflationary impact
because, for instance, resources will not be released from the import-
competing industries. Then the order of liberalization can be also ques-
tioned within the same "account".

Another imbalance needs consideration: higher foreign competition
through a reduction in trade barriers will certainly require that after
several decades of protection, domestic producers start a process of
investments, adopting new technologies or improving their efficiency.
An increase in the demand for working capital is therefore foreseeable
in the transition period towards lower domestic costs. Hence, a rise in
domestic savings must take place as well. Again, if higher foreign indebtedness wants to be avoided, a significant increase in domestic savings is required. This is generally achieved by a relative increase in
the return of domestic financial assets through a liberalization of the
financial market (e.g., interest rates are freely determined or interest
rates ceilings will be changed). Higher interest rates can be an important step in achieving higher savings, although this is not always guarantee as the Argentine experience has shown. That is, giving the fact
that foreign currency can be extensively used, as a store of value,
unit of account, and medium of exchange; a consistent exchange-inter-

est-rate policy is necessary to discourage capital flights or the holding of foreign financial and real assets. By consistent, it is meant, for instance: a (passive) crawling-peg with modifications in interest rate ceilings or a flexible rate with freely determined interest rates. However, it is more appropriate that the burden of adjustment (e.g., due to changes in expectation) during the transition period falls on both variables rather than only on the exchange rate (assuming fixed interest rates) or only on the interest rate (assuming a fixed exchange rate). As pointed out before, since a flexible exchange rate cannot be implemented as long as exchange and capital movements controls are in effect, it follows that during the adjustment period the government should keep under control the exchange and the interest rates. Here, the Argentine authorities made another important mistake by sticking to their exchange rate policy and allowing the full burden of adjustment to fall on the interest rate.

Given the above argument, with total trade liberalization a simultaneous liberalization of the domestic financial market-cum-consistent exchange rate policy must take place. This can also mean to ease restrictions on international capital movements if the financing of the trade deficit plus the need for higher savings, must come from abroad. In other words, trade and capital accounts liberalization should occur together if the country is not able to rely on an increase in domestic savings during the transition period to finance both disequilibria. This implies that a rise in foreign indebtedness is unavoidable during a liberalization process, thus exports must go up more in countries with low savings. Finally, note that if domestic financial liberalization takes place before complete trade liberalization, it can be even more difficult to reduce inflation due to the accumulation of foreign reserves not compensated by a lower trade surplus.

With respect to the third controversial point presented in the introduction, several alternatives are worthwhile to consider: 1) stabilization first and then total liberalization (trade plus capital accounts); 2) stabilization-cum-liberalization (broad liberalization measures are implemented to stabilize the economy); 3) stabilization-cum-partial trade liberalization and then total liberalization.

McKinnon (1982b, p. 160) stressed once again that "control over public finances is a necessary condition for escaping from the repression of domestic financial processes that in turn is necessary for the full liberalization of foreign trade". There are several other reasons why stabilization must occur before liberalization: 1) part of government revenues come from taxing exports and imports, thus a decline in these sources of revenues must be compensated by a decline in expenditure; 2) the impact of the government deficit, financed through public bonds can set a floor to the domestic interest rate which can encourage a net "undesirable" inflow of capital, in turn, a non-sterilized accumulation of international reserves can bring about higher domestic inflation; 3) the diversion of financial resources from the private sector at a time when the latter is in an urging need to finance new projects and working capital, can soar interest rates, and 4) if the government decides to implement some kind of unemployment compensation during the transition period, this will increase the government deficit which can undermine the liberalization process.

The characteristics of the Argentine economic program during the second phase can be categorized within the second alternative. However, it can be considered that the case of stabilization-cum-partial trade liberalization has the twofold advantage of reducing the recessionary impact of the decline in government expenditures, and in building-up international reserves with the purpose of financing a further push in trade liberalization to avoid an increase in foreign indebtness. Thus, a stabilization program coupled with a transfer of resources towards the export sector through a clear export promotion policy may avoid the unstable accumulation of reserves due to short-term capital inflows. The effect of this approach on inflation will depend on how close the economy is to the full-employment level.

APPENDIX FOR CHAPTER 5

THE INFLUENCE OF THE ARGENTINE PESO EXPECTED DEVALUATION RATE ON US DOLLAR DEPOSITS IN URUGUAY, II-1977/II-1981

Another approach that may be undertaken to prove the significance of the CS phenomenon in Argentina, is to see if foreign currency deposits in Uruguay were affected by changes in the expected rate of devaluation of the Argentine peso relative to the US dollar. That is, an increase in the expected rate of devaluation in Argentina would encourage asset-holders in that country to shift into foreign currency deposits in Uruguay. The latter has been generally considered a safe place for investments by Argentinians. Besides, its capital-city is very close to Buenos Aires and this makes it easier to transfer foreign currency personally without the need for intermediaries and legal paper-work.

The central bank of Uruguay publishes data on foreign currency deposits classified by ownership as: residents and non-residents. In 1976, 80 percent of the deposits were owned by residents. In 1981, half of the deposits were owned by non-residents. If most of the classified as non-residents were Argentinians, they would have deposits of almost US\$ 900 million in the Uruguayan banking system in 1981. These figures should be read with care for two reasons: (1) other Latin-Americans may also own part of the foreign currency deposits, and (2) until 1979, it was not carefully checked whether the owner of a deposit classified as resident was really one. Therefore, the amount of foreign currency owned by non-residents could be underestimated.

Our next step was to estimate the demand for foreign currency deposits in Uruguay as a function of: (1) the real ex-post interest rate on local currency deposits, (2) the real ex-post interest rate on foreign currency deposits, (3) the expected rate of devaluation of the Argentine peso, and (4) M_2 (broad definition of money) as a proxy for income since no quarterly data were available for this variable. The expected sign of the domestic interest rate coefficient is negative, for foreign interest rate positive, and for the expected rate of devaluation and for the income both positive [see Tables U-2 and U-5]. The econometric result is presented below:

$$LnTDFC_t = -3.6287 - 0.0706 \ LLnTDFC_t + 1.3876 \ LlnM_{2t} -$$
$$(-3.2142) \quad (-0.1763) \quad\quad (2.8914)$$

$$-3.2599 \ LnRILC_t + 2.5720 \ LnRIFC_t + 0.1404 \ X_t^e$$
$$(-1.2780) \quad\quad (0.8045) \quad\quad (2.7875)$$

$$\bar{R}^2 = 0.9586 \quad dw = 2.1712 \quad s.e.e. = 0.0654$$

where

LnTDFC= Ln of total foreign currency deposits in the Uruguayan banking system expressed in constant Uruguayan pesos,

LLnTDFC = LnTDFC lagged one period,

$LLnM_2$ = M_2 lagged one period expressed in constant Uruguayan pesos,

LnRILC = the real ex-post interest rate of local currency deposits in Uruguay calculated as: $[Ln (1+i_{dt}) - ln (1+\pi_t)]$, where the nominal interest rate (i) and the wholesale inflation rate (π) are average in the period,

LnRIFC = the real ex-post interest rate of foreign currency deposits in Uruguay. The nominal deposit interest rate is the sum of the ex-post average rate of the Uruguayan peso devaluation in the period and the average international interest rate paid on foreign currency time deposits in Uruguay. The wholesale inflation rate is also the average in the period. The real interest rate on foreign currency time deposits was calculated the same as LnRILC.

X^e = the Argentine peso expected rate of devaluation (the same variable was used to estimate the monetary sector equations for Argentina).

The estimated time period was from the second quarter of 1977 to the second quarter of 1981 and a partial adjustment approach was used. The method of estimation was OLS.

The above results confirm the relevant effect of the Argentine expected rate of devaluation on foreign currency deposits in Uruguay. The coefficient of the dependent variable lagged one period indicates a very low value for the average adjustment period (0.07); this result suggests that the adjustment between the desired and the actual demand for foreign currency is almost instantaneous. This implies that the estimated short-run and long-run coefficients are practically the same because   is almost equal to one. However, since our sample is very small the estimated value of long-run coefficients may be biased. Also note that the estimated coefficients of both interest rates, although of the expected sign, are statistically insignificant, which can indicate that most of the foreign currency deposits in Uruguay were owned by Argentinians during the period of analysis.

NOTES

[1] Some articles that based the failure particularly on implementation errors and other inconsistencies can be found in Barletta, Blejer and Landan (eds., 1983). For authors that criticized the liberalization attempts in the Southern Cone, see: Felix (1981, 1983), Foxley (1983), French-Davis (1983), Ledesma (1981), Ramos (1984). Other related articles are by Noguès (1984), Mathieson (1982), Frenkel (1981), Diaz-Alejandro (1981), Dornbusch (1984), Dagnino-Pastore (1983), Fernández (1982). For an official account of the "success" of the Argentine Program, see Martinez de Hoz (1982).

[2] See Eshaz and Thorp (1965), Maynard and van Rijckeghen (1968), Calvo (1981), Dornbusch (1982), Cardoso (1982), Khan and Knight (1982), and in particular, <u>Economic Stabilization in Developing Countries</u>, a book edited by Cline (1981) for an extensive theoretical and empirical research on that topic.

[3] The preannounced schedule of exchange rate devaluation was popularly known as "la tablita".

[4] During the first phase real wages were declining and the real effective exchange rate was depreciating for primary products according to calculations presented by Noguès (1984). Therefore, it was expected that the country experienced a recession, a balance of payments surplus, and high inflation.

[5] It was assumed that "q" was a constant equal to zero. This assumption was not so incorrect since "q" was a policy instrument that did not vary ramdonly. However, it may have overestimated the expected rate of devaluation before 1979, without affecting its trend. On the other hand, the exclusion of a risk term can be considered a more serious mistake; Blejer (1982) suggested that this may not be so. See also note [7] in Chapter four.

[6] Quasi-money (time and savings deposits in real terms, TD) was also estimated. The results obtained are shown below (t-values between parenthesis):

$$LnTD_t = 2.8571 + 0.7226 \ LnTD_{t-1} - 0.084 \ LnX_t^e +$$
$$ (5.4200) \quad (13.6378) \phantom{LnTD_{t-1}} (-1.3596)$$

$$0.1522 \ Ln \ (1 + i_{dt}/1 + \pi_t)$$
$$(2.1843)$$

$\bar{R}^2 = 0.9401 \qquad DW = 2.2191 \qquad$ average adjustment period = 2.60

The income coefficient turned out to be positive but again statistically insignificant when included in the regression.

[7] The implementation in 1977 of an account of monetary regulation (cuenta de regulación monetaria) during the financial reform was a terrible mistake according to this argument. Through this account, the central bank would pay an interest rate on the amount of the legal reserves of time deposits while commercial banks would pay an interest rate for that use of sight deposits as credit. There-

fore, the government was paying back the inflationary tax to financial entities, reducing its revenue and hindering the fight against inflation. For further details on this account see Fischer and Trapp (1984).

[8] Recall that the Argentine government allowed the public to buy and sell foreign currency with very few restrictions at a time when domestic inflation still remained at a very high rate.

[9] Jacob Frenkel (1982) comment of the McKinnon (1982b) paper.

6 The southern cone liberalization experience: a comparison of macroeconomic events, 1976-81

6.1. INTRODUCTION

Around the mid-1970's the Southern Cone countries implemented similar economic programs, not only in their goals but also in the policies chosen to achieve them as shown in the Figure 6.1 below. One of the most important reforms introduced in these countries took place in their financial system. Among other things, this reform was aimed at allowing domestic interest rate to be freely determined. This was expected to make the real interest rate positive, which would increase the demand for domestic interest-bearing monetary assets and improve the allocation of resources by stopping the explicit subsidy that a negative real interest rate offered the borrower. One should bear in mind that previously the interest rate was controlled by the authorities and it was generally set at a rate below the domestic inflation rate. Another measure implemented in this reform was to lift restrictions on capital movement in order to facilitate borrowing by local firms in the international financial market.

We will discuss here the interest and exchange rate policies implemented in Argentina, Chile, and Uruguay in order to find points in common and similar outcomes under the same institutional framework. We are concerned with:

(1) the relationship between manufacturing output and the real lending interest rate,
(2) the relationship between the demand for financial assets denominated in local currency and their real deposit interest rate,
(3) the relationship between the demand for foreign currency the exchange rate and the domestic interest rate policy.

It is assumed that: (1) there is a negative relationship between the level of the real lending interest rate and the level of industrial activity, (2) a positive one between the demand for local monetary assets and their own rate of return and a negative one with respect to alternative assets rate of return, and (3) the demand for foreign currency is mainly affected by its return through the exchange rate policy, other things being equal [1].

FIGURE 6.1

SOUTHERN CONE COUNTRIES – ECONOMIC PROGRAM

Problems
———— a high and persistent rate of inflation
———— recurrent balance of payments crises
———— very slow economic growth

Economic program

objectives
———— to better allocation of resources
———— to strengthen the balance of payments position
———— to reduce inflation
———— to sustain economic growth

instruments
———— reduction in public sector deficit (particularly through lower government expenditures)
———— free determination of prices and domestic interest rates (open-up capital account)
———— trade liberalization (reduction in tariffs) (open-up trade account)
———— exchange rate:

    ———— Argentina ———— crawling-peg (1976-77)
    ———— flexible (1978)
    ———— preannounced (1979-81)

    ———— Chile ———— crawling-peg (1973-78)
    ———— preannounced (1978)
    ———— fixed (1979-1982)

    ———— Uruguay ———— crawling-peg: dual exchange market (1972-78)
    ———— preannounced (1979-82)

outcome
———— high real domestic interest rates – unstable growth –
———— overvaluation – balance of payment crisis

6.2. FIRST RELATIONSHIP

This relationship is graphically shown in the Figures 6.2 below. In the Argentine case, as expressed before, the business cycle experienced from 1977 to 1981 can be clearly related to the changes in the real lending interest rate. In 1977, manufacturing output grew by 7.7 percent in real terms with respect to the previous year while the average lending real interest rate was -2.5 percent in the same year. However, after the financial reform took place in June 1977, the real interest rate showed a tendency to become positive. During the last quarter of 1977, it became drastically positive (52.2 percent annual rate), following the same trend in 1978. In the latter year, industrial production declined by 10.5 percent and the net purchases of foreign currency by the central bank reached a maximum of US$ 1,130.3 million in the second quarter, while it was US$ 404.2 million in the same quarter of 1977 (See Table A.3). This suggests that the higher real return on domestic monetary assets encouraged people to dishoard foreign currency and also encouraged an inflow of foreign capital by non-residents. Again, 1979 showed a higher level of economic activity associated with a negative or slightly positive interest rate while the contrary happened in 1980-1981.

In the Chilean case, the negative relationship between the real lending interest rate and industrial activity is less evident. The interest rate remained highly positive from 1976 to 1981, at 35 percent average annual rate in each year, while production grew by an average annual rate of 6 percent. Uruguay seems to support the fact that having moderate positive real lending interest rates (e.g. less than 10 percent real annual rate), made it possible to have acceptable growth rates (e.g. industrial production grew by an average of 5.1 percent from 1976 to 1980 while the average real lending interest rate was 1.2 percent over the same years), without the need to subsidize economic activity with a negative real interest rate. Consequently, there seems to be no support for the need of a negative real lending interest rate to encourage industrial production. Positive real interest rates have been associated with more than historical average growth in Chile and Uruguay with the exception of Argentina. However, this can be a misleading conclusion.

In Chile and Uruguay, around 50 percent of the commercial bank loans to the private sector were made in foreign currency from 1975 to 1982. When it is weighted the real interest rate according to the percentage of loans made in local and foreign currency by commercial banks; in 1978 the Chilean real weighted lending interest rate was equal to 14.3 percent average in the year, quite below the 33.0 percent reported for the cost of domestic credit. In Argentina, loans in foreign currency represented only 15 percent of total credit granted to the private sector by commercial banks from the second quarter of 1977 to the first quarter of 1981. When the real cost of foreign borrowing is also considered, the real weighted interest rate becomes negative or slightly positive. We need to emphasize that our analysis involves ex-post rates and does not take into account all the taxes and fees that were included in contracting a foreign loan, therefore the cost of foreign borrowing may be underestimated.

FIGURE 6.2.A

ARGENTINA - MANUFACTURING PRODUCTION AND THE REAL LENDING IN-
TEREST RATE[a], 1977-81

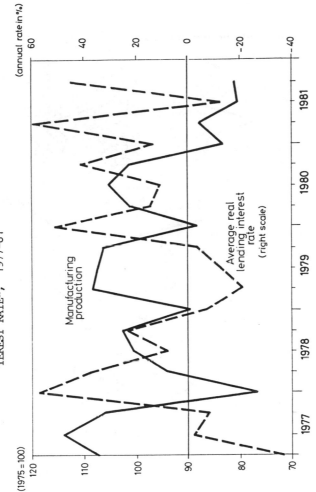

Sources: Tables A-1 and A-1.1

a/ Manufacturing production corresponds to the period 't' and the real
   lending interest rate to 't-1'.

FIGURE 6.2.B

CHILE — MANUFACTURING PRODUCTION AND THE REAL LENDING INTEREST
RATE, 1976–81

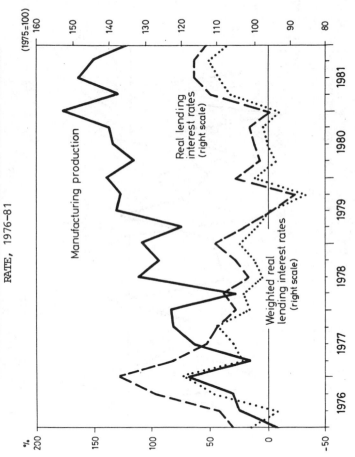

Source: Table C-1

111

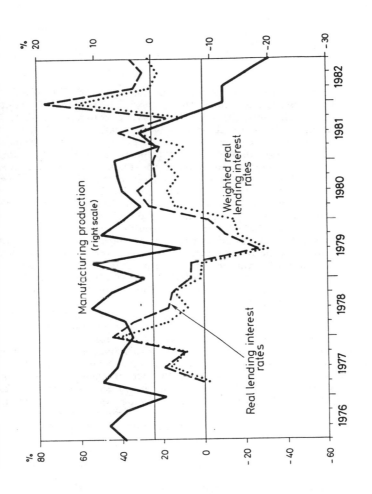

FIGURE 6.2.C

URUGUAY – MANUFACTURING PRODUCTION AND THE REAL LENDING INTEREST RATE, 1978-82

Source: Table U-1

6.3 SECOND AND THIRD RELATIONSHIPS

With respect to our concern with the second relationship, there is no doubt about the positive effect of the interest rate reform in increasing the demand for local interest-bearing monetary assets. Time and savings deposits denominated in local currency experienced a fourfold increase in Argentina and Uruguay in real terms, and an elevenfold rise in Chile (from December 1975 to December 1982). The real ex-post deposit interest rate reached positive levels or was slightly negative during much of the period (See Figures 6.3). However, although we are urged to conclude that by increasing the real return on domestic money, there will be a rise in the demand for local monetary interest-bearing assets, it is important to consider the exchange rate policy implemented at the same time.

In Argentina, while the government implemented the (open devaluations) crawling-peg policy until the second quarter of 1978 coupled with a financial liberalization, it seemed to have encouraged a shift into local monetary assets. The central bank was generally a net buyer of foreign currency. But after the exchange rate policy changed from crawling-peg to a flexible one (in April 1978), there was a tendency for the exchange rate to appreciate, increasing the expectation of a future depreciation. In the third quarter of 1978, the net purchases of foreign currency by the central bank were reduced by half relative to the previous quarter, and it became a net seller in the last quarter before the new exchange rate policy was announced in December 1978 and, a the same time, real time deposits in local currency decreased by 14 percent. According to this new policy, the future path of the devaluation rate was going to be announced some time in advance. CS was discouraged at the beginning of this policy, because the public believed that the government was committed to defend this strategy. However, the fact that the exchange rate was becoming increasingly overvalued made the expectation of a change in plans quite likely. Although, the central bank bought foreign currency from authorized agencies during 1979, every quarter showed a decline in the amount purchased [see Table A-3]. In 1980, the central bank had to sell foreign currency in order to defend the preannouncement of the exchange rate strategy. This suggests that people started to shift into foreign currency. Such a shift was reflected in the real growth rate of time deposits denominated in local currency. In 1979, deposits grew by 35 percent, in 1980 only 6 percent and in 1981 they declined by 23 percent. It is surprising that in spite of a 28.8 percent real average deposit interest rate from the third quarter of 1980 to the first quarter of 1981, real time deposits practically experienced no growth.

The Chilean case shows that the high real deposit interest rate, coupled with a fixed exchange rate policy, encouraged asset-holders to hold time and savings deposits denominated in local currency rather than foreign currency from June 1979 to June 1982: time and savings deposits denominated in local currency grew by 156 percent while foreign currency deposits grew by 41 percent both in real terms. The implementation of the fixed exchange made foreign currency deposits decline as a percentage of total quasi-money from 7.8 percent in March 1979 to 3.0 percent in March 1982. In 1982, when there were expectations of an important devaluation, since the Chilean peso lost almost 40 percent of its value since June 1979, local currency deposits started to

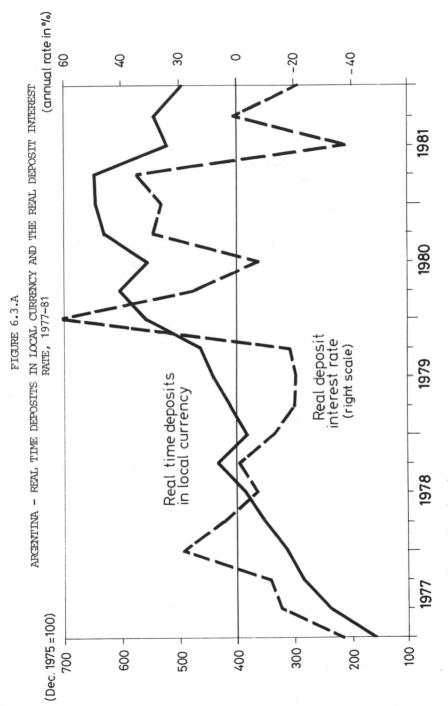

FIGURE 6.3.A

ARGENTINA - REAL TIME DEPOSITS IN LOCAL CURRENCY AND THE REAL DEPOSIT INTEREST
RATE, 1977-81

Source: Tables A-2 and A-4

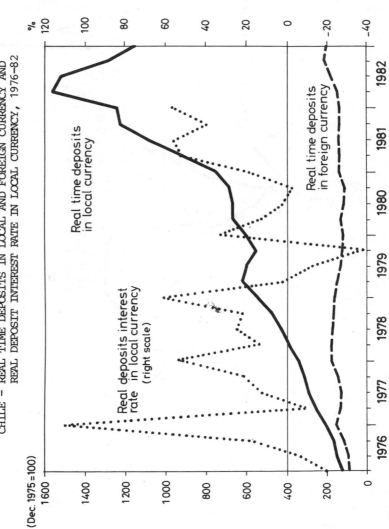

FIGURE 6.3.B

CHILE - REAL TIME DEPOSITS IN LOCAL AND FOREIGN CURRENCY AND
REAL DEPOSIT INTEREST RATE IN LOCAL CURRENCY, 1976-82

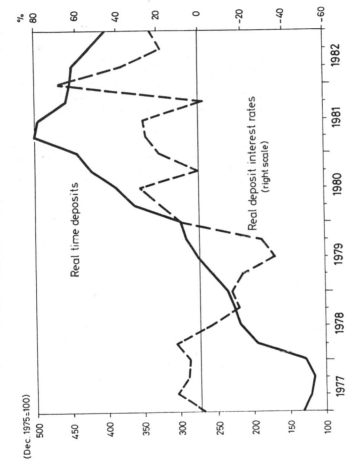

FIGURE 6.3.C

URUGUAY – REAL TIME DEPOSITS IN LOCAL CURRENCY AND REAL
DEPOSIT INTEREST RATE, 1977–82

(Dec. 1975=100)

Real time deposits

Real deposit interest rates
(right scale)

Sources: Tables U-6 and U-2

decline (26 percent in real terms by the end of the year) while foreign currency deposits started to increase (58 percent in real terms by the end of the year). One should stress that this happened in spite of the fact that the annual real deposit interest rate at commercial banks reached 50.6 percent. Also note that when the fixed rate was established in June 1979, the nominal lending as well as the deposit interest rates remained practically constant for almost four quarters. The same happened in Argentina and Uruguay after the implementation of the preannouncement of the exchange rate. This implies that people believed that there was not going to be a sudden change in policy, and the interest rate was mainly affected by exchange rate expectations.

In the case of Uruguay, local currency deposits grew 28 percent in real terms while foreign currency deposits experienced an almost three-fold increase from December 1975 to December 1977. Ex-post real deposit rates showed that the return on foreign currency deposits was higher than on local currency deposits until the end of 1977. However, it is difficult to assess how the changes in time and savings deposits in Uruguay were related to their reta of return because, it was already stressed in the previous chapter that a great deal of foreign currency deposits were owned by Argentinians.

Once the Uruguayan government implemented the preannouncement of the exchange rate strategy in December 1978 and until the end of 1982, when the policy was suspended, local currency deposits increased much faster than foreign currency deposits (See Table U-5). For instance, in 1980 the former grew by 48 percent against 14 percent for the latter. However, a closer look at foreign currency deposits classified according to ownership residence, showed that resident-foreign currency deposits only grew 5 percent while non-resident deposits increased by 72 percent. In 1981, despite the fact that the real rate of return for local currency deposits was much higher than for foreign currency deposits, the former increased by 2 percent while the latter rose by 73 percent in current dollar amounts (US dollar deposits owned by non-residents increased 65 percent and by residents 84 percent. See Figure 6.4).

In 1982, the appreciation of the Uruguayan peso suffered under the preannouncement of the exchange rate strategy (coupled with the fact in 1981 that the same policy was interrupted in Argentina, and followed by several maxi-devaluations) and the nationalization of foreign currency deposits in Mexico (Argentines were afraid that the Uruguayan government would do the same), brought about expectations of a change in Uruguayan exchange rate policy. In September 1982, foreign currency deposits represented 72 percent of total quasi-money but by the end of the year these deposits declined 30 percent in just three months. The central bank lost almost US$ 500 million, a significant amount given the small size of the domestic financial system. This does not mean that CS was not taking place. On the contrary, this implied that due to the lack of confidence, foreign currency was not coming back to the financial system. Finally, it is important to note that foreign currency deposits in Uruguay more than satisfied the amount of loans made to the private sector by commercial banks in foreign currency during much of the period 1976-1982.

Certainly, the macroeconomic effects of the economic program implemented in the Southern Cone countries were quite similar. However,

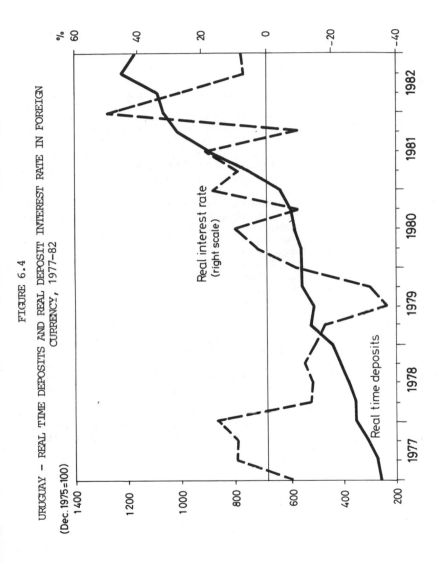

FIGURE 6.4

URUGUAY – REAL TIME DEPOSITS AND REAL DEPOSIT INTEREST RATE IN FOREIGN
CURRENCY, 1977–82

(Dec.1975=100)

Source: Tables U-2 and U-6

since the degree of liberalization was different in each country, with Chile in the extreme of deep liberalization measures, Uruguay in the other extreme and with Argentina in the middle; the microeconomic impact of the program must be also taken into account to judge the outcome of such a program; however, this goes beyond our objective here.

6.4   CONCLUSION

As suggested before, in the presence of CS, a real interest rate rather than a money growth rule would be more appropriate to stabilize domestic income. However, if the real interest rate is going up because the nominal interest rate is increasing due to an increase in the expected rate of devaluation or to a higher risk premium, then not even by following an interest rate rule will the authorities discourage local residents from shifting into foreign currency as well as avoiding the eventual adjustment of the exchange rate that everybody is expecting. But again, not even a freely determined interest rate would help. The only difference between both institutional arrangements would be that in the first one a recession would be avoided for a longer period of time than in the second case, but eventually the adjustment should occur. This is stressed by the fact that a very high real rate of return on local currency deposits did not discourage people from shifting into foreign currency. For instance, in Argentina from June 1980 to June 1981, local currency deposits went down by an average of 3.3 percent a quarter (in real terms) while before they were going up at an average of 10 percent a quarter in spite of a lower real return. Note that foreign currency deposits in Uruguay started to go up faster since June 1980, after several quarters of slow growth. Argentine asset-holders, therefore, shifted into foreign currency almost a year prior to the suspension of the preannouncement of the exchange rate. In Uruguay, quasi-money as well as currency and demand deposits started going down since the second quarter of 1981, while the exchange rate policy was changed at the end of 1982. Chileans increased their holdings of foreign currency deposits since December 1981 and local currency deposits started to go down since March 1982, that is, almost a year in prior to the end of the fixed exchange rate regime and the introduction of a flexible one.

The experience of these countries show that although policy-makers succeeded in increasing the demand for interest bearing denominated in local currency by allowing the domestic nominal interest rate to be freely determined, this policy proved to be successful as long as there was no expectation of an exchange rate change. Once this expectation arose, not even extremely high real rate of return on domestic currency could avoid the shift into foreign currency. Also note, the considerable lag that existed between the moment that the demand for local currency is affected by the change in expectations and the actual moment of the change in the exchange rate policy. This suggests that CS is not just a temporary phenomenon that takes place a short time before a devaluation is expected.

The Chilean experienced with fixed exchange rate was the most successful policy to discourage asset-holders to shift into foreign currency deposits. The credibility of this policy was based on the significant reduction in the rate of inflation that Chile experienced since 1979. The interest rate remained stable for almost one year and manufacturing production grew by 8 percent. But Argentina and Uruguay also experienced stable interest rates, increased economic activity, and apparently a reduction in CS after the implementation of the preannouncement of the exchange rate. This suggests that it is important to establish a credible exchange rate policy or a policy that keeps expectations constant (e.g., if people believe that the exchange rate is undervalued, then there would not be any reason to shift into foreign currency).

A final lesson that may be drawn is that in countries where CS is believed to be a significant phenomenon, the government should allow financial intermediaries to accept foreign currency deposits. This would avoid that asset-holders keep their foreign currency "under the mattress" or send it abroad. This may have a positive effect because the foreign currency will not be an unproductive asset, money supply will not go down (its composition is just changing), and, besides, there will be no effect from a balance of payments point of view since no capital outflows will occur. The stability of this system will depend on the public's expectation of the full convertibility of the deposits at any moment. The Argentine case stressed that not even by allowing local financial intermediaries to accept foreign currency deposits, did residents deposit their foreign currency balances in the local financial sector rather than send them abroad or keep them "under the mattress" (recall that foreign currency deposits were never guaranteed by the government in case of a bank default, as local currency deposits always were) [2].

In sum, policy-makers should recognize the importance of reducing CS. This will be achieved by implementing a credible exchange rate policy and a consistent interest rate policy. However, it seems, according to the experience of the Southern Cone countries, that the most important measure to eradicate CS is through a drastic reduction in the domestic inflation rate. The anti-inflationary program, so-called "plan Austral", implemented in Argentina since June 1985 should be welcome and considered as an indication that the Argentine people and authorities have finally realized that there is no room for sustained economic growth and development within a high-inflation economy [3].

NOTES

[1] The tables refer in this chapter can be found in the Statistical Appendix II.

[2] During the government of President Alfonsin, it was stablished for the first time an official-guarantee to bank deposits in foreign currency however the public's reaction was quite disappointed. Only after the implementation of the "plan Austral" in June 1985 which has a clear and a drastic anti-inflationary purpose, seems to be that a significant reduction in currency substitution has taken place in the Argentine economy according to preliminary figures (rise in bank depositis and capital inflow) and news report.

[3] The implementation of the anti-inflationary program in Brazil, "plan Tropical", since March 1986 seems to be another indication that the high-inflation economies of Latin-America are understanding the need to promote growth and development without embarking in inflationary policies. Note that most of policies implemented in the Argentine and Brazilian plans were quite similar to the ones suggested in this study.

Statistical Appendix I

STATISTICAL APPENDIX I

TABLE 1

ARGENTINA - PRINCIPAL MACROECONOMIC INDICATORS, 1958-1981[a]

Year	GDP	WPI	Agric	Inds	Serv	Intern reserv [b]	Consump	GDI	Exports [c]	Imports [c]	real exch rate [d]
1958	8.0	31.5	4.4	8.4	-4.3	-	5.6	9.6	0.6	-7.3	269
1959	-6.4	133.7	-1.0	-10.3	7.3	-	-7.4	-11.3	1.4	-19.6	137
1960	7.5	15.5	1.7	10.1	7.5	258	3.2	47.3	6.8	25.6	118
1961	6.9	10.0	-0.7	10.0	7.5	-232	10.0	9.6	-10.3	17.3	108
1962	-0.9	27.3	4.1	-5.5	-0.7	1297	-4.2	-8.0	25.8	-7.4	137
1963	-3.7	42.9	2.0	-4.2	-2.6	141	-2.0	-18.0	12.5	-27.4	94
1964	11.7	30.0	7.0	15.5	6.9	-74	10.2	26.0	3.1	9.5	83
1965	8.7	30.8	6.0	17.3	7.6	127	8.2	7.3	3.4	9.3	79
1966	0.8	20.6	-3.7	0.0	1.6	26	0.8	-7.2	3.3	-9.4	86
1967	3.2	25.6	4.3	1.6	2.0	541	2.5	4.5	-8.3	-2.7	116
1968	3.9	9.3	-5.4	8.1	4.5	33	3.9	10.6	-9.9	4.2	106
1969	8.9	6.4	5.5	10.4	6.8	-222	6.0	21.5	13.5	29.7	100
1970	4.1	14.0	5.6	6.8	4.0	185	3.8	7.4	6.0	3.6	100
1971	5.9	39.0	-5.0	10.1	4.5	-384	6.2	10.2	-5.1	6.8	90
1972	3.7	76.7	-7.9	4.6	3.4	-167	2.5	5.2	6.7	-2.4	51
1973	4.8	50.4	16.8	6.6	4.2	921	6.9	0.6	48.8	3.7	34
1974	6.3	19.9	3.6	6.2	6.6	-51	8.9	4.6	1.3	36.8	28
1975	-1.1	192.5	-1.5	-2.9	0.5	-791	0.4	0.1	-31.1	-0.1	118
1976	-1.6	499.1	4.0	-4.0	-2.4	1192	-7.4	8.2	26.5	-24.7	88
1977	4.9	149.5	1.2	4.2	5.3	2226	2.1	19.7	35.9	29.5	77
1978	-3.7	146.0	1.7	-11.0	-1.8	1998	-2.7	-10.1	5.1	-14.9	52
1979	8.7	149.3	5.0	8.7	7.9	4442	12.5	6.4	8.4	53.6	34
1980	-0.5	75.4	-6.5	-4.3	2.9	-2796	5.2	6.1	-9.9	36.7	24
1981	-5.9	109.6	2.5	-14.8	-3.2	-3806	-3.5	-13.5	4.9	-17.7	42

Source: Own calculations based on Banco Central de la Republica Argentina (BCRA). Boletin Estadistico Mensual, and the IFS (the IMF, several numbers).

a/ Gross Domestic Product (GDP), WPI (Wholesale Price Index, general), Agricultrual output (Agric), Industrial output (Inds), Service sector output (Serv), Consumption (total) (Consump), Gross Domestic Investment (GDI) are all expressed in percentage growth rate in real terms with the exception of WPI that is the annual inflation rate.

b/ Intern reserv : international reserves are expressed in current dollar amount and reflect the change from the previous year. A negative sign indicates a decline in international reserves at the Argentine Central Bank.

c/ Exports and Imports indicate percentage change from the previous year, expressed in constant US dollar deflated by the US wholesale price index.

d/ The real exchange rate was obtained by deflating the nominal exchange rate (item RF in IFS) by the WPI, 1970 = 100.

TABLE 2

ARGENTINA - SECTORAL COMPOSITION OF REAL GDP AT FACTOR COST, 1955-80

(In percentage)

Sectors	1955	1960	1965	1970	1971	1972	1973	1974	1975	1976	1977	1978	1979	1980
Agriculture	19.2	16.6	17.0	12.4	11.6	11.3	11.9	11.7	11.7	12.3	11.9	12.5	12.2	11.4
Mining	0.7	1.1	1.4	1.8	1.7	1.7	1.6	1.5	1.5	1.5	1.6	1.7	1.6	1.7
Manufacturing	29.2	31.1	33.9	35.6	36.9	37.7	38.3	38.3	37.5	36.5	36.2	34.4	35.3	34.1
Construction	3.8	4.0	3.2	5.3	5.3	5.1	4.3	4.3	4.6	5.2	5.7	5.9	5.7	6.3
Electricity, gas, and water	1.1	1.2	1.8	2.3	2.4	2.5	2.6	2.6	2.8	2.9	2.9	3.1	3.1	3.4
Commerce, hotel and resteraunts	18.6	18.9	18.1	17.9	18.1	18.0	17.7	18.0	18.0	17.3	17.5	17.0	17.3	17.3
Transport, storage and communication	8.0	7.9	7.7	7.6	7.3	7.2	7.3	7.1	7.1	7.0	7.1	7.1	7.1	7.0
Banking	4.1	4.0	3.6	3.5	3.4	3.2	3.3	3.5	3.2	3.1	3.3	3.8	3.8	4.5
Government and other services	15.3	15.2	14.3	13.6	13.2	13.1	13.1	12.9	13.7	14.2	13.8	14.5	13.9	14.3
total	100.0	100.0	100.0	100.0	100.0	100.0	100.0	100.0	100.0	100.0	100.0	100.0	100.0	100.0

Source: Own calculations based on BCRA: Boletin Estadistico Mensual.

TABLE 3

ARGENTINA - BALANCE OF PAYMENTS IN MILLIONS OF CURRENT US$, 1958-81

Year	Merchandise Exports FOB	Imports CIF	Trade BCE	Current Account	Balance of Payments	Private Capital Movement: Long-term (net)	Private Capital Movement: Short-term (net)
1958	993.9	-1,232.6	-238.7	-256.0	- 214	60.5	-73.8
1959	1,009.0	- 993.0	16.0	14.2	119	73.0	6.0
1960	1,079.2	-1,249.3	-152.1	-197.3	173	245.7	- 29.9
1961	964.1	-1,460.3	-496.2	-572.0	- 140	158.9	125.5
1962	1,216.0	-1,356.5	-140.5	-268.0	- 315	297.9	-329.3
1963	1,365.5	- 980.7	384.8	243.0	- 175	160.1	-243.1
1964	1,410.5	-1,077.4	333.1	35.9	43	10.4	- 39.1
1965	1,488.0	-1,195.0	293.0	194.7	180	15.7	-176.8
1966	1,593.2	-1,124.0	469.2	255.7	104	- 36.7	-176.6
1967	1,464.5	-1,095.5	369.0	183.5	372	- 18.6	250.7
1968	1,367.9	-1,169.2	198.7	- 14.5	65	1.5	128.7
1969	1,612.1	-1,587/1	36.0	-219.3	- 147	71.9	- 78.5
1970	1,773.2	-1,694.1	79.1	-158.9	259.9	143.6	185.2
1971	1,740.4	-1,868.1	-127.7	-388.7	- 560.4	66.1	-397.6
1972	1,941.1	-1,905.7	36.4	-222.9	- 284.7	118.4	- 73.7
1973	3,266.0	-2,229.5	1036.5	720.7	731.2	4.4	150.9
1974	3,930.7	-3,634.9	295.8	127.2	94.7	- 50.2	- 61.6
1975	2,961.3	-3,946.5	-985.2	-1284.6	-1094.5	- 41.4	158.2
1976	3,916.1	-3,033.0	883.1	649.6	124.7	- 51.5	- 46.7
1977	5,651.8	-4,161.5	1490.3	1289.9	2479.0	691.9	458.9
1978	6,399.5	-3,833.7	2565.8	1833.6	3199.0	2269.6	-1555.8
1979	7,809.9	-6,711.5	1098.4	-550.1	4318.1	2734.9	1448.2
1980	8,021.4	-10,540.5	-2519.2	-4767.8	-2514.5	3927.0	-1958.9
1981 I	1,989.9	-2,614.0	-624.1	-2089.6	-2810.2	1901.3	-3946.6

Source: Banco Central de la Republica Argentia (Annual Reports).

a/ - = outflow, or deficit; + = inflow or surplus.

TABLE 4

ARGENTINA - COMPOSITION OF IMPORTS AS PERCENTAGE OF TOTAL IMPORT IN CURRENT US DOLLARS, 1951-1980

Categories	1951a/	1960a/	1970	1971	1972	1973	1974	1975	1976	1977	1978	1979	1980
Capital goods	25.0	45.0	21.5	22.4	24.0	17.1	11.9	14.2	17.0	26.7	18.6	23.4	22.7
Consumer goods	14.0	6.0	4.8	3.7	4.4	3.0	3.7	3.3	2.0	3.3	5.5	10.5	17.6
Raw Materials and Intermediate goods	46.0	37.0	69.0	67.3	67.9	72.4	70.0	69.4	64.0	53.8	53.6	49.8	49.5
Fuel and Lubricants	15.0	12.0	4.7	6.5	3.7	7.5	14.5	13.0	17.0	16.2	12.3	16.4	10.2
Total	100.0	100.0	100.0	100.0	100.0	100.0	100.0	100.0	100.0	100.0	100.0	100.0	100.0

Sources: Diaz-Alejandro (1970) and Ambito Financiero (suplemento estadistico) May 23, 1983 (p. 49).

a/ Diaz-Alejandro (1970), Tables No. 66 and 55.

TABLE 5

SOUTHERN CONE COUNTRIES - VELOCITY COEFFICIENTS, 1960-82

Year (End of Period)	Argentina V_1	V_2	Chile V_1	V_2	Uruguay V_1	V_2
1960	4.3	15.8	—	—	5.7	8.2
1961	4.5	15.4	—	—	5.9	8.5
1962	5.6	17.6	—	—	6.6	8.2
1963	5.8	15.4	—	—	6.1	5.3
1964	5.6	14.3	6.4	12.7	6.2	5.7
1965	6.2	15.3	9.3	17.8	4.9	6.5
1966	5.7	15.5	8.4	24.8	6.7	10.7
1967	5.4	15.5	11.0	16.2	5.4	10.6
1968	5.0	13.0	10.0	13.9	7.7	15.5
1969	6.2	11.4	10.7	13.3	6.5	16.0
1970	5.8	9.7	9.4	14.4	6.9	14.5
1971	5.9	10.3	6.0	10.8	5.4	11.8
1972	7.1	9.8	4.4	7.9	6.2	10.4
1973	6.2	9.0	5.4	4.7	7.0	13.8
1974	5.2	8.2	11.4	7.5	7.8	13.0
1975	5.2	18.7	13.7	9.0	9.8	10.5
1976	7.2	14.1	16.2	12.7	9.3	6.9
1977	9.0	7.0	17.1	11.4	10.1	5.0
1978	8.7	5.8	15.5	8.3	8.4	4.0
1979	10.0	4.7	14.8	7.7	9.3	4.0
1980	10.3	5.1	13.1	6.8	10.3	3.5
1981	11.6	4.2	16.5	5.2	—	—
1982	—	—	15.0	3.9	—	—
Average Velocities:						
1960-69	5.5	13.6	9.3 2/	16.5 2/	5.6	8.7
1970-80	7.3	9.3	11.6	9.2	8.2	8.9
1977-1981	9.9	5.4	—	—	—	—
1974-1981	—	—	14.8	8.6	—	—
1976-81	—	—	—	—	9.5	4.5

Source: Own calculations based on IFS (International Financial Statistics, the IMF).

1/ V_1 = GNP/M where for V_1, M is item 34 in IFS (narrow definition of money) and for V_2 is item 35 (quasi money).

2/ period 1964-1969.

TABLE 6

ARGENTINA - NOMINAL MONETARY INDICATORS EXPRESSED IN MILLIONS OF ARGENTINE PESOS; DOMESTIC AND US WHOLESALE PRICE INDEXES, 1959 - 76

Year	M_1	M1 annual growth	Currency	Demand Deposits	Quasi-Money	QM annual growth	WPI 1960=100	U.S. WPI 1960=100
1959	142.2	43.8	84.4	57.8	44.9	10.2	87	99.9
1960	178.7	25.7	105.4	73.3	60.1	33.9	100	100.0
1961	205.4	15.0	121.7	83.7	74.8	24.5	110	99.7
1962	219.7	6.9	135.4	84.3	85.5	14.3	140	99.8
1963	282.9	28.8	167.1	115.8	123.5	44.4	200	99.6
1964	395.7	39.9	227.8	167.9	178.9	44.9	260	99.8
1965	497.5	25.7	296.6	200.9	233.7	30.7	340	101.8
1966	671.7	35.0	396.9	274.8	289.4	23.8	410	105.2
1967	871.6	29.8	508.7	362.9	385.2	33.1	430	105.4
1968	1,105.0	26.8	591.5	513.5	528.4	37.2	470	108.0
1969	1,223.1	10.7	658.9	564.2	628.4	18.9	500	112.2
1970	1,467.8	20.0	761.7	706.1	799.0	27.2	570	116.3
1971	2,003.4	36.5	993.4	1,010.0	1,145.2	43.3	792	120.1
1972	2,882.4	43.9	1,315.7	1,566.7	1,905.8	66.4	1,400	125.5
1973	5,622.1	95.1	2,640.6	2,981.5	3,577.8	87.7	2,105	141.9
1974	8,888.0	58.1	4,312.5	4,575.5	5,647.1	57.8	2,524	168.7
1975	25,027.3	192.5	12,384.3	13,643.0	11,556.1	104.6	7,383	184.3
1976	92,733.7	256.2	41,162.5	51,571.2	61,663.8	433.6	44,229	192.8

Sources: BCRA (Boletin Estadistico Mensual) and IFS.

TABLE 7

ARGENTINA – MEAN AND STANDARD DEVIATION OF PRINCIPAL INDICATORS IN DIFFERENT PERIODS, 1959–81

Period (years)	WPI %	CPI %	GDP %	Agricul Prod %	Industr Prod %	Service Sector %	Consump %	GDI %	Constru %	Wages %	V_1	V_2	M_1	Q M	Monetary Base	Credit to the Public sector	Credit to the Private sector	X	M
1959-1981																			
mean	81.5	81.7	2.9	1.7	2.8	3.0	2.9	5.5	4.3	66.3	6.6	11.7	69.5	93.0	76.1	83.3	87.4	6.1	6.1
s	106.9	98.4	5.1	5.4	8.6	3.9	5.6	14.4	10.8	58.6	2.0	4.4	66.3	113.2	86.5	83.8	95.9	16.7	21.5
1959-63																			
mean	45.9	41.4	0.7	1.2	0.0	1.4	-0.1	3.9	-2.7	35.0	4.9	15.6	24.0	25.5	20.7	25.4	22.5	7.2	-2.3
s	50.7	40.8	6.3	2.1	9.4	5.6	6.8	26.3	16.6	23.7	0.7	1.4	14.1	14.0	17.7	14.0	11.6	23.4	23.0
1964-66																			
mean	27.1	27.4	7.1	3.1	10.9	5.4	6.4	8.7	4.8	32.8	5.8	15.2	33.5	33.1	35.7	38.2	29.6	3.3	3.1
s	5.7	4.9	5.6	5.9	9.5	3.3	5.0	16.6	1.3	3.5	0.3	0.8	7.2	10.8	7.3	13.3	4.3	0.2	10.9
1967-70																			
mean	13.8	16.7	5.0	2.5	6.7	4.3	4.1	11.0	14.9	15.3	5.6	12.4	21.8	29.1	18.7	9.6	28.8	5.8	8.7
s	8.5	9.2	2.6	5.3	3.7	2.0	1.5	7.4	4.6	11.0	0.5	2.5	8.5	7.9	16.9	2.7	11.3	11.0	14.3
1971-75																			
mean	75.7	72.0	3.9	1.2	4.9	3.8	5.0	4.1	1.0	71.9	5.9	11.2	85.2	72.0	100.1	105.6	83.4	4.1	9.0
s	68.5	63.7	3.0	9.7	4.8	2.2	3.5	4.1	8.4	58.4	0.8	4.3	64.1	24.3	84.2	77.6	66.6	28.9	16.0
1976-81																			
mean	188.2	193.3	0.3	1.3	-3.5	1.5	1.0	2.8	5.5	138.5	9.5	6.8	143.9	239.4	160.5	184.5	212.6	11.8	10.4
s	155.2	127.0	5.5	4.1	8.9	4.6	7.2	12.4	8.3	43.0	1.5	3.7	65.5	139.8	104.7	64.3	94.4	16.6	33.4

Source: Own calculations based on Tables 1, 5 and 6.

TABLE 8

ARGENTINA - ACTUAL AND POTENTIAL REAL GDP IN MILLIONS OF 1960
PESOS, 1955-80

YEAR	Actual GDP	Potential GDP [1]	GAP (3)-(2)	Internat Reserves In Months of Imports
1955	7,995.4	7,844.9	-150.50	5
1956	8,217.7	8,080.3	-137.40	4
1957	8,639.2	8,322.7	-316.50	3
1958	9,167.6	8,572.4	-595.20	1
1959	8,576.9	8,829.5	252.60	0
1960	9,249.4	9,182.7	- 66.70	5
1961	9,908.3	9,550.0	-358.30	3
1962	9,747.8	9,932.0	184.20	1
1963	9,514.3	10,329.3	815.00	3
1964	10,498.5	10,742.5	244.00	2
1965	11,457.8	11,172.2	-285.60	2
1966	11,529.6	11,619.1	89.50	2
1967	11,840.7	12,083.8	243.10	8
1968	12,345.1	12,567.2	222.10	8
1969	13,403.7	13,195.5	-207.20	4
1970	13,964.7	13,987.3	22.60	5
1971	14,785.0	14,826.5	41.50	2
1972	15,347.8	15,716.1	368.30	3
1973	16,070.6	16,659.1	588.50	7
1974	17,053.2	17,658.6	605.40	4
1975	16,905.2	18,541.5	1,636.30	1
1976	16,616.5	19,839.4	3,222.90	6
1977	17,437.4	21,426.6	3,989.20	10
1978	16,838.3	23,140.7	6,302.40	15
1979	18,248.0	24,529.2	6,281.20	17
1980	18,219.0	25,755.6	7,536.60	8

Source: BCRA (Boletin Estadistico Mensual) and own
estimations.

1/ the full-employment growth rate = $\dfrac{\text{average propensity to save}}{\text{capital-output ratio}}$

capital output ratio was assumed to be: 1955-59 = 6; 1960-69 =
5; 1970-80 = 4.

TABLE 9

ARGENTINA - OFFICIAL AND BLACK MARKET EXCHANGE RATE,
1958-75

YEAR (1)	OFFICIAL RATE 1/ (2)	BLACK RATE 1/ (3)	DIFFERENCE (%) (4)=[(3) - (2)]/(2)	OFFICIAL DEVALUATION RATE (5) =Δ(2) (%)	BLACK MKT DEVALUATION RATE (6) =Δ(3) (%)
1958	48.04	50.05		-	-
1959	79.19	79.57	0.5	64.8	59.0
1960	82.94	82.74	-0.2	4.7	4.0
1961	82.83	82.62	-0.2	- 0.1	- 0.2
1962	113.73	120.29	6.0	37.3	45.6
1963	138.29	138.02	-0.2	21.6	14.7
1964	139.88	157.52	12.6	1.2	14.1
1965	168.49	244.00	45.0	20.5	54.9
1966	207.45	243.79	18.0	23.1	- 0.1
1967	333.35	340.42	2.1	60.7	39.6
1968	350.00	350.50	0.1	5.0	3.0
1969	350.00	350.75	0.2	0.0	0.1
1970*	3.79	3.89	2.6	8.3	10.9
1971 2/	5.84	6.35	8.7	54.1	63.2
1072	9.85	11.88	20.6	68.7	87.1
1973	9.98	11.42	14.4	1.3	- 3.9
1974	9.98	17.00	70.3	0.0	48.9
1975	31.98	75.20	135.2	220.4	342.4

Source: BCRA (Boletin Estadistico Mensual) and Pick's
Currency Yearbook (several issues).

1/ defined as Argentine pesos per US$ 1.00 and corresponds to the
average exchange rate in the year.

2/ corresponds to the Financial Market rate from 1971 to 1975.

* the "new" peso was introduced in January 1970 by chopping
off two zeros.

TABLE 10

ARGENTINA - QUARTERLY GROWTH RATE OF PRINCIPAL INDICATORS, 1975-8

(In percent)

YEAR/ QUARTER	G.D.P. at market price 2/	Agricult. sector GDP	Industrial sector GDP	Banking sector GDP	Gross 3/ Domestic Investment	Average 4 inflation rate
1975	-0.8	-3.8	-2.6	-8.4	0.1	334.9
I	2.8	-2.6	1.7	0.9	3.9	5.2
II	1.0	-8.7	2.4	-5.3	6.6	11.3
III	-2.3	-1.5	-6.0	-14.5	-5.9	22.3
IV	-4.5	-2.0	-7.6	-14.3	-2.9	14.0
1976	-0.5	4.6	-3.0	- 4.2	8.2	347.5
I	-1.6	7.7	-4.5	-12.9	2.8	21.3
II	-2.4	1.2	-5.9	-11.6	9.1	15.5
III	2.0	3.7	-1.1	3.3	20.1	6.7
IV	0.3	6.3	-0.6	6.5	2.2	10.2
1977	6.4	2.7	7.8	13.9	19.7	160.4
I	3.1	5.9	1.1	5.6	25.4	7.9
II	8.2	9.3	6.4	18.6	29.7	6.7
III	10.0	-0.3	17.4	18.4	21.8	9.0
IV	4.4	-4.3	5.9	12.8	3.9	9.6
1978	- 3.5	1.4	-10.5	6.7	-10.1	169.8
I	- 2.7	4.1	-14.8	12.9	- 6.3	9.7
II	- 5.9	-0.3	-12.7	5.2	-18.8	8.8
III	- 4.8	-1.2	-11.7	3.8	-13.6	6.9
IV	- 0.2	3.4	- 3.4	5.8	0.3	9.2
1979	7.1	4.1	10.2	7.8	6.4	139.8
I	8.4	10.6	16.7	5.4	- 1.9	9.3
II	8.4	1.3	15.4	7.7	4.2	7.9
III	5.6	1.6	7.1	6.9	5.8	8.5
IV	6.3	2.7	3.6	11.7	16.6	4.6
1980	1.1	-6.6	- 3.8	12.3	6.1	87.9
I	1.8	-5.2	- 1.2	15.5	7.9	6.1
II	-2.1	-8.7	- 6.5	11.7	- 1.0	5.9
III	1.9	-6.1	- 2.2	14.3	8.8	4.2
IV	2.9 .	-6.3	- 4.8	8.2	8.3	5.4
1981	-5.9	2.5	-16.0	- 5.3	-13.5	131.3
I	0.7	-0.5	- 5.5	3.4	- 3.8	5.0
II	-0.1	11.4	-13.2	- 2.5	- 5.1	8.3

Source: FIDE (April 1983, Anexo Estadistico XIV) and BCRA
(Annual Reports).

1/ with respect to the same quarter of the previous year;
GDP at factor cost in real terms.

2/ GDP in real terms (in 1970 prices)

3/ includes: durable equipment (transport material and machinery) and total construction.

4/ consumer prices (general).

TABLE 11

ARGENTINA - INDEX OF AVERAGE WAGE PER EMPLOYEE
IN THE INDUSTRIAL SECTOR, 1976 - 81

(1976, 2nd quarter = 100)

		Nominal Wage (1)	Consumer Price Index (2)	Real Wage 2/ (3)	Unemploy- ment rate 3/ (4)
1976	II	100.0	100.0	100.0	4.8
	III	112.8	118.2	95.4	4.5
	IV	150.9	153.7	98.2	4.1
1977	I	186.3	200.9	92.7	..
	II	267.0	245.2	108.9	3.2
	III	297.0	311.7	95.3	3.4
	IV	440.2	415.3	106.0	2.2
1978	I	499.7	544.9	91.7	..
	II	700.6	708.2	98.9	3.9
	III	806.0	868.6	92.8	2.6
	IV	1216.9	1110.3	109.6	1.7
1979	I	1433.0	1467.4	97.7	..
	II	2034.5	1823.4	110.5	2.1
	III	2424.3	2336.2	104.0	1.5
	IV	3704.2	2766.7	133.0	2.0
1980	I	3684.8	3083.3	119.5	..
	II	4433.2	3654.8	121.3	2.3
	III	5324.3	4173.6	127.6	..
	IV	6092.5	4934.1	123.5	2.2
1981	I	6097.6	5644.3	122.4	..
	II	7984.1	6904.3	115.4	4.0
	III	9354.0	8859.3	105.6	5.0
	IV	11557.8	10993.0	105.1	5.0

Source: National Statistical Institute (INDEC)

1/ total remuneration (wages and salaries plus supple-
ments) from a sample of 1,300 firms.

2/ (3) = $[(1)/(2)]$ x 100

3/ Buenos Aires only. Unemployment rate corresponds to
April, July and October.

TABLE 12

ARGENTINA – AVERAGE INDUSTRIAL SALARIES, 1975-80 1/

(1975 = 100)

YEAR	Average Forman Salary (2)	Average Peon Salary (3)	CPI (4)	Real Foreman Salary (5)=(2)/(4)	Real Peon Salary (6)=(3)/(4)
1975	100.0	100.0	100.0	100.0	100.0
1976	304.9	312.9	433.5	70.3	72.2
1977	661.6	652.7	1,455.5	45.5	44.8
1978	1,302.4	1,167.2	4,011.4	32.5	29.1
1979	3,197.5	2,413.4	10,410.0	30.7	23.2
1980	7,796.7	5,797.2	20,899.6	37.3	27.7

Source: Ledesma (1981), Table 1.8, p. 143.

1/ annual average.

TABLE 13

ARGENTINA - COMMODITY EXPORTS (MILLIONS OF US DOLLARS), 1975-80

concept	1975	1976	1977	1978	1979	1980	1975-80[a]
Total	2,961	3,916	5,652	6,400	7,810	8,022	171.0
Agricultural Prod	1,635	2,152	3,125	3,449	4,541	4,170	155.1
Meat	240	478	621	798	1,154	892	271.7
Beef	112	251	331	426	752	587	424.1
Cereals & Others	1,285	1,465	2,072	2,200	2,775	2,688	109.2
Vegetables and Animal oils	92	176	370	391	540	524	469.6
Others	18	33	62	60	82	66	266.7
Mineral Products	22	28	38	74	70	315	1331.8
Industrial Prod.	1,304	1,736	2,489	2,877	3,199	3,537	171.2
Feed, Beverages & Tobacco	444	574	857	845	1,014	1,184	164.4
Chemicals	113	133	156	200	242	367	224.8
Plastics&Rubber	10	11	23	31	26	26	160.0
Leather goods	92	201	307	433	670	555	503.3
Paper Products	28	32	130	54	59	69	146.4
Textiles	153	239	387	473	363	474	209.8
Ceramics, glass	6	12	25	35	34	28	366.7
Metal Products	61	131	129	302	305	325	432.8
Electrical Mach	222	202	244	286	304	345	55.4
Transport Mat'l	175	201	231	218	182	174	-

Source: Banco Central de la República Argentina Boletín Estadístico Mensual

a/ growth rate between 1975 and 1980, in percent.

TABLE 14

ARGENTINA - STRUCTURE OF COMMODITY EXPORTS, 1975-80

Concept	1975	1976	1977	1978	1979	1980
Total	100	100	100	100	100	100
Agricultural Products	55	55	55	54	58	52
Meat	8	12	11	12	15	11
Beef	4	6	6	7	10	7
Cereals & Others	43	37	37	35	36	34
Vegetables & Animal oils	3	4	7	6	7	7
Others	1	1	1	1	1	1
Mineral Products	1	1	1	1	1	4
Industrial Products	44	44	44	45	42	44
Feed, Beverages & Tobacco	15	15	15	13	13	15
Chemicals	4	3	3	3	3	5
Plastics & Rubber	-	-	-	-	-	-
Leather goods	3	5	5	7	9	7
Paper Products	1	1	2	1	1	1
Textiles	5	6	7	7	5	6
Ceramics, glass	-	-	-	-	-	-
Metal Products	2	3	2	5	4	4
Electrical Mach	7	5	4	4	4	4
Transport Material	6	5	4	3	2	2

Source: Table 13.

TABLE 15

ARGENTINA - NOMINAL MONETARY BASE AND MONEY SUPPLY, 1977 - 1981

concept	December 1977	December 1978	1979				1980				March 1981
			March	June	September	December	March	June	September	December	
I. Monetary Base	3,246	7,034	8,201	10,189	11,972	13,310	13,415	16,258	18,332	21,896	23,219
(% increase with respect to previous period)	-	116.7	16.6	24.2	17.5	11.2 (89.2)1/	0.8	21.2	12.8	19.4 (64.5)1/	6.0
Sources:											
1. External sector (net)	1,592	3,607	4,495	6,169	7,447	8,655	8,831	5,129	5,725	1,437	-4,598
(% participation) 2/	(49.0)	(51.0)	(54.8)	(63.5)	(62.2)	(65.0)	(65.8)	(32.0)	(31.2)	(7.0)	(-19.8)
2. Domestic sector (net)	1,654	3,427	3,706	4,020	4,525	4,655	4,584	11,129	12,607	20,459	27,817
a. Public sector 2/	1,083	1,676	1,678	1,642	1,822	1,620	1,912	2,309	4,754	10,633	15,117
(% participation) 2/	(33.0)	(24.0)	(20.5)	(39.5)	(15.2)	(12.0)	(14.3)	(14.0)	(25.9)	(49.0)	(65.1)
(% increase) 3/	-	107.2	0.2	-2.2	11.0	-11.1	18.0	20.8	105.9	123.7	42.2
b. Financial sector	606	419	547	626	706	786	641	7,712 4/	8,132	11,135	15,295
(% participation)	(19.0)	(6.0)	(6.7)	(6.1)	(5.9)	(4.8)	(4.7)	(44.4)	(44.4)	(51.0)	(65.9)
c. Account of Monetary Regulation	242	1,660	1,886	2,152	2,517	2,926	2,731	2,240	1,802	1,312	565
(% participation)	(7.5)	(23.6)	(23.0)	(21.1)	(21.0)	(22.2)	(20.4)	(13.8)	(9.8)	(6.0)	(2.4)
d. Other accounts	-277	-328	-405	-400	-520	-607	-700	-1,132	-2,081	-2,621	-3,160
Uses:											
1. Currency	1,450	3,253	4,531	5,513	6,627	9,258	10,266	12,528	14,092	18,104	18,298
2. Financial Institution deposits at the Central Bank	1,796	3,253	3,670	4,676	5,345	4,052	3,149	3,730	4,240	3,792	4,930

cont.

TABLE 15 cont.

concept	December 1977	December 1978	1979				1980				March 1981
			March	June	September	December	March	June	September	December	
II. Secondary Expansion	2,990	10,801	14,819	19,691	27,321	38,187	49,268	53,985	67,214	76,425	83,195
reserve requirement (%)	44	29	27	27	24	16.5	11.5	12	11.5	10	12
III. Money Supply (M_2)	6,236	17,835	23,020	29,880	39,293	51,497	62,683	70,243	85,546	98,327	106,414
(% increase)	-	(186.0)	(29.1)	(29.8)	(31.5)	(31.1)	(21.7)	(12.1)	(21.8)	(14.9)	(8.2)
a. Currency in hands of public	865	2,662	3,001	3,633	4,316	6,367	7,512	9,033	10,465	13,729	13,322
b. Demand and Time Deposits	5,371	15,167	20,019	26,247	34,977	45,130	55,171	61,210	75,081	84,598	93,092

Source: BCRA (Boletin Estadistico Mensual, several numbers)

1/ from December to December.

2/ participation over Monetary Base (I).

3/ with respect to previous period.

4/ financial crisis.

TABLE 16

ARGENTINA – THE BANKING SECTOR, 1976 – 1980

(1976 I = 100)

Year	Index of Employment in the Sector					Number of Banks and Others in the Sector					Index of GDP of Banking sector e/	Index of Productivity f/
	official banks	private national banks a/	foreign banks	financial firms b/	total	commercial banks	financial firms	loans & savings associat c/	others d/	total		
	(1)	(2)	(3)	(4)	(5)	(6)	(7)	(8)	(9)	(10)	(11)	(12)
1976												
I	100.0	100.0	100.0	100.0	100.0	-	-	-	-	-	100.0	100.0
IV	-	-	-	-	-	111	80	424	69	684	-	-
1977												
II g/	90.8	104.7	99.2	143.6	99.2	110	79	423	69	681	115.1	116.0
III	85.3	105.1	97.3	183.9	100.3	-	-	-	-	-	123.0	123.0
IV	85.4	105.0	95.5	235.4	100.3	-	-	-	-	-	122.2	122.0
1978												
III	83.1	109.5	97.6	239.3	103.4	-	-	-	-	-	127.0	123.0
IV	82.8	109.3	96.4	248.7	104.2	157	138	377	14	686	129.4	124.0
1979												
IV	80.0	128.1	90.9	312.6	108.7	219	142	104	-	465	145.0	133.4
1980												
IV	79.2	134.0	94.5	335.3	112.4	107	135	92	-	434	156.0	138.8

Source: BCRA (Annual Reports)

a/ only in Buenos Aires
b/ compañías financieras
c/ cajas de crédito
d/ sociedades de crédito para consumo
e/ in real terms (1970 prices)
f/ (12) = [(11)/(5)] x 100

TABLE 17

ARGENTINA – STRUCTURE OF GROSS DOMESTIC INVESTMENT, 1970-81 1/

(In percent)

	1970	1971	1972	1973	1974	1975	1976	1977	1978	1979	1980	1981 2/
TOTAL	100.0	100.0	100.0	100.0	100.0	100.0	100.0	100.0	100.0	100.0	100.0	100.0
1. Durable Equip.	37.6	37.9	39.4	41.9	40.3	37.5	36.1	41.1	35.7	37.8	38.2	37.6
a. Transp. Material	(31.2)	(31.5)	(34.1)	(35.4)	(31.4)	(30.1)	(27.1)	(27.8)	(29.3)	(32.8)	(30.8)	(27.8)
b. Machinery	(68.8)	(68.5)	(65.9)	(64.6)	(68.6)	(69.9)	(72.9)	(72.2)	(70.7)	(67.2)	(69.2)	(72.2)
2. Construction	62.4	62.1	60.6	58.1	59.7	62.5	63.9	58.9	64.3	62.2	61.8	62.4
a. Public	(39.9)	(41.4)	(43.3)	(40.4)	(40.0)	(33.6)	(41.2)	(50.5)	(49.5)	(45.4)	(46.5)	(60.6)
b. Private	(60.1)	(58.6)	(56.7)	(59.6)	(60.0)	(66.4)	(58.8)	(49.5)	(50.5)	(54.6)	(53.5)	(39.4)
TOTAL DURABLE EQUIPMENT:	100.0	100.0	100.0	100.0	100.0	100.0	100.0	100.0	100.0	100.0	100.0	100.0
a. National	(69.7)	(70.4)	(73.1)	(80.0)	(80.2)	(77.2)	(80.5)	(72.5)	(70.2)	(67.8)	(56.5)	(47.4)
b. Imported	(30.3)	(29.6)	(26.9)	(20.0)	(19.8)	(22.8)	(19.5)	(27.5)	(29.8)	(32.2)	(43.1)	(52.6)

Source: Own calculations based on FIDE (April 1983, Anexo Estadístico XIV).

1/ calculations based on real Gross Domestic Investment in 1970 prices.

2/ corresponds to first quarter.

TABLE 18

ARGENTINA – EXTERNAL DEBT, 1975–80

Concept	1975	1976	1977	1978	1979	1980
TOTAL	7,875.1	8,279.5	9,678.2	12,496.1	19,034.7	27,162
Public Sector	4,021.3	5,189.0	6,043.7	8,357.0	9,960.3	14,459
(% Participation)	(51.1)	(62.7)	(62.4)	(66.9)	(52.3)	(53.2)
Annual growth rate		29.0	16.5	38.3	19.2	45.2
1. Import Financing	n.a.	n.a.	n.a.	3,125.6	3,173.3	3,335
a. Short-term 1/	-	-	-	399.9	570.6	974
b. Long-term 2/	-	-	-	3,525.5	2,602.7	2,361
2. Finacial Leans	n.a.	n.a.	n.a.	5,191.7	6,699.7	11,044
a. Short-term	-	-	-	1,209.4	1,076.7	3,178
b. Long-term	-	-	-	3,982.3	5,623.0	7,866
3. Other Finance Obl.	n.a.	n.a.	n.a.	39.7	87.3	80
a. Short-term	-	-	-	0.7	47.6	23
b. Long-term	-	-	-	39.0	39.7	57
4. Total short-term debt	n.a.	n.a.	n.a.	1,610.0	1,694.9	4,175
% Paticipation	-	-	-	(19.3)	(17.0)	(18.9)
annual growth rate	-	-	-	-	5.3	146.3
5. Total long-term debt	n.a.	n.a.	n.a.	6,747.0	8,265.4	10,284
% Participation	-	-	-	(80.7)	(83.0)	(71.1)
annual growth rate	-	-	-	-	22.5	24.4
Private Sector	3,853.8	3,090.5	3,634.5	4,139.1	9,074.4	12,703
% Participation	(48.9)	(37.3)	(37.6)	(33.1)	(47.7)	(46.8)
annual growth rate	-	-19.8	17.6	13.9	119.2	40.0
1. Financial Leans	1,954.9	1,453.7	1,719.2	2,207.2	5,621.1	8,710
a. Short-term	n.a.	n.a.	n.a.	93.4	1,471.7	3,559
b. Long-term	n.a.	n.a.	n.a.	2,113.4	4,149.4	5,151
2. Import Financing	1,441.0	1,181.7	1,393.1	1,796.0	3,278.6	3,791
a. Short-term	n.a.	n.a.	n.a.	900.1	2,070.2	2,452
b. Long-term	n.a.	n.a.	n.a.	895.9	1,208.4	1,339
3. Other Financial Obl.	457.9	455.1	522.2	135.9	174.7	202
a. Short-term	n.a.	n.a.	n.a.	43.6	93.7	99
b. Long-term	n.a.	n.a.	n.a.	92.3	81.0	103
4. Total short-term debt	n.a.	n.a.	n.a.	1,037.1	3,635.6	6,110
% Participation 4/				(25.1)	(40.1)	(48.1)
Annual growth rate				-	250.6	68.1
5. Total long-term debt	n.a	n.a	n.a	3,102.0	5,438.8	6,593.0
% Participation 4/				(74.9)	(59.9)	(51.9)
Annual growth rate				-	75.3	21.2
Total Debt/Exports (FOB)	2.7	2.1	1.7	2.0	2.4	3.4

Source: BCRA (Annual Reports).

1/ up to one year.
2/ more than one year.
3/ total public sector external debt.
4/ total private sector external debt.

TABLE 19

ARGENTINA - STRUCTURE OF REAL GDP BY SECTORAL ORIGIN, 1971-1980 1/

(In percent)

Sectors	1971	1972	1973	1974	1975	1976	1977	1978
Agriculture	11.6	11.3	11.9	11.7	11.7	12.3	11.9	12.5
Mining	1.7	1.7	1.6	1.5	1.5	1.5	1.6	1.7
Manufacturing	36.9	37.7	38.3	38.3	37.5	36.5	36.2	34.4
Construction	5.3	5.1	4.3	4.3	4.6	5.2	5.7	5.9
Services	44.5	44.2	43.9	44.2	44.7	44.5	44.6	45.5
Electricity, gas & water	2.4	2.5	2.6	2.6	2.8	2.9	2.9	3.1
Commerce, restaurants & hotels	18.1	18.0	17.7	18.0	17.9	17.3	17.5	17.0
Transport & Communications	7.3	7.2	7.3	7.1	7.1	7.0	7.1	7.1
Banking, Insurance and Real State	3.4	3.2	3.3	3.5	3.2	3.1	3.3	3.8
Government & other services	13.2	13.1	13.1	12.9	13.7	14.2	13.8	14.5
GDP at factor cost	100.0	100.0	100.0	100.0	100.0	100.0	100.0	100.0

cont.

TABLE 19 cont.

Sectors	1979	1980	average participation in			structure of the service sector		
			1971-1975	1976-1980		1971	1975	1980
Agriculture	12.2	11.4	11.6	12.1	4.3			
Mining	1.6	1.7	1.6	1.6	-			
Manufacturing	35.3	34.1	37.7	35.3	-6.4			
Construction	5.7	6.3	4.7	5.8	23.4			
Services	45.2	46.5	44.3	45.3	2.2	100.0	100.0	100.0
Electricity, gas & water	3.1	3.4	2.6	3.2	15.2	5.3	6.2	7.3
Commerce, restaurants & hotels	17.3	17.3	17.9	17.3	-3.4	40.7	40.2	37.2
Transport & Communications	7.1	7.0	7.2	7.1	-1.4	16.6	15.9	15.1
Banking, Insurance and Real State	3.8	4.5	3.3	3.7	12.1	7.7	7.2	9.7
Government & other services	13.9	14.3	13.2	14.1	6.6	29.8	30.6	30.7
GDP at factor cost	100.0	100.0	100.0	100.0	100.0			

Source: Own calculations based on FIDE (April 1983, Anexo Estadistico XIV).

1/ GDP at factor cost in 1970 prices.

TABLE 20

ARGENTINA - ANNUAL GROWTH RATE OF REAL GDP BY SECTORAL ORIGIN, 1971-1980 [1]/

Sectors	1971	1972	1973	1974	1975	1976	1977	1978
Agriculture	- 0.1	1.3	10.2	4.4	- 1.5	4.0	1.2	1.7
Mining	3.6	2.3	- 3.9	2.9	-4.6	1.8	9.5	1.3
Manufacturing	9.7	6.0	6.4	6.1	- 2.8	-4.5	4.2	-7.9
Construction	6.6	-1.4	-12.6	7.4	5.1	11.9	14.6	0.4
Services								
Electricity, gas & water	9.0	10.6	7.2	6.5	5.8	3.4	4.9	3.1
Commerce, restaurants & hotels	6.6	3.7	2.7	8.2	- 1.0	-5.7	6.1	-5.8
Transport & Communications	2.5	1.8	5.8	4.2	- 1.4	-3.2	6.1	-2.6
Banking, Insurance and Real State	2.5	-1.1	5.9	14.1	- 9.4	-6.6	14.8	8.9
Government & other services	2.6	3.6	4.5	3.9	5.4	2.3	1.9	1.7
GDP at factor cost	5.9	3.8	4.7	6.1	- 0.9	-1.7	4.9	-3.2

cont.

TABLE 20 cont.

Sectors	1979	1980	average growth rate in: 1971-1975	1976-1980 2/
Agriculture	5.0	-5.5	2.9 (4.7)	1.3 (4.1)
Mining	4.3	4.7	0.1 (4.0)	4.3 (3.3)
Manufacturing	11.0	-3.8	5.1 (4.7)	-0.2 (7.7)
Construction	4.9	7.8	1.0 (8.4)	7.9 (5.6)
Services:				
Electricity, gas & water	9.9	7.5	7.8 (2.0)	5.8 (2.9)
Commerce, restaurants & hotels	11.9	-0.5	4.0 (3.6)	1.2 (7.7)
Transport & Communications	8.5	0.4	2.6 (2.7)	1.8 (5.2)
Banking Insurance and Real State	10.5	17.7	2.4 (8.7)	9.1 (9.4)
Government & Other services	2.5	3.3	4.0 (1.0)	2.3 (0.6)
GDP at factor cost	8.5	-0.2	3.9 (2.9)	1.7 (4.9)

Source: Own calculations based on FIDE (April 1983, Anexo Estadistico XIV).

1/ GDP at factor cost in 1970 prices.

2/ Standard deviation between parenthesis.

TABLE 21

ARGENTINA - ANNUAL GROWTH RATE OF THE MANUFACTURING SECTOR, 1970- 1981

Industry	1971	1972	1973	1974	1975	1976	1977	1978
Food, Beverages & Tobacco	- 1.7	5.2	1.7	8.9	0.7	- 0.5	- 1.5	- 2.6
Textiles, Shoes & Clothing	3.8	0.8	1.9	10.3	- 4.6	- 5.4	3.7	-14.2
Wood & Wood Products	4.1	7.3	0.7	14.6	- 8.4	-18.2	4.8	- 1.2
Paper, Printing & Publishing	2.0	4.2	5.7	6.2	0.7	-12.4	0.0	3.2
chemicals, Rubber Petroleum Derivatives & Plastics	9.5	6.2	6.8	- 5.4	1.4	1.7	1.5	- 8.0
Non-Metallic Minerals	7.4	3.2	- 6.0	7.8	1.9	- 3.5	- 1.3	0.4
Basic Metals	11.9	7.2	4.4	2.7	- 4.1	- 9.6	14.9	- 5.5
Metal Products, Machinery& Equipment, Transport Vehicles	11.7	3.4	7.0	7.3	- 6.5	- 1.8	22.2	-20.3
Other Industries	6.1	4.0	4.0	5.9	- 2.6	- 3.1	7.8	-10.5
All Industries (simple average)	6.1	4.0	4.0	5.9	- 2.6	- 3.0	7.8	-10.5

cont.

TABLE 21 cont.

Industry	1979	1980	1981 [1]	average growth rate in: 1971-1975	1976-1980 [2]
Food, Beverages & Tobacco	5.2	1.8	- 3.3	2.9 (4.1)	0.5 (3.1)
Textiles, Shoes & Clothing	10.8	-15.1	-12.4	2.4 (5.4)	-4.0 (11.3)
Wood & Wood Products	11.1	- 3.0	16.1	3.7 (8.5)	-1.3 (10.9)
Paper, Printing & Publishing	1.8	- 6.7	-13.2	3.8 (2.4)	-2.8 (6.6)
Chemicals, Rubber Petroleum Derivitives Plastics	12.3	0.9	8.6	3.7 (5.9)	1.7 (7.2)
Non-Metallic Minerals	7.1	- 3.5	-11.0	2.9 (5.6)	-0.2 (4.4)
Basic Metals	17.0	- 7.9	-12.2	4.4 (5.9)	1.8 (13.0)
Metal Products, Machinery & Equipment, Transport Vehicles	13.5	- 4.5	-10.0	4.6 (6.9)	1.8 (16.5)
Other Industries					
All Industries	10.2	- 3.8	- 5.5	3.5 (3.5)	0.1 (8.6)

Source: Own calculations based on FIDE (April 1983, Anexo
        Estadistico XIV).

1/ corresponds to the first quarter.
2/ standard deviation between parenthesis.

TABLE 22

ARGENTINA - STRUCTURE OF THE MANUFACTURING SECTOR, 1970-1981

(In percent)

Industry	1970	1971	1972	1973	1974	1975	1976	1976 1st quarter
Food, Beverages & Tobacco	21.7	20.1	20.3	19.3	20.4	21.1	21.6	25.8
Textiles, Shoes & Clothing	13.2	12.9	12.5	12.2	12.8	12.5	12.2	11.9
Wood & Wood Products	2.1	2.1	2.0	1.9	2.1	2.0	1.7	1.7
Paper, Printing & Publishing	5.7	5.4	5.4	5.5	5.5	5.7	5.2	5.9
Chemicals, Rubber Petroleum Derivatives & Plastics	13.6	14.0	14.3	14.7	13.1	13.6	14.3	13.9
Non-Metallic Minerals	5.6	5.7	5.6	5.1	5.2	5.4	5.4	5.4
Basic Metals	5.0	5.3	5.4	5.5	5.3	5.2	4.9	4.6
Metal Products, Machinery & Equipment, Transport Vehicles	26.3	27.7	26.6	28.3	28.7	27.6	27.9	23.9
Other Industries	6.8	6.9	6.9	6.9	6.9	6.9	6.9	6.9
Total	100.0	100.0	100.0	100.0	100.0	100.0	100.0	100.0

cont.

TABLE 22 cont.

Industry	1977	1978	1979	1980	1981 1st quarter	average participation		percentage change of participation
						1971-1975	1976-1980	
Food, Beverages & Tobacco	19.8	21.5	20.5	21.7	25.7	20.4	21.0	3.0
Textiles, Shoes & Clothing	11.7	11.2	11.3	10.0	8.9	12.6	11.3	-10.0
Wood & Wood Products	1.6	1.8	1.8	1.8	1.9	2.0	1.7	-15.0
Paper, Printing & Publishing	4.8	5.5	5.1	5.0	4.7	5.5	5.1	- 7.3
Chemicals, Rubber Petrol-eum Derivatives & Plastics	13.5	13.8	14.1	14.8	16.3	13.9	14.1	1.4
Non-Metallic Minerals	4.9	5.5	5.4	5.4	5.3	5.4	5.3	- 1.9
Basic Metals	5.2	5.5	5.8	5.6	5.1	5.3	5.4	1.9
Metal Products, Machinery & Equipment, Trans-port Vehicles	31.6	28.2	29.0	28.8	25.2	27.9	29.2	47
Other Industries	6.9	6.9	6.9	6.9	6.9	6.9	6.9	-
Total	100.0	100.0	100.0	100.0	100.0	100.0	100.0	

Source: Own calculations based on FIDE (April 1983, Anexo Estadistico XIV).

TABLE 23

ARGENTINA – OUTPUT, EMPLOYMENT, AND PRODUCTIVITY IN DIFFERENT INDUSTRIES, 1971–80

INDUSTRIES	output	1971 employment	hours worked per worker	productivity	output	1975 employment	hours worked per worker	productivity
Cigarettes & Tobacco	101.9	97.5	99.4	102.5	120.2	112.4	140.6	91.0
Printing & Publishing	99.4	98.8	98.8	100.6	115.6	97.7	107.8	107.2
Pharmaceuticals & Other Chemicals	110.7	107.0	102.0	108.5	139.4	114.3	103.4	134.8
Petroleum Refineries	105.2	101.6	102.9	102.2	95.1	137.4	135.5	70.2
Petroleum Derivatives & Coal	89.3	91.7	87.1	102.5	75.6	96.1	88.3	85.6
Rubber Products	112.5	106.7	111.3	101.1	133.3	141.5	137.6	96.9
Non-Ferrous Metals	119.1	123.3	130.3	91.4	119.2	147.0	140.6	84.8
Vehicles & Transport Material	114.6	103.5	103.7	110.5	108.0	137.6	123.8	87.2
Food	99.1	106.2	105.5	93.9	114.6	120.3	120.6	95.0
Beverages	95.6	100.3	101.9	93.8	121.0	126.5	129.4	93.5
Textiles	104.5	100.5	101.7	102.8	114.2	109.2	110.2	103.6
Clothing	106.9	104.8	100.2	106.7	125.0	119.1	112.5	111.1
Leather & Leather Products	97.8	109.6	104.1	93.9	104.1	149.2	137.8	75.5
Shoes	45.2	97.8	96.2	47.0	74.9	90.8	97.1	77.1
Wood & Wood Products	110.4	103.6	104.9	105.2	115.8	139.3	128.0	90.5
Paper&Paper Products	106.3	103.9	106.1	100.2	125.2	122.0	111.8	112.0
Chemicals	115.2	99.9	101.8	113.2	130.1	121.3	117.4	110.8
Plastics	109.9	99.5	99.4	110.6	127.8	207.2	187.7	67.7
Porcelin, Clay and Ceramic Products	104.8	106.5	110.8	95.6	109.7	113.7	112.2	97.8
Glass & Glass-ware	97.2	95.9	98.4	98.8	119.7	113.6	116.5	102.7
Other Mineral Products	109.9	101.7	101.7	108.1	113.4	107.0	100.4	112.9
Iron & Steel	113.8	107.8	107.5	105.9	115.9	134.2	125.1	92.6
Metal Products	113.7	104.2	106.6	106.7	126.9	119.0	118.3	107.3
Non-Electric Machinery	112.8	99.4	99.5	113.4	139.1	116.5	106.9	130.1
Electrical Machinery & Apparatus	114.2	102.3	103.8	110.0	124.2	99.4	93.1	133.4
TOTAL	106.9	103.0	103.5	103.3	118.4	119.2	115.5	102.5

(continued)

TABLE 23 cont.

INDUSTRIES	1978				1980			
	output	employ-ment	hours worked per worker	product-ivity	output	employ-ment	hours worked per worker	product-ivity
Cigarettes & Tobacco	123.2	92.7	111.6	110.4	126.9	90.8	100.7	126.0
Printing & Publishing	100.4	70.6	80.9	124.1	98.5	74.9	88.9	110.8
Pharmaceuticals & Other Chemicals	112.2	95.5	89.6	125.2	127.0	88.5	83.0	153.0
Petroleum Refineries	108.1	139.8	143.8	75.2	119.0	108.6	117.1	102.4
Petroleum Derivatives & Coal	76.1	87.5	91.4	83.3	89.7	81.0	81.2	110.5
Rubber Products	130.7	125.7	121.0	108.0	151.2	125.1	132.6	114.0
Non-Ferrous Metals	95.9	127.2	138.2	79.4	139.0	126.1	138.2	100.6
Vehicles & Transport Material	93.3	101.7	101.0	92.4	124.0	101.7	101.6	116.0
Food	111.7	105.0	114.1	97.9	110.6	99.4	107.7	102.7
Beverages	95.9	111.1	116.0	82.7	139.5	116.9	123.8	112.7
Textiles	102.0	84.7	89.8	113.6	94.7	60.3	66.7	142.0
Clothing	85.2	87.9	86.1	99.0	89.0	65.0	63.4	140.0
Leather & Leather Products	129.3	161.9	154.3	83.8	93.5	118.0	109.9	85.1
Shoes	49.8	58.7	59.8	83.3	48.2	53.7	53.8	89.6
Wood & Wood Products	94.8	114.3	113.9	83.2	92.8	93.0	92.1	100.8
Paper & Paper Products	118.7	119.0	121.0	98.1	108.9	100.7	101.3	107.5
Chemicals	120.2	106.6	107.4	111.9	131.8	95.5	99.9	131.9
Plastics	109.3	136.4	125.4	87.2	136.4	149.1	142.5	95.7
Porcelin, Clay and Ceramic Products	81.5	87.0	89.7	90.9	94.7	95.4	107.8	87.8
Glass & Glass-ware	105.4	109.0	118.9	88.6	106.9	91.6	94.7	112.9
Other Mineral Products	115.8	91.8	92.8	124.8	118.4	85.6	91.7	129.1
Iron & Steel	101.3	117.5	118.1	85.8	180.2	112.6	113.2	159.2
Metal Products	115.0	97.8	102.7	112.0	123.4	91.5	96.8	127.5
Non-Electric Machinery	149.4	95.6	93.4	160.0	140.0	71.5	72.5	193.1
Electrical Mach-inery & Appara-tus	95.8	81.3	77.6	123.5	96.9	71.7	74.9	129.4
TOTAL	108.1	97.7	101.0	107.0	122.2	88.1	93.3	131.0

Source: FIDE (April 1983, Anexo Estadistico).

TABLE 24

ARGENTINA - PROFITS, SIZE OF ENTERPRISE, AND COSTS, 1976-80

Sample of Industrial Corporations	1976	1977	1978	1979	1980
I. All Firms					
1. Sales	100.0	100.0	100.0	100.0	100.0
2. Production Costs	68.6	72.9	71.4	73.8	78.8
3. Gross Margins	31.4	27.1	28.6	26.2	21.2
4. Financial Costs	9.3	10.4	13.0	9.8	8.5
5. Other Costs 1/	18.0	15.1	18.6	17.8	18.9
6. Net Profit	4.1	1.6	-3.0	-0.9	-5.3
II. LARGE FIRMS 2/					
1. Sales	100.0	100.0	100.0	100.0	100.0
2. Production Costs	68.9	73.6	72.1	74.3	79.5
3. Gross Margins	31.1	26.4	27.9	25.7	20.5
4. Financial Costs	9.5	10.1	1?.3	9.0	8.1
5. Other Costs 1/	18.0	14.7	18.3	17.0	17.6
6. Net Profit	3.6	1.6	-2.7	-0.3	-5.2
III. MEDIUM-SIZED FIRMS					
1. Sales	100.0	100.0	100.0	100.0	100.0
2. Production Costs	63.0	59.7	56.3	60.7	62.5
3. Gross Margins	37.0	40.3	43.7	39.3	37.5
4. Financial Costs	6.0	17.6	27.8	29.7	17.2
5. Other Costs 1/	19.7	22.0	24.3	25.5	28.1
6. Net Profit	11.3	0.7	-8.4	-15.9	-7.8
IV. IMPORT COMPETING FIRMS 3/					
1. Sales	100.0	100.0	100.0	100.0	100.0
2. Production Costs	65.6	73.1	71.9	72.9	78.0
3. Gross Margins	34.4	26.9	28.1	27.1	22.0
4. Financial Costs	8.9	10.7	14.3	11.3	10.5
5. Other Costs 1/	19.3	15.5	17.8	18.3	19.8
6. Net Profit	6.2	0.7	-4.0	-2.5	-8.3
V. FIRMS WITH NON TRADED PRODUCTS					
1. Sales	100.0	100.0	100.0	100.0	100.0
2. Production Costs	72.8	72.7	70.4	75.1	80.0
3. Gross Margins	27.2	27.3	29.6	24.9	20.0
4. Financial Costs	9.9	9.9	10.7	7.6	5.6
5. Other Costs 1/	16.3	14.6	20.0	15.8	15.6
6. Net Profit	1.0	3.2	-1.1	1.5	-1.2

Source: Cavallo and Petrei (1983).

1/   Outlays for marketing, organization and other miscellaneou:
     items.
2/   Firms, which sold over the equivalent of US$ 7 million per
     year.
3/   The distinction between industries producing traded or non-
     traded goods was made on the basis of a correlation of ann
     price increases and the rate of devaluation. The dividing
     line was a correlation coefficient of 0.5.

TABLE 25

ARGENTINA - PRICE MOVEMENTS, NON-TRADED AND GOVERNMENT CONTROLLED
GOODS AND SERVICES, 1977-1979
(percentage change from previous period)

	CPI weights	1977 III	1977 IV	1978 I	1978 II	1978 III	1978 IV	1979 I	1979 II	1979 III	1979 IV
TRADED GOODS & SERVICES	73.8										
Cereals and cereal products	5.0	21	22	54	31	17	14	22	30	27	20
Meat and meat products	15.2	31	28	12	35	22	52	32	33	49	-4
Fish and fish products	.6	37	23	37	14	24	17	52	29	36	-3
Oils	1.0	16	6	51	37	8	29	6	15	21	10
Dairy products	5.7	10	21	32	30	3	24	52	36	18	7
Fruit and vegetables	5.7	26	41	29	21	51	42	25	3	23	22
Sugar and sugar products	1.3	21	40	13	33	12	19	39	18	18	10
Coffee and tea	.9	20	11	15	13	14	15	23	22	24	19
vinegar and spices	.3	30	31	45	29	21	31	22	28	25	19
Other processed foods	.7	34	36	33	26	16	32	32	24	30	19
Outside meals	5.1	33	30	28	31	27	28	33	27	30	14
Beverages and liquors	4.9	48	45	38	36	20	31	50	19	16	23
Garments	10.9	22	38	16	31	18	41	24	29	11	26
Furniture and household goods	4.6	32	33	31	31	22	23	27	27	27	19
Pharmaceutical products	2.1	27	41	40	31	20	22	32	22	26	24
Vehicles for private use	1.1	32	32	31	30	33	31	26	22	18	25
Toys and related items	1.4	35	11	29	33	23	17	24	31	13	13
Vacations and tourism	1.4	26	51	36	5	20	26	14	12	32	21
Books and magazines	1.6	20	48	30	29	21	27	24	27	30	21
Tobacco	2.5	52	31	42	29	28	24	29	21	26	21
Goods for personal care	1.2	30	45	44	39	20	23	21	21	22	24
Various goods (n.e.i.)	.6	28	25	26	23	27	24	22	26	25	22
Quarterly weighted average increase		28	32	27	31	21	34	31	26	27	15

cont.

TABLE 25 cont.

	CPI Weights	1977		1978				1979			
		III	IV	I	II	III	IV	I	II	III	IV
NON-TRADED GOODS AND SERVICES	10.4										
Rent and related items.	3.4	43	36	29	23	29	24	26	30	28	18
Dry cleaning	.3	32	29	33	38	26	22	20	27	28	18
Household help	.4	20	--	50	30	22	23	35	37	72	12
Medical services	2.3	36	22	38	33	27	25	39	38	34	24
Car repairs	.9	28	59	25	29	51	25	29	21	27	26
Car washing	.4	37	42	42	28	85	31	35	23	26	18
Football, movies and photo	1.0	26	32	53	23	46	11	32	26	13	12
Education services	1.1	20	16	34	27	14	17	64	31	28	15
Barber shop and beauty salon	.6	30	38	42	37	39	33	25	25	23	22
Quarterly weighted average increase		33	31	36	28	33	24	34	30	29	19
GOVERNMENT CONTROLLED GOODS AND SERVICES	9.0										
Electricity	2.5	49	35	53	19	26	39	30	24	18	13
Fuel	1.6	34	15	49	16	16	26	41	19	18	9
Transportation	4.5	40	51	42	24	45	30	24	25	24	32
Communication	.4	18	30	56	18	42	15	19	15	15	11
Quarterly weighted average increase		52	39	46	32	45	42	39	34	32	33
CONSUMER PRICE INDEX		29	32	32	29	22	30	31	25	28	15

Source: INDEC (Boletin Mensual, several issues).

TABLE 26

ARGENTINA - GOVERNMENT EXPENDITURE, 1975-80

YEAR	In Millions of 1960 $	% of GDP
1975	7,356.3	39.5
1976	6,604.1	36.5
1977	6,461.5	34.1
1978	7,558.7	41.4
1979	7,522.5	37.0
1980	7,703.0	37.1

Source: Ledesma (1981) Table
A.1, p. 101.

TABLE 27

ARGENTINA - TREASURY DEFICIT FINANCING, 1975-80

Financing	1975	1976	1977	1978	1979	1980
Credit (net)	16.3	44.3	19.9	68.2	58.9	-37.0
a. Domestic	15.0	37.2	19.0	23.6	44.7	46.9
b. Foreign	1.3	7.2	0.9	44.6	14.2	9.9
Central Bank Operations	71.7	38.3	35.3	-	2.1	124.4
a. Transitory Drawings	11.5	15.5	- 3.4	-	-	70.2
b. Others	60.2	22.8	35.7	-	-	54.2
Unified Fund	11.7	16.8	26.2	45.7	41.8	19.8
Others	0.3	0.5	18.5	-13.9	- 2.8	- 5.3
TOTAL	100	100	100	100	100	100
Fiscal deficit as % of GDP	14.4	9.4	3.1	3.6	3.9	4.0

Source: Ledesma (1981), table A.6, p. 105.

TABLE 28

ARGENTINA - EFFECTIVE PROTECTION IN DIFFERENT INDUSTRIES

SECTOR	without peso overvaluation			peso overvalued by	
	Oct 80	Jan 84	Jan 86	30% Oct 80	40% Oct 80
Agriculture, Hunting and Fishing	- 29.30	- 22.93	- 25.56	- 54.61	- 62.14
Mining	31.94	22.57	18.66	- 14.27	- 28.24
Food, Beverage, and Tobacco	152.16	150.18	131.52	9.42	- 16.76
Textiles	214.88	82.82	70.24	14.89	- 15.07
Clothing, and Shoes	299.05	76.24	63.41	20.17	- 13.44
Wood, and Wood Products	77.07	37.35	30.49	- 10.00	- 29.31
Paper, and Printing	53.67	41.27	34.79	'- 14.85	- 31.75
Leather	- 62.56	- 41.17	- 43.05	- 74.93	- 78.82
Rubber	136.08	53.45	44.81	5.04	- 19.72
Chemical Products	35.62	38.18	31.95	- 22.69	- 37.60
Oil, and Oil Derivatives	- 17.47	- 0.92	- 4.50	- 47.56	- 56.39
Non-Metal Minerals	53.14	42.68	35.68	- 17.65	- 34.48
Metals	61.37	39.41	33.42	- 8.81	- 26.55
Machinery	66.74	45.50	38.49	- 10.94	- 29.25
Electrical Apparatus	64.94	42.97	36.18	- 11.36	- 29.48
Transport Material	96.03	39.88	33.96	7.32	- 14.24
Others	62.41	47.17	39.41	- 16.47	- 34.22
Electricity, Gas, and Water	- 4.92	- 5.01	- 4.15	11.11	22.59
Construction	- 15.92	- 13.56	- 11.96	15.75	46.37
Commerce, Restaurants, and Hotels	- 1.31	- 1.23	- 1.05	1.61	3.31
Transport	- 13.15	- 11.46	- 9.87	19.03	49.90
Housing	- 0.16	- 0.29	- 0.21	1.18	1.94
Personal Services, and Financing	- 3.31	- 2.74	- 2.39	2.32	5.74

Source: Fernandez (1982), Table 1, p. 266.

TABLE 29

ARGENTINA - WHOLESALE NON-AGRICULTURAL MONTHLY PRICE INCREASES, US AND INTERNATIONAL PRICE MOVEMENTS WEIGHTED BY ARGENTINE WPI WEIGHTS, AND RATE OF DEVALUATION, 1977-81

1977	Jan	Feb	Mar	Apr	May	June	July	August	Sept	Oct	Nov	Dec
U.S. Producer Prices	0.5	1.1	1.0	1.3	0.4	-0.4	0.2	-0.2	0.4	0.5	0.4	0.6
U.S.& International Prices weighted by Argentine WPI weights (non-agricul)	0.6	1.0	0.9	1.3	0.9	-0.2	0.0	0.0	0.5	0.2	0.4	0.8
Domestic WPI (non-argicultural)	14.4	2.7	2.7	6.2	5.0	7.0	6.0	14.2	8.4	14.7	8.9	4.9
Rate of Devaluation	6.4	6.8	7.6	4.7	5.6	4.8	6.1	5.5	8.0	8.4	8.5	7.2
International inflation adjusted for rate of devaluation 1/	7.1	7.9	8.6	6.1	6.1	4.6	6.1	5.5	8.5	8.6	8.9	8.0
Difference 2/	7.3	- 5.2	- 5.8	0.	- 1.5	2.4	-0.1	8.7	-0.1	6.3	0.0	-3.1

cont.

TABLE 29 cont.

1978	Jan	Feb	Mar	April	May	June	July	August	Sept	Oct	Nov	Dec
U.S. Producer Prices	1.0	1.0	0.8	1.4	0.7	0.8	0.5	-0.1	0.9	1.2	0.3	0.8
U.S.& International Prices weighted by Argentine WPI weights (non-agricult)	1.1	1.4	0.7	1.0	0.7	0.8	0.5	0.4	1.1	0.9	0.4	0.9
Domestic WPI (non-agricultural)	11.3	6.5	8.1	8.7	9.2	5.9	5.5	6.8	5.9	9.0	8.5	8.0
Rate of Devaluation	7.4	6.2	5.3	5.5	2.2	1.5	2.2	3.1	4.3	4.7	5.5	4.8
International inflation adjusted for rate of devaluation 1/	8.5	7.9	6.0	6.5	2.9	2.3	2.7	3.5	5.4	5.6	5.9	5.7
Difference 2/	2.8	- 1.4	2.1	2.2	6.3	3.6	2.8	3.3	0.5	3.4	2.6	2.3

cont.

TABLE 29 cont.

1979	Jan	Feb	Mar	April	May	June	July	August	Sept	Oct	Nov	Dec
U.S. Producer Prices	1.5	1.5	1.2	1.5	0.9	0.7	1.3	0.6	1.5	1.5	0.8	1.0
U.S.& International Prices weighted by Argentine WPI weights (non-agricult)	1.4	1.2	1.6	1.3	0.9	0.3	1.2	0.3	1.2	0.8	0.4	0.7
Domestic WPI (non-argicultural)	11.3	8.4	8.9	6.6	8.8	9.4	6.9	12.6	5.7	3.8	3.3	3.5
Rate of Devaluation	5.2	4.8	4.7	4.6	4.5	4.2	4.0	3.8	3.6	3.4	3.2	3.0
International inflation adjusted for rate of devaluation 1/	6.7	6.1	6.4	6.0	5.4	4.5	5.2	4.1	4.8	4.2	3.6	3.7
Difference 2/	4.6	2.3	2.5	0.6	3.4	4.9	1.7	8.5	0.9	-0.4	-0.3	-0.2

cont.

TABLE 29 cont.

1980

	Jan	Feb	March	April	May	June	July	August	Sept	Oct	Nov	Dec
(1) U.S. Producer Prices	2.1	2.1	0.7	0.3	0.5	0.5	1.8	1.0	0.4	1.4	0.5	0.6
(2) U.S.& International Prices weighted by Argentine WPI weights (non-agricult)	1.7	1.5	0.5	0.1	1.7	0.4	1.6	1.2	0.2	0.9	0.5	-0.9
(3) Domestic WPI (non-argicultural)	4.3	4.5	4.8	3.7	4.5	6.6	3.3	3.2	3.0	8.2	2.9	2.7
(4) Rate of Devaluation	2.9	2.7	2.5	2.3	2.1	2.0	1.9	1.5	1.3	1.1	1.0	1.0
(5) International Inflation adjusted for rate of devaluation 1/	4.6	4.2	3.0	2.4	2.8	2.4	3.5	2.9	1.5	2.0	1.5	0.1
(6) Difference 2/	-0.3	0.3	1.8	1.3	1.7	4.2	-0.2	0.3	1.5	6.2	1.4	2.6

1981

	Jan	Feb	March
(1) U.S. Producer Prices	1.4	1.0	0.9
(2) U.S.& International Prices weighted by Argentine WPI weights (non-agricult)	1.2	0.0	0.6
(3) Domestic WPI (non-argicult-ural)	3.4	4.9	5.2
(4) Rate of Devaluation	2.0	12.0	2.0
(5) International Inflation adjusted for rate of deval-uation 1/	2.7	11.5	4.6
(6) Difference 2/	0.7	-6.6	0.6

Source: Own calculations based on BCRA (Boletin Estadistico Mensual) and IFS.

1/ $(1 + (2)) \times (1 + (4)) = (5)$

2/ $(3) - (5) = (6)$

Statistical Appendix II

TABLE A-1

ARGENTINA – QUARTERLY INDUSTRIAL PRODUCTION, INFLATION AND
SHORT-TERM LENDING INTEREST RATES, 1977-81

| | Manufact-uring Pro-duction 1/ | Inflation Rate 2/ | Nominal Lending Interest Rate | | | | | | Cost of Foreign Borrowing in Peso Terms 5/ |
| | | | Average Rate 3/ | Banco Nacion | Private National. Bank Financial Companies | | | | |
					Prime Rate	Other	Prime Rate	Other	
1977	104.5	153.6	147.2	≡	≡	≡	≡	≡	132.3
I	90.3	167.9	69.6	—	—	—	—	—	138.9
II	107.6	96.7	93.0	—	—	—	—	—	93.1
III	114.0	179.1	157.5	—	—	—	—	—	129.6
IV	106.4	181.6	342.8	—	—	—	—	—	174.4
1978	93.5	139.5	173.9	≡	≡	≡	≡	≡	85.2
I	76.9	160.9	259.4	—	—	—	—	—	133.3
II	94.0	145.2	165.3	—	—	—	—	—	60.1
III	100.6	98.1	144.4	119.2	121.5	146.3	123.7	148.7	63.2
IV	102.8	159.5	141.7	130.3	136.9	163.3	148.8	176.9	105.0
1979	103.1	133.5	134.6	132.3	125.9	150.4	137.4	165.0	84.2
I	89.7	190.4	131.1	126.2	123.0	140.3	130.1	156.1	97.8
II	108.4	161.2	129.6	127.0	124.5	144.6	135.3	161.5	84.9
III	107.7	157.2	147.1	147.1	147.7	175.7	159.8	189.1	77.1
IV	106.4	52.3	131.1	129.3	110.1	142.7	125.7	154.6	74.6
1980	99.2	66.7	98.7	97.2	90.7	112.2	99.8	122.9	42.7
I	88.6	77.5	103.5	97.4	91.2	113.2	94.5	122.5	61.5
II	101.3	65.5	93.8	99.4	91.9	115.3	101.5	126.2	42.8
III	105.4	45.9	104.9	100.8	86.7	106.5	100.3	117.0	34.2
IV	101.3	69.6	93.0	91.2	93.2	113.9	102.8	126.2	33.8
1981	83.3	167.0	223.7	168.4	246.1	299.0	281.2	389.5	
I	83.7	69.6	170.6	149.0	235.4	282.3	288.8	376.2	136.2
II	88.0	281.3	233.6	162.4	329.3	368.8	358.0	528.3	40.8*
III	80.4	192.3	324.2	219.0	249.5	326.1	291.7	445.7	19.6*
IV	81.1	168.7	186.8	148.8	185.0	231.4	202.7	251.7	17.4*

Sources: Central Bank of Argentina; FIDE (April 1983); and FIEL (Coyuntura Económica)

* Monthly average rate in the quarter.
1/ Index 1975 = 100 in real terms.
2/ Wholesale non-agricultural national inflation rate.
3/ Controlled interest rate until June 1977.
4/ Correspond to September 1978.
5/ Ex-post cost of foreign borrowing. It was assumed a spread of 1 percent annual over the eurodollar 90 days deposit rate and it was added additional cost according to R. Frenkel (1979, page 35).

TABLE A-1.1

ARGENTINA - REAL SHORT-TERM LENDING INTEREST RATES, 1977-81

| Year | Average Rate (1) | Banco Nacion (2) | Private National Bank | | Financal Companies | | Cost of Foreign Borrowing (7) |
			Prime Rate (3)	Other (4)	Prime Rate (5)	Other (6)	
1977	-2.5	-	-	-	-	-	-8.4
I	-36.7	-	-	-	-	-	-10.8
II	-1.9	-	-	-	-	-	-1.8
III	-7.7	-	-	-	-	-	-17.7
IV	57.2	-	-	-	-	-	-2.6
1978	14.4	-	-	-	-	-	-22.7
I	37.8	-	-	-	-	-	-10.6
II	8.2	-	-	-	-	-	-34.7
III	23.4	10.7	11.8	24.3	12.9	25.5	-17.6
IV	-6.9	-11.2	-8.7	1.5	-4.1	6.7	-21.0
1979	0.8	-0.5	-3.3	7.2	1.7	13.5	-21.1
I	-20.4	-22.1	-23.2	-17.3	-20.8	-11.8	-31.9
II	-12.1	-13.1	-14.1	-6.4	-9.9	0.1	-28.1
III	-3.9	-3.9	-3.7	7.2	1.0	12.4	-31.1
IV	51.7	50.6	38.0	59.4	48.2	67.1	14.6
1980	19.2	18.3	14.4	27.3	19.9	33.7	-14.4
I	14.7	11.2	7.7	20.1	9.6	25.4	-9.0
II	10.4	13.6	9.3	22.7	14.8	28.9	-18.6
III	40.4	37.6	28.0	41.5	37.3	48.7	-8.0
IV	13.8	12.7	13.9	26.1	19.6	33.4	-21.1
1981	21.2	3.3	29.6	49.4	42.8	83.3	...
I	59.6	46.8	97.8	125.4	129.2	180.8	39.3
II	-12.5	-31.2	12.6	22.9	20.1	64.8	25.9*
III	45.1	9.1	19.6	45.8	34.0	86.7	9.4*
IV	6.7	-7.4	6.1	23.3	12.6	30.9	8.1*

Source: Table A-1

* Monthly average rate in the quarter.
1/ Deflated by column (2), Table A-1. The real interest rate was calculated as:
   (i - Π /1 + Π) where i = interest rate, Π = inflation rate.

TABLE A-2

ARGENTINA - NOMINAL AND REAL SHORT-TERM DEPOSIT INTEREST RATES
AND EXCHANGE RATE, 1977-81

	Nominal Interest Rates 1/ (1)	Wholesale (general) Inflation Rate (2)	Real Interest Rate 1/2/ (3)	Devaluation Rate 3/ (4)	Real Exchange Rate 4/ (5)
1977	112.7	145.7	-13.4	116.3	113
I	60.5	156.1	-37.3	124.4	118
II	73.7	104.2	-14.9	80.6	118
III	133.7	163.0	-11.1	113.4	109
IV	214.2	165.0	18.6	152.9	107
1978	130.6	140.8	-4.2	68.1	89
I	167.9	154.9	5.1	112.3	103
II	123.5	141.1	-7.3	44.0	94
III	116.1	117.5	-0.6	45.6	84
IV	118.5	151.5	-13.1	79.5	75
1979	117.6	127.7	-4.6	62.4	58
I	113.6	169.1	-20.	76.1	66
II	113.6	167.6	-20.3	67.7	62
III	131.1	183.1	-18.4	56.6	53
IV	111.2	31.8	60.2	50.3	52
1980	79.3	57.0	14.2	23.2	46
I	85.2	60.7	15.2	36.1	50
II	75.5	89.3	-7.3	26.8	48
III	81.7	40.9	29.0	18.2	44
IV	74.9	41.8	23.3	12.8	42
1981	153.3	180.4	-9.6	...	52
I	119.2	63.1	34.4	100.4	43
II	167.9	331.2	-37.9	34.9 5/	55
III	207.6	204.8	0.9	14.0 5/	54
IV	127.8	188.2	-21.0	13.0 5/	54

Source: Central Bank of Argentina (Monthly Bulletin and Annual

1/ From 1977-1981 figures correspond to 30-days deposit interest rates
paid by commercial banks.
2/ The real interest rate was calculated as: $(i - \Pi /1 + \Pi)$ where
i = interest rate (column (1)) and Π = inflation rate, column (2).
3/ Average official rate of Peso devaluation against U.S. dollar
(Banco Nacion, selling rate).
4/ Index 1976 = 100. Deflated by W.P.I. (general).
5/ Monthly average rate in the quarter.

TABLE A-3

ARGENTINA - FOREIGN EXCHANGE MOVEMENT, 1975-81

	Changes in International Reserves (total) + = increase (1)	Current Account + = surplus (2)	Autonomous Capital Movement - = outflow (3)	Sources of International Reserves (CBA) (4)	Net Purchases of Foreign Currency by CBA from Authorized Agencies (5)	Uses of International Reserves (CBA) (6)	Net sale of International Currency to Authorized Agencies by CBA (7)
1976							
I	64.0	32.0	-114.0	644.3	—	551.0	246.1
II	479.0	261.0	5.0	772.6	38.9	392.1	72.9
III	131.0	155.0	-142.0	620.5	42.6	488.4	54.8
IV	518.0	202.0	-265.0	1,394.5	164.4	846.2	3.8
1977							
I	291.0	334.0	-19.0	584.1	401.8	346.1	—
II	440.0	536.0	-48.0	744.2	404.2	328.7	—
III	693.0	327.0	442.0	882.5	635.7	174.5	—
IV	802.0	90.0	901.0	1,167.4	850.6	438.4	—
1978							
I	1,184.0	337.0	1,030.0	1,518.9	1,095.2	405.4	—
II	546.0	857.0	391.0	1,538.8	1,130.3	974.9	—
III	546.0	857.0	391.0	1,113.2	522.5	562.6	—
IV	-213.0	109.0	-326.0	1,131.0	—	1,397.0	756.0
1979							
I	996.6	-63.8	1,054.2	1,454.7	679.3	529.8	—
II	1,478.7	467.9	970.6	1,762.3	1,314.0	239.5	—
III	1,181.1	-57.1	1,274.3	1,243.3	639.4	125.8	—
IV	786.0	-883.4	1,378.8	1,245.0	463.8	501.5	261.2
1980							
I	187.3	-757.4	1,226.5	1,218.5	—	1,030.4	334.5
II	-1,477.0	-1,023.1	-690.7	868.8	—	2,338.0	2,120.6
III	301.5	1,146.1	1,571.2	...	1,233.0	...	725.6*
IV	-1,807.9	-1,868.9	491.1	...	—	...	2,176.8*
1981							
I	-2,985.3	-1,939.6	-907.4	...	—	...	3,998.4*
II	30.0	-65.5	788.6	...	—	...	...
III							
IV							

Source: Central Bank of Argentina (Statistical Bulletin)

* Estimated.

CBA = Central Bank of Argentina

TABLE A-4

ARGENTINA - REAL MONEY AND QUASI-MONEY, 1975-81

	Money			Time and Savings Deposits in L/C (4)	Foreign Currency Deposits 2/ (5)	Quasi-Money (6)	FC/QM (percentage) (7)	Money and Quasi-Money (8)
	Curr-ency (1)	Sight Deposits (2)	Total (3)					
1975								
December	124	136	260	78	49*	127	--	387
1976								
March	63	89	152	41	—	41	—	193
June	60	106	166	58	—	58	—	223
September	63	107	170	79	--	79	—	249
December	102	128	229	132	27*	159	—	388
1977								
March	69	101	169	125	--	125	—	294
June	81	112	193	187	—	187	—	381
September	74	92	166	224	--	224	—	390
December	89	84	173	243	17*	260	--	433
1978								
March	76	81	157	275	--	275	—	432
June	86	89	175	302	--	302	—	477
September	82	75	157	339	—	339	--	496
December	114	79	193	297	22	319	7.0	512
1979								
March	86	83	169	321	16	337	4.7	506
June	88	84	172	343	18	361	4.9	533
September	76	71	147	361	17	378	4.5	525
December	118	89	207	435	21	456	4.5	663
1980								
March	106	99	205	471	23	494	4.7	699
June	112	97	209	435	23	458	5.0	667
September	114	93	207	494	30	524	5.8	731
December	156	104	259	501	37	538	6.8	797
1981								
March	112	70	182	503	29	532	5.5	714
June	94	59	153	409	42	451	9.4	604
September	77	53	130	423	37	460	8.1	590
December	102	54	156	385	40	425	9.5	581

Source: Central Bank of Argentina (Monthly Bulletin).

1/ Deflated by W.P.I. (general).
2/ The figures in this column over estimate the amount of foreign currency deposits by residents since they also include other types of deposits in local currency.
* Deposits in L/C only.

TABLE A-5

ARGENTINA - INDEX OF REAL MONEY AND QUASI-MONEY, 1975-81

		Money		Time and savings deposits Private Banks		Quasi-	Money and
	Currency	Sight Deposits	Total	L/C	F/C	Money	Quasi-Money
1975							
December	100	100	100	100	100	100	100
1976							
March	51	65	59	53	...	32	50
June	48	78	64	74	...	46	58
September	51	79	65	101	...	62	64
December	82	94	88	169	55	125	100
1977							
March	56	74	65	160	...	98	76
June	65	82	74	240	...	147	99
September	60	68	64	287	...	176	101
December	72	62	67	312	35	205	112
1978							
March	61	60	60	353	...	217	112
June	69	65	67	387	...	238	123
September	66	55	60	435	...	267	128
December	92	58	74	381	45	251	132
1979							
March	69	61	65	412	33	265	131
June	71	62	66	440	37	284	138
September	61	52	57	463	35	298	136
December	95	65	80	558	43	359	171
1980							
March	86	73	79	604	45	389	181
June	90	71	80	558	45	361	172
September	92	68	80	633	61	413	189
December	126	77	100	642	76	424	206
1981							
March	90	52	70	645	59	419	185
June	76	43	59	524	86	355	156
September	62	39	50	542	76	362	152
December	82	40	60	494	82	335	150

Source: Table A-4.

TABLE A-6

ARGENTINA - COMMERCIAL BANKS LOANS TO THE PRIVATE SECTOR, 1976-81

	Local Currency (1)	Foreign Currency (2)	Total Banking System (3) = (1+2)	FC/TBS Percentage (4)=(2)/(3)	Index Dec. 1975 = 100		
					Local Currency (5)	Foreign Currency (6)	Total (7)
1975							
December	196	29	225	12.9	100	100	100
1976							
March	100	22	122	18.0	51	76	54
June	108	20	128	15.6	55	69	57
September	133	19	152	12.5	68	66	66
December	222	26	248	10.5	113	90	110
1977							
March	178	28	206	13.6	91	97	92
June	232	34	266	12.8	118	117	118
September	272	36	308	11.7	139	124	137
December	309	48	357	13.4	158	166	159
1978							
March	245	76	321	23.7	125	262	143
June	265	70	335	20.9	135	241	149
September	293	60	353	17.0	150	207	157
December	367	47	414	11.4	187	162	184
1979							
March	350	57	407	14.0	179	197	181
June	370	66	436	15.1	189	228	194
September	386	68	454	15.0	197	235	202
December	501	94	595	15.8	256	324	264
1980							
March	553	103	656	15.7	282	355	292
June	584	100	684	14.6	298	345	304
September	632	111	743	14.9	322	383	330
December	676	113	789	14.3	345	390	351
1981							
March	655	115	810	14.2	334	397	360
June	506	215	721	29.8	258	741	320
September	451	188	639	29.4	230	648	284
December	408	199	607	32.8	208	686	270

Source: Central Bank of Argentina (Monthly Bulletin).

TABLE C-1

CHILE - QUARTERLY INDUSTRIAL PRODUCTION, INFLATION, AND SHORT-TERM LENDING INTEREST RATE, 1976-81

Year	Manufacturing Production 1/ (1)	Inflation Rate 2/3/ (2)	Nominal Lending Interest Rate 3/4/ (3)	Real Lending Interest Rate 5/3/ (4)	Cost of Foreign Borrowing in Peso Terms 6/3/ (5)	Cost of Foreign Borrowing in Real Terms 5/7/ (6)
1976	105.0	166.2	352.2	69.9	119.0	-17.7
I	93.0	293.8	413.1	30.3	316.7	5.8
II	104.0	265.3	418.5	41.9	69.3	-49.8
III	106.0	92.3	281.3	98.3	105.3	6.8
IV	118.0	79.6	311.0	128.8	109.1	16.4
1977	116.0	70.9	157.5	50.7	72.2	0.8
I	101.0	101.2	261.4	79.6	33.0	-34.0
II	116.0	62.0	146.3	52.9	66.8	3.0
III	122.0	44.2	108.2	44.2	106.3	43.1
IV	123.0	81.6	132.9	28.3	92.0	5.7
1978	124.0	39.7	85.8	33.0	33.6	-4.4
I	105.0	44.2	101.2	39.5	47.5	2.3
II	132.0	51.1	79.6	18.2	38.11	-8.6
III	126.0	34.5	73.5	28.3	26.7	-5.8
IV	131.0	29.8	90.1	46.5	23.4	-4.9
1979	134.0	54.9	62.0	4.9	30.0	-16.1
I	120.0	40.9	67.7	19.6	33.9	-5.0
II	138.0	67.7	60.1	-4.9	63.0	2.8
III	137.0	96.7	60.1	-22.4	12.8	-42.7
IV	141.0	23.9	60.1	29.8	15.9	-6.5
1980	141.0	34.1	45.5	8.7	15.5	-13.9
I	133.0	51.1	62.0	7.4	18.3	-21.7
II	139.0	26.8	42.6	12.7	12.3	-11.4
III	140.0	21.0	40.9	16.8	13.2	-6.5
IV	153.0	39.3	37.7	-1.2	18.3	-15.1
1981	142.0	-0.7	52.0	56.0	17.7	18.5
I	138.0	1.2	52.9	51.1	17.5	16.1
II	149.0	-1.6	51.1	63.8	18.6	20.3
III	145.0	-1.6	51.1	63.8	19.6	21.4
IV	134.0	-0.8	52.9	54.6	14.9	15.8

Source: Central Bank of Chile (monthly bulletin).

1/ Index 1975 = 100
2/ Average inflation rate over previous period of domestic manufactured products (wholesale).
3/ Annual rates
4/ Banking system
5/ The real interest rate was calculated as: $(i - \pi / 1 + \pi)$
6/ The sum of the ex-post annual rate of peso depreciation and short-term eurodollar interest rate. Since the information available corresponds to 90-day period eurodollar deposit rate, it was assumed a one percent differential between the deposit and the lending eurodollar rate. The cost is underestimated since no taxes, fees, and/or capital movements restrictions were considered.
7/ Column (5) deflated by column (2).

TABLE C-2

CHILE – NOMINAL AND REAL SHORT TERM DEPOSIT INTEREST RATE AND THE EXCHANGE RATE, 1976–81

Year	Nominal Deposit Interest Rate in L/C	Wholesale (General) Inflation Rate	Real Deposit Interest Rate	Devaluation Rate	Real Exchange Rate 2/
1976	197.8	152.5	17.3	104.3	100.0
I	217.6	273.2	-20.4	197.1	117.0
II	265.3	289.6	-6.3	58.3	105.0
III	151.8	115.3	17.0	92.3	89.0
IV	169.1	29.8	107.3	96.7	97.0
1977	93.8	65.3	17.2	60.8	89.0
I	125.2	149.0	-9.6	25.3	93.0
II	83.7	63.8	12.2	56.4	83.0
III	71.5	40.9	21.7	92.3	86.0
IV	99.0	29.8	53.3	77.5	94.0
1978	78.6	38.4	29.1	21.7	92.0
I	71.5	51.1	13.5	36.1	97.0
II	79.6	44.2	24.6	26.8	93.0
III	73.5	42.6	21.7	15.4	90.0
IV	90.1	18.2	60.8	10.0	86.0
1979	45.1	58.2	-8.3	—	73.0
I	47.6	45.9	1.2	19.6	84.0
II	44.2	67.7	-14.0	45.9	77.0
III	42.6	132.9	-38.8	-- 3/	68.0
IV	45.9	10.0	32.6	—	63.0
1980	37.3	28.3	7.0	—	54.3
I	51.1	34.5	12.3	—	60.0
II	32.9	29.8	2.4	—	56.0
III	31.4	36.1	-3.5	—	52.0
IV	34.5	14.0	18.0	--	49.0
1981	45.5	-3.4	50.6	—	49.4
I	52.9	1.2	51.1	—	48.7
II	51.1	-3.7	56.7	—	49.1
III	39.3	...	39.3	—	49.4
IV	39.3	-11.4	57.2	—	50.5

Source: Central Bank of Chile (Monthly Bulletin).

1/ Average period.
2/ Index, 1976 = 100. Deflated by wholesale price index (general).
3/ A fixed exchange rate regime was implemented in June 1979.

TABLE C-3

CHILE - COMMERCIAL BANKS LOANS TO THE PRIVATE SECTOR; 1975-82

	Local Currency	Foreign Currency 2/	Total Banking System (3) = (1+2)	(4) = (2/3) Percentage	Index Dec. 1975 = 100 3/		
					Local Currency	Foreign Currency	Total
1975							
December	1,437.7	1,409.1	2,846.8	49.5	100.0	100.0	100.0
1976							
March	1,169.9	1,713.4	2,883.3	59.4	81.4	121.6	101.3
June	1,487.7	1,750.7	3,238.4	54.1	103.5	124.2	113.8
September	1,894.8	2,232.4	4,127.2	54.1	131.8	158.4	145.0
December	2,654.5	2,583.0	5,237.5	49.3	184.6	183.3	184.0
1977							
March	3,188.2	3,237.7	6,425.9	50.4	221.8	229.8	225.7
June	4,038.1	3,707.6	7,745.7	47.9	280.9	263.1	272.1
September	5,185.5	4,337.9	9,523.4	45.5	360.7	307.9	334.5
December	6,421.6	5,445.9	11,867.5	45.9	446.7	386.5	416.9
1978							
March	7,080.4	6,839.4	13,919.8	49.1	492.5	485.4	489.0
June	7,911.1	6,889.1	14,800.2	46.5	550.3	488.9	520.0
September	8,893.7	7,575.6	16,469.3	46.0	618.6	537.6	578.5
December	9,897.8	6,783.4	16,681.2	40.7	688.5	481.4	586.0
1979							
March	9,906.0	7,270.2	17,176.2	42.3	689.0	516.0	603.4
June	10,167.8	7,492.8	17,660.6	42.4	707.2	531.7	620.4
September	9,629.1	8,850.9	18,480.0	47.9	669.8	628.1	649.2
December	11,464.3	9,691.8	21,156.1	45.8	797.4	687.8	743.2
1980							
March	12,264.3	10,513.8	22,778.1	46.2	853.1	746.1	800.0
June	13,518.2	13,183.5	26,701.7	49.4	940.3	935.6	938.0
September	14,274.2	15,534.7	29,808.9	52.1	992.9	1,102.5	1,047.1
December	16,385.0	18,673.7	35,058.7	53.3	1,139.7	1,325.2	1,231.5
1981							
March	19,134.0	20,870.4	40,004.4	52.2	1,330.9	1,481.1	1,405.2
June	23,066.7	23,514.3	46,581.0	50.5	1,604.4	1,668.8	1,636.6
September	25,000.3	27,015.4	52,015.4	51.9	1,738.9	1,917.2	1,827.3
December*	34,059.8	32,091.1	66,150.9	48.5	—	2,277.4	—
1982							
March	32,454.5	32,360.3	64,814.8	49.9	—	2,296.5	—
June	28,591.7	32,505.5	61,097.2	53.2	—	2,306.8	—
September	24,530.4	28,570.4	53,100.8	53.8	—	2,027.6	—
December	23,531.3	25,294.4	48,825.7	51.8	—	1,795.1	—

Source: Central Bank of Chile (monthly bulletin).

* Total financial system (includes commercial banks, Ificoop, Banco del Estado de Chile and Financieras) from December 1981 to December 1982..

1/ Deflated by the wholesale price index (general).
2/ Valued at the exchange rate of December 1975 and deflated by the U.S. wholesale price index December 1975 = 100.
3/ Based on columns (1) - (3).
4/ There were no foreign currency deposits in Financieras.

TABLE C-4

CHILE - REAL MONEY AND QUASI-MONEY, 1975-82

	Money			Time and Savings Deposits in L/C (4)	Foreign Currency Deposits (5)	Quasi-Money (6)	FC/QM (percentage) (7) = (5/6)	Money and Quasi-Money (8) = (3+6)
	Currency (1)	Sight Deposits (2)	Total (3)					
1975								
December	1,374.0	1,621.0	2,995.0	1,639.0	579.0	2,218.0	26.1	5,213.0
1976								
March	1,131.8	1,568.4	2,700.2	1,946.7	520.9	2,467.6	21.1	5,167.8
June	1,109.0	1,314.0	2,333.0	2,337.1	539.8	2,876.9	18.8	5,209.9
September	1,129.0	1,399.2	2,528.2	2,681.4	641.5	3,322.9	19.3	5,851.1
December	1,781.3	1,715.7	3,497.0	3,283.1	865.6	4,148.7	20.9	7,645.7
1977								
March	1,626.8	1,898.8	3,525.6	4,171.7	756.2	4,927.9	15.3	8,453.5
June	1,588.5	1,899.2	3,477.7	4,736.5	687.0	5,423.5	12.7	8,901.2
September	1,793.4	1,872.8	3,666.2	5,119.0	796.2	5,915.2	13.5	9,581.4
December	2,250.4	2,162.7	4,413.1	5,556.9	1,015.7	6,572.5	15.5	10,985.6
1978								
March	2,377.6	2,492.8	4,870.4	6,276.7	1,024.1	7,300.9	14.0	12,171.2
June	2,215.8	2,380.3	4,596.1	7,008.5	985.9	7,994.4	12.3	12,590.5
September	2,232.9	2,132.8	4,365.7	7,804.2	952.2	8,756.4	10.9	13,122.1
December	2,842.8	2,462.2	5,305.0	8,916.4	915.0	9,831.4	9.3	15,136.4
1979								
March	2,713.5	2,663.5	5,377.0	10,190.1	865.2	11,055.3	7.8	16,432.3
June	2,507.1	2,433.1	4,940.7	9,740.7	736.5	10,477.2	7.0	15,417.4
September	2,150.5	2,391.4	4,541.9	8,907.5	669.1	9,576.6	7.0	14,118.5
December	2,728.1	2,785.1	5,513.2	9,926.5	653.7	10,580.2	6.2	16,093.4
1980								
March	2,569.3	3,578.4	6,147.7	10,983.7	763.7	11,747.4	6.5	17,895.1
June	2,440.6	3,162.8	5,603.4	10,873.1	638.8	11,511.9	5.5	17,115.3
September	2,224.5	3,404.9	5,629.4	11,143.9	636.2	11,780.1	5.4	17,409.5
December	3,046.7	3,698.7	6,745.4	12,213.3	787.5	13,000.8	6.1	19,746.2
1981								
March	2,841.7	3,927.2	6,768.9	14,822.9	777.6	15,600.5	5.0	22,369.4
June	2,897.3	3,679.1	6,576.4	17,815.8	775.7	18,591.5	4.2	25,167.9
September	3,082.5	3,389.7	6,472.2	20,042.4	736.6	20,779.0	3.5	27,251.2
December	3,982.2	2,615.7	6,597.9	20,328.1	766.8	21,094.9	3.6	27,692.8
1982								
March	3,420.0	3,542.2	6,962.2	25,511.6	798.1	26,309.7	3.0	33,271.9
June	3,361.8	2,695.3	6,057.1	24,915.5	1,035.0	25,950.5	4.0	32,007.6
September	2,590.1	2,550.2	5,140.3	21,088.6	1,183.3	22,271.9	5.3	27,412.2
December	2,198.9	2,105.4	4,304.3	18,881.8	1,262.5	20,144.3	6.3	24,448.6

Source: IFS.
  Column (1) = 34-24
  Column (2) = 24
  Column (3) = 34
  Column (4) = 25 a
  Column (5) = 25 b at commercial banks (State Bank is included)
  Column (6) = 35

1/ Deflated by wholesale price index.

TABLE C-5
CHILE - INDEX OF REAL MONEY AND QUASI-MONEY, 1975-82

| | Money | | | Time and savings deposits Private Banks | | Quasi-Money | Money and Quasi-Money |
	Currency	Sight Deposits	Total	L/C	F/C		
1975							
December	100	100	100	100	100	100	100
1976							
March	82	97	90	119	90	111	99
June	74	81	78	143	93	130	100
September	82	86	84	164	111	150	112
December	130	106	117	200	150	187	147
1977							
March	118	117	118	255	131	222	162
June	116	117	116	289	119	245	171
September	131	116	122	312	138	267	184
December	164	133	147	339	175	296	211
1978							
March	173	154	163	383	177	329	234
June	161	147	154	428	170	360	242
September	163	132	146	476	165	395	252
December	207	152	177	544	158	443	290
1979							
March	198	164	180	622	149	498	315
June	183	150	165	594	127	472	296
September	157	148	152	544	116	432	271
December	199	172	184	606	113	477	309
1980							
March	187	221	205	670	132	529	343
June	178	195	187	663	110	519	328
September	162	210	188	680	110	531	334
December	222	228	225	745	136	586	379
1981							
March	207	242	226	904	134	703	429
June	211	227	220	1,087	134	838	483
September	224	209	216	1,223	127	937	523
December	290	161	220	1,240	132	951	531
1982							
March	249	219	233	1,557	138	1,186	638
June	245	166	202	1,520	179	1,170	614
September	189	157	172	1,287	205	1,004	526
December	160	130	144	1,152	218	908	469

Source: Table C-4

TABLE C-6

CHILE – FOREIGN CURRENCY DEPOSITS IN THE BANKING SYSTEM, 1973–82

	1973	1974	1975	1976	1977	1978	1979	1980	1981	1982
Foreign currency deposits	116.4	117.1	128.0	179.1	232.5	247.3	270.9	369.6	387.3	411.8
National banks	--	--	--	--	--	172.3	178.8	281.7	257.2	248.2
Banco del Estado de Chile	61.7	50.3	50.0	46.5	62.7	73.0	75.5	83.2	74.0	74.3
Foreign Banks	--	--	--	--	--	2.0	16.6	17.4	56.1	89.3
F/C deposits as percent of imports c.i.f.	10.6	6.1	8.3	10.9	10.3	8.2	6.4	7.2	6.1	11.7
F/C deposits as percent of GNP	3.5	2.3	2.7	2.2	2.1	1.8	1.4	1.4	1.2	2.5

Sources: Central Bank of Chile (Monthly Bulletin); and IFS.

1/ At the end of period.

TABLE U-1

URUGUAY - QUARTERLY INDUSTRIAL PRODUCTION, INFLATION, AND SHORT-TERM LENDING INTEREST RATES, 1976-82

Year	Manufac- turing Produc- tion 1/ (1)	Inflation Rate 2/3/ (2)	Nominal Lending Interest Rate 3/				Real Lending Interest Rate 3/4/			
			Loans in L/C		Loans in F/C in peso terms 5/		Loans in L/C		Loans in F/C in peso terms 5/	
			Prime rate (3)	Other (4)	Prime rate (5)	Other (6)	Prime rate (7)	Other (8)	Prime rate (9)	Other (10)
1976	4.0	44.4	—	—	—	69.4	—	—	—	17.3
I	4.9	18.2	—	—	—	98.6	—	—	—	68.0
II	8.0	22.4	—	—	—	46.3	—	—	—	19.5
III	5.1	92.3	45.0	61.5	—	82.0	-24.6	-16.0	—	-5.4
IV	-2.0	56.4	47.5	62.0	—	55.8	-5.7	3.6	—	-0.4
1977	6.1	41.8	52.7	65.5	—	56.8	7.7	16.7	—	10.6
I	8.9	63.0	45.9	62.0	—	51.8	-10.5	-0.6	—	-6.9
II	6.5	35.8	49.6	62.0	—	48.5	10.2	19.3	—	9.4
III	5.5	48.7	50.3	62.0	—	69.1	1.2	8.9	—	6.7
IV	3.5	22.9	65.8	76.6	68.8	69.1	34.9	43.7	37.4	37.6
1978	6.0	49.3	63.5	74.2	45.0	47.0	9.5	17.8	-2.9	-1.5
I	4.8	31.3	67.2	77.1	22.9	24.0	27.3	34.9	-6.4	-5.6
II	10.6	52.7	63.2	78.9	40.6	42.0	6.9	17.2	-7.9	-7.0
III	7.1	51.1	62.0	74.1	67.9	71.0	7.2	15.2	11.1	13.2
IV	1.5	63.5	61.3	72.7	52.5	55.0	-1.5	5.6	-6.7	-5.2
1979	4.6	82.7	48.9	65.5	38.6	41.0	-18.5	-9.4	-24.1	-22.8
I	10.4	60.6	51.3	69.6	51.0	53.3	-5.8	5.6	-6.0	-4.6
II	-4.8	123.6	47.7	64.1	40.1	43.0	-34.0	-26.6	-37.3	-36.1
III	8.8	81.8	47.2	62.3	37.8	40.7	-19.0	-10.7	-24.2	-22.6
IV	5.1	71.2	49.4	66.2	26.7	28.0	-12.7	-2.9	-26.0	-25.2
1980	4.9	32.9	50.1	66.6	37.9	40.2	12.9	25.4	3.8	5.5
I	1.8	33.4	50.0	67.4	32.6	35.5	12.4	25.5	-0.6	1.6
II	5.2	28.8	51.2	68.2	33.2	35.3	17.4	30.6	3.4	5.1
III	5.8	35.9	50.2	65.9	36.7	39.2	10.5	22.1	0.6	2.4
IV	6.6	33.9	49.1	65.0	49.6	51.3	11.4	23.2	11.7	13.0
1981	-4.6	17.8	47.4	60.4	35.7	37.5	18.3	36.4	15.2	16.7
I	-1.0	36.1	49.6	63.8	32.7	34.0	9.9	20.4	-2.5	-1.5
II	2.0	14.0	47.5	59.6	36.8	39.1	29.4	40.0	20.0	22.0
III	-6.0	35.0	46.5	58.7	37.2	39.5	8.5	17.6	1.6	3.3
IV	-12.5	-8.6	45.9	59.5	36.3	37.4	59.6	74.5	49.1	50.3
1982		38.0		58.1	—	—	—	14.6	—	—
I	-12.3	12.7	42.3	49.2	34.5	36.1	26.3	32.4	19.3	20.8
II	-16.5	18.2	44.7	51.6	35.2	36.3	22.4	28.3	14.4	15.3
III	-20.6	21.0	49.6	62.3	43.4	44.6	23.6	34.1	18.5	19.5
IV	—	125.2	—	70.4	—	52.2 6/	—	-24.3	—	42.2 6/

Source: Central Bank of Uruguay (Monthly Bulletin and Economic and Financial Indicators).

1/ Over corresponding period of previous year.
2/ Average inflation rate over corresponding previous period of domestic manufactures products (wholesale).
3/ Annual rates.
4/ The real interest rate was calculated as: $(i - \Pi/1 + \Pi)$ where i = interest rate, Π = inflation rate [column (2)].
5/ The sum of the ex post annual rate of peso depreciation as measured by the commercial market (buying rate) and short-term lending interest rates.
6/ Average monthly rate in the quarter.

TABLE U-2

URUGUAY - NOMINAL AND REAL SHORT-TERM DEPOSIT INTEREST RATES AND
EXCHANGE RATE, 1976-82

(Annual Rates in percent)

Year	Nominal Deposit Interest Rate 1/ in L/C (1)	F/C 2/ (In peso terms) (2)	Wholesale (general) Inflation Rate (3)	Real Deposit Interest Rate 3/ L/C (4)	F/C (5)	Devaluation Rate 4/ (6)	Real Exchange Rate Index 5/ (7)
1976			44.9			51.3	100.0
I			18.2			77.3	101.0
II			20.0			30.6	102.0
III	30.0*	74.9*	95.2	-33.4	-10.4	62.5	101.0
IV	30.2*	49.4*	59.9	-18.1	-6.0	39.1	96.0
1977	48.8	50.2	41.6	5.1	6.1	39.5	93.5
I	54.8	45.7	58.0	-2.0	-7.8	35.5	94.0
II	45.7	42.7	30.7	11.5	9.2	32.6	94.0
III	48.2	52.9	39.8	6.0	9.4	41.7	93.0
IV	46.6	60.3	39.1	5.4	15.2	48.6	93.0
1978	47.6	38.3	59.6	-7.5	-13.4	28.4	82.5
I	50.7	16.3	34.4	12.1	-13.5	8.2	88.0
II	45.1	33.7	55.2	-6.5	-13.9	24.4	83.0
III	48.2	60.9	81.4	-18.3	-11.3	49.1	82.0
IV	46.5	46.2	71.4	-14.5	-14.7	35.5	77.0
1979	41.9	33.5	77.3	-20.0	-24.7	22.2	60.5
I	41.4	44.1	75.5	-19.4	-17.9	33.1	72.0
II	37.6	34.4	113.9	-35.7	-37.2	23.9	63.0
III	40.5	33.3	96.2	-28.4	-32.0	22.5	56.0
IV	48.5	23.1	34.1	10.7	-8.2	10.4	51.0
1980	50.1	35.0	28.9	16.5	4.7	19.2	48.8
I	49.2	29.9	25.8	18.6	3.3	15.2	51.0
II	52.7	30.6	18.6	28.8	10.1	14.8	50.0
III	48.8	34.0	47.8	0.7	-9.3	19.3	47.0
IV	49.6	46.0	25.2	19.5	16.6	28.6	47.0
1981	46.1	32.1	15.1	27.0	15.0	15.1	46.3
I	48.4	28.6	.18.2	25.6	8.8	12.6	47.0
II	43.1	33.6	12.7	27.0	18.6	16.5	47.0
III	44.8	34.7	47.6	-2.0	-8.7	16.1	45.0
IV	48.1	31.6	-12.0	68.3	49.6	15.2	46.0
1982	49.6	—	33.2	13.5	—	—	52.3
I	4.16	30.8	4.1	36.0	25.7	14.8	48.0
II	44.7	30.6	21.8	18.8	7.2	14.3	48.0
III	53.7	34.5	24.8	23.2	7.8	21.1	48.0
IV	59.1	49.9 6/	98.9	-20.0	26.2 6/	46.1 6/	65.0

Source: Central Bank of Uruguay (Monthly Bulletin).

* End of the period.
1/ Time deposits nominal interest rates up to three months (average annual).
2/ The sum of the ex post annual rate of peso devaluation (commercial market, buying rate) and interest rates paid on foreign currency time deposits.
3/ Deflated by column (3):$(i - \pi/1 + \pi)$ where i = interest rate, π = inflation rate.
4/ Commercial market buying exchange rate. Percentage change in terms of NUr$ per US$ (average rate in the period).
5/ Deflated by W.P.I. (general), 1976 = 100.
6/ Average monthly rate in the quarter.

TABLE U-3

URUGUAY - CREDIT TO THE PRIVATE SECTOR IN REAL TERMS; 1975-82

| | Local Currency | | Foreign Currency 2/ | | Total | Total | Total | |
	Official banks (1)	Private banks (2)	Official banks (3)	Private banks (4)	Local Currency (5)	Foreign Currency 3/ (6)	Banking System (7)	(6)/(7)= (8)
1975								
December	706.3	470.3	144.9	274.1	1,176.6	419.0	1,595.6	26.0
1976								
March	724.3	472.0	183.5	289.5	1,196.3	469.7	1,666.0	28.0
June	768.0	487.1	200.6	298.8	1,255.1	488.6	1,743.7	28.0
September	737.7	461.0	208.8	337.7	1,198.7	526.5	1,725.2	30.5
December	793.9	480.7	208.0	414.2	1,274.6	594.3	1,868.9	31.8
1977								
March	714.2	472.9	225.5	535.2	1,187.1	710.3	1,897.4	37.4
June	685.9	487.7	253.9	550.7	1,173.6	716.2	1,862.9	38.4
September	669.8	490.2	245.5	596.4	1,160.0	761.2	1,921.2	39.6
December	729.9	522.6	295.7	785.3	1,252.5	966.9	2,219.4	43.6
1978								
March	674.1	579.5	324.1	838.4	1,253.6	1,018.8	2,272.4	44.8
June	664.2	684.0	375.0	899.9	1,348.2	1,085.9	2,431.1	44.6
September	628.5	706.5	411.8	959.8	1,335.0	1,144.9	2,479.9	46.2
December	684.6	792.2	444.0	1,062.3	1,476.8	1,234.7	2,711.5	45.5
1979								
March	668.9	806.7	537.9	1,223.8	1,475.6	1,401.5	2,877.1	48.7
June	660.3	1,041.8	534.9	1,449.3	1,702.1	1,524.0	3,226.1	47.2
September	666.6	1,098.1	551.3	1,704.1	1,653.7	1,679.4	3,333.1	50.4
December	615.1	1,168.9	636.4	2,117.5	1,784.0	1,992.8	3,776.7	52.8
1980								
March	607.0	1,301.4	791.6	2,241.8	1,908.4	2,136.0	4,012.0	53.2
June	567.8	1,369.8	947.1	2,493.3	1,937.6	2,312.1	4,249.7	54.4
September	532.9	1,478.3	1,001.1	2,700.0	2,011.3	2,446.3	4,457.6	54.9
December	556.6	1,660.2	1,147.7	3,090.9	2,216.8	2,600.4	4,817.2	54.0
1981								
March	525.1	1,705.0	1,217.6	3,153.8	2,230.1	2,657.4	4,887.5	54.4
June	525.3	1,790.3	1,257.0	3,240.0	2,315.6	2,672.0	4,987.6	53.6
September	531.7	1,765.6	1,223.6	3,590.7	2,297.3	2,778.0	5,075.3	54.7
December	594.3	1,702.1	1,244.4	4,151.3	2,296.4	3,090.3	5,386.7	57.4
1982								
March	569.3	1,628.9	1,244.9	4,169.7	2,198.2	3,083.5	5,281.7	58.4
June	583.2	1,571.2	1,294.3	4,228.7	2,154.4	3,063.2	5,217.6	58.7
September	571.4	1,422.6	1,346.5	4,462.3	1,994.0	3,193.4	5,187.4	61.6
December	633.9	1,300.8	1,561.0	4,231.3	1,934.7	3,137.8	5,072.5	61.9

Source: Central Bank of Uruguay (Monthly Bulletin).

1/ Deflated by the cost-of-living index December 1975 = 100.
2/ Valued at the financial exchange rate of December 1975.
3/ Valued at the financial exchange rate of December 1975 and deflated by the U.S. cost-of-living index.

TABLE U-4

URUGUAY — REAL MONEY AND QUASI-MONEY, 1975-82

	Money			Time and Savings Deposits		Other Deposits		Quasi-Money	Money and Quasi-Money	FC/QM
	Currency (1)	Sight Deposits (2)	Total (3)	L/C (4)	F/C 2/ (5)	L/C (6)	F/C 2/ (7)	(8)	(9)	(percentage) (10)
1975										
December	469.8	351.5	821.3	361.6	323.0	80.9	9.6	775.1	1,596.4	42.9
1976										
March	504.3	399.3	903.6	438.5	396.4	94.1	8.4	937.4	1,841.0	43.2
June	549.2	401.9	951.1	524.4	488.9	92.8	8.9	1,115.0	2,066.1	44.6
September	493.2	357.9	851.1	487.0	591.6	109.4	12.4	1,200.4	2,051.5	50.3
December	558.8	387.9	946.7	481.2	679.6	125.7	24.9	1,311.4	2,258.1	53.7
1977										
March	515.7	388.7	904.4	481.7	825.4	138.6	38.6	1,484.3	2,388.7	58.2
June	449.6	352.5	802.1	437.7	873.8	90.2	62.0	1,463.7	2,265.8	63.9
September	402.3	326.6	728.9	418.2	784.7	109.0	89.9	1,601.8	2,330.7	54.6
December	506.5	338.6	845.1	462.2	1,124.8	109.0	107.6	1,803.6	2,648.7	68.3
1978										
March	475.4	364.8	840.2	709.1	1,138.5	71.1	38.5	1,957.2	2,797.4	60.1
June	513.2	355.5	868.7	791.8	1,220.2	50.2	29.6	2,091.8	2,960.5	59.7
September	453.0	319.2	772.2	821.1	1,309.5	87.4	35.6	2,253.6	3,025.8	59.7
December	564.2	393.8	958.0	950.4	1,403.9	63.0	28.4	2,345.7	3,303.7	61.6
1979										
March	487.7	420.3	908.3	922.2	1,668.7	53.5	37.4	2,681.8	3,590.1	63.6
June	498.2	449.2	947.4	998.1	1,634.2	55.8	24.1	2,712.2	3,659.6	61.1
September	440.9	384.0	824.9	1,049.3	1,779.4	29.2	26.5	2,884.4	3,709.3	62.6
December	541.4	444.2	985.6	1,074.4	1,780.2	56.8	33.4	2,944.8	3,930.4	61.6
1980										
March	563.3	393.2	956.5	1,298.3	1,792.4	36.9	29.5	3,157.1	4,113.6	57.7
June	471.3	381.9	853.2	1,397.8	1,865.9	53.6	32.2	3,349.5	4,202.7	56.7
September	435.3	375.2	810.5	1,520.7	1,903.0	28.1	51.9	3,503.7	4,314.2	55.8
December	607.0	433.1	1,040.2	1,594.3	2,038.6	38.3	70.3	3,741.5	4,781.7	56.4
1981										
March	527.1	411.1	938.2	1,807.5	2,415.4	45.3	62.7	4,330.9	5,269.1	57.2
June	551.3	366.5	917.8	1,795.9	2,883.2	27.8	...	4,706.9	5,624.7	61.3
September	478.7	319.3	798.0	1,646.9	3,266.2	26.2	...	4,939.3	5,737.3	66.1
December	565.3	339.6	904.9	1,631.0	3,439.6	41.7	...	5,112.3	6,017.2	67.3
1982										
March	501.3	295.9	797.2	1,622.6	3,513.4	40.9	...	5,176.9	5,974.1	67.9
June	475.2	266.3	741.5	1,529.8	3,942.9	37.5	...	5,510.2	6,251.7	71.6
September	438.9	218.5	657.4	1,449.1	3,774.8	38.3	...	5,262.2	5,919.6	71.7
December	614.9	299.8	914.7	1,409.2	2,651.8	34.3	...	4,095.3	5,010.0	64.8

Source: Central Bank of Uruguay (Monthly Bulletin).

1/ Deflated by the cost-of-living index.
2/ Valued at the financial exchange rate of December 1975 and deflated by the U.S. cost-of-living index.
L/C = Local currency.
F/C = Foreign currency.

TABLE U-5

URUGUAy - FOREIGN CURRENCY DEPOSITS IN THE BANKING SYSTEM, 1972-82

| At the End of (1) | BROU (2) | Time and savings deposits Private Banks | | | Total (6) | Other | | | Total (10) | As Percent of GNP m.p. (11) | As Percent of Import C.I.F. (12) |
		Resi-dents (3)	Non-Residents (4)	Sub-total (5)		BROU (7)	Private Banks (8)	Sub-total (9)			
1972	4.0	5.5	6.9	12.4	26.4	0.6	23.0	23.6	40.0	2.4	18.9
1973	3.3	29.3	5.6	34.9	38.2	0.6	3.6	4.2	42.4	1.6	14.9
1974	4.7	42.6	8.6	51.2	55.9	0.7	5.7	6.4	62.3	2.3	12.8
1975	12.2	85.0	22.5	107.5	119.7	0.7	2.9	3.6	123.3	4.1	22.2
1976	33.4	187.8	46.1	233.9	267.3	0.8	9.0	9.8	277.1	8.7	47.2
1977	57.4	346.6	62.6	409.2	466.6	2.7	33.3	36.0	502.6	13.8	68.9
1978	71.5	407.4	161.1	568.5	640.0	3.9	12.9	16.8	656.8	15.3	84.8
1979	96.5	539.5	274.7	814.2	910.7	1.2	17.2	18.4	929.1	13.6	75.5
1980	137.9	566.4	473.3	1,039.7	1,177.6	2.4	44.3	46.7	1,224.3	13.1	76.0
1981	235.3	932.1	871.6	1,803.7	2,039.0	2.5	94.1	96.6	2,135.6	20.4*	123.6
1982	--	--	--	1,582.0*	--	--	--	--	--	17.3*1/	140.8 1/

Sources: Central Bank of Uruguay (Monthly Bulletin); and IFS.

BROU = Banco de la Republica Oriental del Uruguay.
* Preliminary figure
1/ As percent of column (5), 1982.

TABLE U-6

URUGUAY - INDEX OF REAL MONEY AND QUASI-MONEY, AND OF CREDIT
TO THE PRIVATE SECTOR, 1975-82

	Money	Time and Savings Deposits		Other Deposits	Quasi-Money	Total Money and Quasi-Money	Credit to the Private Sector		
		L/C	F/C 2/				Local Currency	Foreign Currency 2/	Total
1975									
December	100.0	100.0	100.0	100.0	100.0	100.0	100.0	100.0	100.0
1976									
March	110.0	121.2	122.7	113.3	120.9	115.3	101.7	112.1	104.4
June	115.8	145.0	151.4	112.4	143.9	129.4	106.7	116.6	109.3
September	102.4	134.7	183.2	134.6	157.5	128.5	101.9	125.7	108.1
December	115.3	133.1	210.4	166.4	169.2	141.4	108.3	141.8	117.1
1977									
March	110.1	133.2	255.5	195.8	191.5	149.6	100.9	169.5	118.9
June	97.7	121.0	270.5	168.2	188.8	141.9	99.7	170.9	116.7
September	88.7	115.7	304.9	219.8	206.9	146.0	98.6	181.7	120.4
December	102.9	127.8	348.2	239.3	232.7	165.4	106.5	230.8	139.0
1978									
March	102.3	196.1	352.5	121.1	252.5	175.2	106.6	243.1	142.4
June	105.8	219.0	377.8	88.2	269.9	185.4	114.7	258.2	152.6
September	94.0	227.1	405.4	135.9	290.8	189.5	113.5	273.2	155.4
December	116.6	235.2	434.6	101.0	302.6	206.9	125.5	294.7	170.0
1979									
March	110.6	255.0	516.6	100.4	346.0	224.9	125.4	334.5	180.3
June	115.4	276.0	505.9	88.3	349.9	229.2	144.7	363.7	202.2
September	100.4	290.1	550.9	61.5	372.1	232.4	140.5	400.7	208.8
December	120.0	297.1	551.1	99.7	379.9	246.2	151.6	475.6	236.7
1980									
March	116.5	359.9	554.9	73.4	407.3	257.7	162.2	502.0	251.4
June	103.9	386.6	577.7	94.8	432.1	263.3	164.7	551.8	266.4
September	98.6	420.5	589.2	88.4	452.0	270.2	170.9	583.8	279.4
December	126.7	440.9	631.1	120.0	482.7	299.5	188.4	620.6	301.9
1981									
March	114.2	499.9	747.8	119.3	558.8	330.1	189.5	634.1	306.3
June	111.7	496.6	892.6	...	607.2	352.3	196.8	637.7	312.6
September	97.2	455.5	1,011.2	...	637.2	359.4	195.2	663.0	318.1
December	110.2	451.0	1,064.9	...	659.5	376.9	188.4	620.6	301.9
1982									
March	97.1	448.1	1,087.7	...	667.9	374.2	186.8	735.9	331.0
June	90.3	423.1	1,220.7	...	710.9	391.6	183.1	731.1	327.0
September	80.0	400.7	1,168.7	...	678.9	370.8	169.5	762.1	325.1
December	111.4	389.7	821.0	...	528.3	313.8	164.4	748.9	317.9

Source: Central Bank of Uruguay (Monthly Bulletin).

1/ Deflated by cost-of-living index (December 1975 = 100).
2/ Valued at the financial exchange rate of December 1975 and deflated by the U.S. cost-of-living index.

References

Arango, Sebastian and M. Ishaq Nadiri, "The Demand for Money in Open Economies", Journal of Monetary Economics, Vol. 7 (1981), pp. 69-83.

Argentine Central Bank: Annual Reports (several numbers).

Argentine Economic Development (AED), April 1976 - December 1980, Ministry of Economy.

Arnaudo, Aldo and J.A. Bartolemei, "Devaluation under Inflationary Expectations: Argentina, 1967-1971", Applied Economics, Vol. 10 (1978), pp. 115-124.

Arriazu, Ricardo H., "Policy Interdependence from a Latin-American Perspective", IMF Staff Papers, Vol. 30 (1983a), pp. 113-163.

--, Panel Discussion on Southern Cone, IMF Staff Papers, Vol. 30 (1983b), pp. 177-184.

Baer, Werner, "ISI in Latin America: Experiences and Interpretations", Latin American Research Review, (Spring 1972).

--, and Larry Samuelson, "Toward a Service-Oriented Growth Strategy", World Development, Vol. 9 (1981), pp. 499-514.

Baez, Juan C., "Estimation of Money Demand Components", Discussion Paper No. 6, Center of Monetary and Banking Studies of the Central Bank of the Argentine Republic, (Buenos Aires, September 1979).

Baliño, Tomas J.T., "The Demand for Money and its Components in Argentina. Annual Estimations, 1935-1969", in Money and Monetary Policy in Less-Developed Countries, Warren L. Coats and Deena Khatkhate (eds.), New York: Pergamon Press, 1980, pp. 279-296.

Banda, Ariel, "Una Aproximación Empírica al Estudio de Los Sustitutos del Dinero en el Uruguay", Paper presented at the XIX reunión de tecnicos de bancos centrales del continente americano, Vina del Mar (Chile), 1982.

Behrman, Jere, Macroeconomic Policy in a Developing Country: The Chilean Experience, Amsterdam: North-Holland Publ. Co., 1977.

Bhandari, Jagdeep S., Exchange Rate Determination and Adjustment, New York: Praeger, 1982.

Bilson, John, "Recent Developments in Monetary Models of Exchange Rate Determination", IMF Staff Papers, Vol. 26 (1979), pp. 201-223.

--, "The Monetary Approach to the Exchange Rate: Some Empirical Evidence", IMF Staff Papers, Vol. 25 (1978), pp. 48-75.

Blejer, Mario, "Interest Rate Differentials And Exchange Risk: Recent Argentine Experience", IMF Staff Papers, Vol. 29 (1982), pp. 270-279.

--, "Black Market Exchange Rate Expectations and the Domestic Demand for Money: Some Empirical Evidence", Journal of Monetary Economics, Vol. 4 (1978), pp. 767-774.

--, and Don Mathieson, "The Preannouncement of the Exchange Rate as a Stabilization Instrument", IMF Staff Papers, Vol. 28 (1981), pp. 760-792.

Bordo, Michael and Eshan Choudhri, "Currency Substitution and the Demand for Money: Some Evidence for Canada", Journal of Money, Credit, and Banking, Vol. 14 (1982), pp. 48-57.

Boughton, James M., "Recent Instability of the Demand for Money: an International Perspective", Southern Economic Journal, Vol. 47 (1981), pp. 579-597.

Boyer, Russel, "Currency Mobility and Balance of Payments Adjustment", in The Monetary Approach to International Adjustment, B.H. Putman and D. Sykes Wilford (eds.), New York: Praeger Publishers (1978a), pp. 23-51.

--, "Optimal Foreign Exchange Market Intervention", The Journal of Political Economy, Vol. 86 (1978b), pp. 23-51.

Brillembourg, Arturo and Susan Schadler, "A Model of Currency Substitution in Exchange Rate Determination", IMF Staff Papers, Vol. 26 (1979), pp. 513-543.

Brittain, Bruce, "International Currency Substitution and the Apparent Instability of Velocity in Some Western European Economies and in the United States", Journal of Money, Credit, and Banking, Vol. 13 (1981), pp. 135-155.

Brodersohn, Mario, "Conflictos entre Objetivos de Política Económica de Corto Plazo de la Economía Argentina", Documento de Trabajo No. 77, Buenos Aires: Instituto Torcuato di Tella, 1977.

--, "Estrategias de Estabilización y Expansión en La Argentina: 1959-1967", in Los Planes de Estabilización en La Argentina, Buenos Aires: Editorial Paidos, 1967.

Calvo, Guillermo A., "Reflexiones Teóricas Sobre El Problema de Estabilización en La Argentina", Documento de Trabajo No. 29, Buenos Aires: Centro de Estudios Macroeconómicos Argentinos (CEMA), October 1981.

--, and Roque Fernandez, "Pauta Cambiaria y Déficit Fiscal", in Inflacion y Estabilidad, Roque Fernandez and Carlos Rodriguez (eds.), Buenos Aires: Editorial Macchi, 1982, pp. 175-179.

--, and Carlos Rodriguez, "A Model of Exchange Rate Determination Under Currency Substitution and Rational Expectations", Journal of International Economics, Vol. 86 (1977), pp. 617-625.

Canitrot, Adolfo, "Teoría y Práctica del Liberalismo. Política Anti-Inflacionaria y Apertura Económica en La Argentina, 1976-1981", Estudios CEDES (Buenos Aires), Vol. 3, No. 10 (1980).

--, "La Disciplina como Objectivo de la Política Económica. Un Ensayo sobre el Programa Economico del Gobierno Argentino desde 1976", Estudios CEDES, Vol. 2, No. 6 (1979).

Canto, Victor A., "Monetary Policy, 'Dollarization', and Parallel Market Exchange Rates: The Case of the Dominican Republic", Journal of International Money and Finance, Vol. 4 (1985), pp. 486-506.

Cardoso, Eliana, "Stabilization in Latin America: Popular Models and Unhappy Experiences", manuscript, Boston University, 1982.

--, "The Burden of Exchange Rate Adjustment in Brazil", in Export Diversification and The New Protectionism, Werner Baer and Malcolm Gillis (eds.), University of Illinois at Urbana-Champaign, Bureau of Economic and Business Research, 1981, pp. 168-179.

Cavallo, Domingo, "Los Efectos Recesivos e Inflationarios Iniciales de las Políticas Monetaristas de Estabilización", Ensayos Económicos, No. 4, Banco Central de la Republica Argentina, 1977.

--, and A. Humbero Petrei, "Financing Private Business in an Inflationary Context: The Experience of Argentina Between 1967 and 1980", in Financial Policies and the World Capital Market: The Problem of Latin-American Countries, Pedro Aspe Armella, Rüdiger Dornbusch, and Maurice Obstfeld (eds.), The University of Chicago Press, 1983, pp. 153-220.

Chan, Kenneth S., "Currency Substitution Theory Reconsidered", Research Report No. 20, McMaster University (Ontario, Canada), 1982.

Corden, William M., Inflation, Exchange Rate, and The World Economy, University of Chicago Press, 1977.

Crockett, A., "Stabilization Policies in Developing Countries: Some Policy Considerations", The IMF Staff Papers, Vol. 28 (1981), pp. 54-79.

Cuddington, John, "Currency Substitution, Capital Mobility and The Demand for Money", Working Paper, Stanford University, 1982.

Day, William H., "Domestic Credit and Money Ceilings Under Alternative Exchange Rate Regimes", IMF Staff Papers, Vol. 26 (1979), pp. 490-512.

de Melo, Jaime and Shurijo Urata, "The Impact of Trade Reforms on Industry Performance in Chile", Paper presented at The Allied Social Science Association Conference, San Francisco (USA), December 28-30, 1983.

de Pablo, Juan Carlos, Política Anti-inflacionaria en La Argentina, 1967-1970, Buenos Aires: Amorrortu Editores, 1970.

--, Economía Potítica del Peronismo, Buenos Aires: Editorial El Cid, 1980.

Deaver, John V., "The Chilean Inflation and The Demand for Money", in Varieties of Monetary Experience, David Meiselman (ed.), The University of Chicago Press, 1970.

Dervis, Kemal, Jaime de Melo, and Sherman Robinson, General Equilibrium Models for Development Policies, The World Bank Research Publication, Cambridge University Press, 1982.

Diamand, Marcelo, Doctrinas Económicas, Desarrollo, e Independencia, Buenos Aires: Editorial Paidos, 1973.

Diaz-Alejandro, Carlos, "No Less Than One Hundred Years of Argentine Economic History Plus Some Comparisons", Economic Growth Center, Yale University, Discussion Paper No. 392 (New Haven, January 1982).

--, "Southern Cone Stabilization Plans", in Economic Stabilization in Developing Countries, W. Cline and S. Weintraub (eds.), Washington D.C.: Brookings Institution, 1981.

--, "Exchange Rates and Terms of Trade in the Argentine Republic, 1913-1976", Economic Growth Center, Yale University, Discussion Paper No. 341, (New Haven, March 1980).

--, Essays on the Economic History of the Argentine Republic, Yale University Press (1970).

--, "A Note on the Impact of Devaluation and the Redistributive Effect", Journal of Political Economy, Vol. 71 (1963), pp. 577-580.

Diz, Adolfo C., "Money and Prices in Argentina, 1935-1967", in Varieties of Monetary Experience, op.cit. (1970), pp. 68-137

Dooley, Michael P., and Peter Isard, "Capital Controls, Political Risk, and Deviations from Interest-Rate Parity", Journal of Political Economy, Vol. 88 (1980), pp. 370-384.

Dornbusch, Rüdiger, "Panel Discussion On Southern Cone", IMF Staff Papers, Vol. 30 (1983), pp. 173-176.

Dornbusch, Rüdiger, Argentina since Martinez de Hoz, NBER Working Paper Series No. 1466, 1984.

--, "Stabilization Policies in Developing Countries: What Have We Learned?", World Development, Vol. 10 (1982), pp. 701-708.

--, Open Economy Macroeconomics, New York: Basic Books Inc. Publisher, 1980a.

--, "Exchange Rate Economics: Where Do We Stand?", Brookings Papers On Economic Activity (1980b), pp. 143-185.

--, "Monetary Policy under Exchange Rate Flexibility", in The Functioning of Floating Exchange Rates: Theory, Evidence and Policy Implications, David Bigman and Teizo Taya (eds.), Cambridge, Mass.: Ballinger Publishers, 1980c, pp. 3-31.

--, "Devaluation, Money and Non-traded Goods", American Economic Review, Vol. 63 (1973), pp. 871-880.

Edwards, Sebastian, The Order of Liberalization of the Balance of the Balance of Payments, World Bank Staff Working Papers No. 710 (Washington D.C., December 1984)

--, "Stabilization with Liberalization: An Evaluation of Ten Years of Chilese Experiment with Free Market Policies, 1973-1983", Economic Development and Cultural Change, Vol. 33 (1985), pp. 224-254.

Emminger, O., "The Exchange Rate as an Instrument of Policy", in The Functioning of Floating Exchange Rates: Theory, Evidence and Policy Implications, op.cit., chapter 16.

Eshag, E. and R. Thorp, "Economic and Social Consequences of Orthodox Economic Policies in Argentina in the Post-War Years", Bulletin of the Oxford University Institute of Economic and Statistics, Vol. 27, No. 1 (1965)

Fasano-Filho, Ugo, "Currency Substitution, Fixed Exchange Rates and Income Stabilization; the Case of the European Monetarv Union", Graduate Student Working Paper No. 5, University of Illinois at Urbana-Champaign, 1984.

--, "Currency Substitution and the Demand for Money: the Argentine Case, 1960-76 (forthcoming in Weltwirtschaftliches Archiv, 1986).

--, and Maria Isabel Horta-Correia, "Increase in Foreign Debt and Exchange Rate Regime - in the Presence of Currency Substitution and Wage Rigidities - A Theoretical Approach", manuscript, Kiel Institute of World Economics, 1985.

Felix, David, "Latin-American Monetarism in Crisis", IDS Bulletin, Vol. 13, (1981), pp. 6-13.

Fernandez, Roque, "Consideraciones Ex-Post Sobre El Plan Económico de Martinez de Hoz", in Inflación y Estabilidad, op.cit., pp. 255-271.

Fernandez, Roque, and James A. Hanson, "El Rol de la Indexación en los Procesos Inflacionarios de America Latina", Buenos Aires: Fundación Banco de Boston, Agosto 1978.

Ffrench-Davis, Ricardo, "The Monetarist Experiment in Chile: A Critical Survey", World Development, Vol. 11 (1983), pp. 905-926.

Fischer, Bernhard, Ulrich Hiemenz, and Peter Trapp, Economic Crisis in Argentina and No Way Out? Kiel Institute of World Economics Working Paper No. 210 (Kiel, September 1984) (revised version forthcoming as Kieler Studien).

--, and Peter Trapp, "The Argentine Financial Sector: Performance, Problems, and Policy Issues", Kiel Working Paper No. 226, February 1985.

Fischer, Standley, "Seignorage and the Case for a National Money", The Journal of Political Economy, Vol. 90 (1982), pp. 295-313.

Flood, Robert P., "Capital Mobility and the Choice of Exchange Rate System", International Economic Review, Vol. 20 (1979), pp. 405-416.

Foxley, Alejandro, Latin-American Experiments in Neo-Conservative Economics, University of California Press, 1983.

Frenkel, Jacob, "The Forward Rate, Expectations, and The Demand for Money: The German Hyperinflation", The American Economic Review, Vol. 67 (4) (September, 1977).

--, "Panel Discussion on Southern Cone", IMF Staff Papers, Vol. 30 (1983), pp. 164-173.

--, "Purchasing Power Parity", Journal of International Economics, Vol. 8 (1978a), pp. 169-191.

--, "A Monetary Approach to the Exchange Rate: Doctrinal Aspects and Empirical Evidence", in The Economics of Exchange Rate, Jacob Frenkel and Harry Johnson (eds.), Mass.: Addison-Wesley Publishing Company, 1978b, pp. 1-26.

Frenkel, Roberto, "Mercado Financiero, Expectativas Cambiarias y Movimientos de Capitales", Estudios CEDES, Vol. 4, No. 3 (1981).

--, "Decisiones de Precios en Alta Inflacion", Estudios CEDES, Vol. 2, No. 3 (1979).

--, and Guillermo O'Donnell, "Los Programas de Estabilizacion Convenidos con el FMI y sus Impactos Internos", Estudios CEDES, Vol. 1, No. 1 (1978)

Friedman, Milton, "The Quantity Theory of Money. A Restatement", In Studies in the Quantity Theory of Money, Milton Friedman (ed.), University of Chicago Press, 1956.

--, "The Demand for Money: Some Theoretical and Empirical Results", Journal of Political Economy, Vol. 67 (1959).

Gaba, Ernesto, "La Reforma Financiera Argentina", Ensayos Economicos, Banco Central de la Republica Argentina (september 1981).

Galbis, Vincent, "Inflation and Interest Rates in Latin America, 1967-1976", manuscript, The International Monetary Fund (January, 1979).

Girton, Lance, and Don Roper, "Theory and Implications of Currency Substitution", Journal of Money, Credit and Banking, Vol. 13 (1981), pp. 12-30.

--, --, "The Theory of Currency Substitution and Monetary Unification", Economie Applique, Vol. 23 (1980), pp. 135-160.

Guitián, Manuel, "Credit versus Money as an Instrument of Control", in The Monetary Approach to the Balance of Payments, International Monetary Fund, 1977.

Henderson, D.W., "Financial Policies in Open Economies", American Economic Review, Vol. 69 (1979), pp. 232-239.

Husted, Steven, The Theory and Empirical Estimation of Currency Substitution, Unpublished Ph.D. dissertation, Michigan State University, 1980.

Isard, P., "How Far Can We Push The Law Of One Price", American Economic Review, Vol. 67 (1977), pp. 942-948.

Johnson, Harry, "The Monetary Approach to the Balance of Payments: a Non-Technical Guide", Journal of International Economics, Vol. 7 (1977), pp. 251-268.

Johnston, J., Econometric Methods, New York: McGraw-Hill Book Co. (second edition), 1972.

Joines, Douglas H., "International Currency Substitution and the Income Velocity of Money", Journal of International Money and Finance, Vol. 4 (1985), pp. 303-316.

Judd, John P., and John L. Scadding, "The Search for a Stable Money Demand Function: a Survey of the Post-1973 Literature", Journal of Economic Literature, Vol. 20 (1982), pp. 993-1023.

Kahn, M.S., "Variable Expectations and The Demand for Money in High Inflation Countries", in Money and Monetary Policy in Less Developed Countries, op. cit., 1980, pp. 307-323.

Kiguel, Miguel A., Three Essays on the Theory of Exchange Rate Regimes, Ph.D. Dissertation, Columbia University, 1983.

King, Davig, Bluford H. Putnam, and D. Sykes Wilford, "A Currency Portfolio Approach to Exchange Rate Determination: Exchange Rate Stability and the Independence of Monetary Policy", in The Monetary Approach to International Adjustment, B.H. Putnam and D. Sykes Wilford (eds.), New York: Praeger (Special Studies), 1978.

Kouri, Pentti J.K., and Michael G. Porter, "International Capital Flows and Portfolio Equilibrium", Journal of Political Economy, Vol. 82 (1974), pp. 443-467.

Kreinin, Mordechai E., and Lawrence Officer, "The Monetary Approach to the Balance of Payments: a Survey", Princeton Studies in International Finance, No. 43, 1978.

Krueger, Anne O., Exchange Rate Determination, Cambridge University Press, 1983.

Landy, Laurie, "Eurodollars in Canada and Domestic Monetary Control", Research Paper No. 8212, Federal Reserve Bank of New York, 1982.

Ledesma, Joaquin R., Cinco Años de Política Económica: Abril 1976 - Marzo 1981, Buenos Aires: Editorial FEPA, 1981.

Loser, Claudio, "The Role of Economy Wide Prices in the Adjustment Process", Paper presented at The Seminar on the Role of the IMF in the Adjustment Process, Viña del Mar (Chile), April 5-8, 1983.

Mallon, Richard, "Exchange Policy - Argentina", in Development Policy: Theory and Practice, Gustav Papanek (ed.), Harvard University Press, 1968.

Mantel, Rolf, and Ana Martirena-Mantel, "Exchange Rate Policies in a Small Economy: the Active Crawling-peg", Journal of International Economics, Vol. 13 (1982), pp. 301-320.

Marshall, Jorge, Jose L. Madones, and Isabel Marshall, "IMF Conditionality: the Experience of Argentina, Brazil and Chile", in IMF Conditionality, John Williamson (ed.), Institute of International Economics, MIT-Press, 1983.

Martinez de Hoz (h), José A., Bases para una Argentina Moderna: 1976-1980, Buenos Aires: Compañía Impresora Argentina S.A., 1982.

Martirena-Mantel, Ana, "The Crawling-peg: Argentina", in Exchange Rate Rules: the Theory, Performance and Prospects of the Crawling-peg, John Williamson (ed.), The MacMillan Press Ltd., 1981.

--, "Politica de Intervención Oficial en el Mercado de Cambio Futuro: Análisis de su Estabilidad", Economica, Vol. 18, No. 2 (La Plata, Argentina), (March-April 1972), pp. 215-235.

Mathieson, Don, "Estimating Models of Financial Market Behavior During Periods of Extensive Structural Reform: the Experience of Chile", IMF Staff Papers, Vol. 30 (1983), pp. 350-393.

--, "Inflation, Interest Rates, and the Balance of Payments during a Financial Reform: The Case of Argentina", World Development, Vol. 10 (1982), pp. 812-827.

Maynard, Geoffrey, and Willy van Rijckeghen, "Stabilization Policy in an Inflationary Economy - Argentina", in Development Policy: Theory and Practice, op.cit., 1968, pp. 207-235.

McKinnon, Ronald, "Currency Substitution and Instability in the World Standard", American Economic Review, Vol. 7 (1982a), pp. 320-333.

--, "The Order of Economic Liberalization: Lessons from Chile and Argentina", in Economic Policy in a World of Change, K. Brumer and A. Metzler (eds.), (Amsterdam: North-Holland Publishing Col, 1982b).

--, Money and Capital in Economic Development, Washington D.C.: Brookings Institution, 1973.

--, and Donald I. Mathieson, How to Manage a Repressed Economy, Essays in International Finance No. 145 (Princeton University, December 1981).

Melvin, Michael, "Currency Substitution and Western European Monetary Unification", manuscript, Arizona State University, 1982.

Miles, Marc, "Currency Substitution, Flexible Exchange Rates, and Monetary Independence", The American Economic Review, Vol. 68, (1978), pp. 428-436.

--, and Marion B. Stewart, "The Effects of Risk and Return on the Currency Composition of Money Demand", Weltwirtschaftliches Archiv, Vol. 116 (1980), pp. 613-626.

Nogués, Julio, Nature of Argentina's Economic Policy Reforms During 1976-1981, manuscript, the World Bank Research Department, June 1984.

Ortiz, Guillermo, "Currency Substitution in Mexico", Journal of Money, Credit and Banking, Vol. 15 (1983), pp. 174-185.

Poole, William, "Optimal Choice of Monetary Policy Instruments in a Simple Stochastic Macro-Model", The Quarterly Journal of Economics, Vol. 85 (1971), pp. 197-216.

Prachowny, Martin F., "Sectorial Conflicts over Stabilization Policies in Small Open Economies", Queen's University Discussion Paper No. 364 (Canada, 1979).

Ramos, Joshep, "Inflacion Persistente, Inflacion Reprimida e Hiperinflacion, Lecciones de Inflacion y Estabilizacion en Chile", Desarrollo Economico, Vol. 18 (1978).

Rietti, Mario, Money and Banking in Latin-America, New York: Praeger Publishers, 1979.

Robichek, Walter, "Financial Programing Exercised of the IMF in Latin-America", The International Monetary Fund (unpublished lectures), 1967.

Rodriguez, Carlos and Larry Sjaastad, "El Atraso Cambiario en Argentina, Mito o Realidad?" in Inflacion y Estabilidad, op.cit., 1982, pp. 285-327.

Rodriguez, Carlos and Larry Sjaastad, "Relación entre Salarios Reales y Tipo de Cambio", in Inflacion y Estabilidad, op.cit, 1982, pp. 329-335.

--, "El Plan Argentino de Estabilización del 20 de Diciembre", Documento de Trabajo No. 9 (Buenos Aires: CEMA, 1979).

Roper, Don and Stephen Turnovskiy, "Optimal Exchange Market Intervention in a Simple Stochastic Macro-Model", Canadian Journal of Economics, Vol. 13 (1980), pp. 296-309.

Rubli, Federico, "An Analysis on the Theory and Implications of the Currency Substitution Phenomenon", Columbia University (unpublished manuscript), 1981.

Salama, Elias, "Demanda de Dinero y Formación de Expectativas. Algunos Resultados Empíricos", Serie de Estudios Técnicos No. 32, Banco Central de la República Argentina, 1978.

Simone, Dante, "Politica Monetaria en Alta Inflación", Económica (La Plata, Argentina), Vol. 19 (1972), pp. 55-118.

Sjaastad, Larry, "Failure of Economic Liberalism in the Cone of Latin-America", The World Economy, Vol. 6, No. 1 (1983), pp. 5-26.

--, "Estabilizacion y Tipo de Cambio: el Contraste entre Chile y Argentina", Documento de Trabajo No. 1, Santiago de Chile: Centro de Estudios Publicos, October 1981.

Swoboda, Alexander, "Monetary Policy under Fixed Exchange Rates: Effectiveness, the Speed of Adjustment, and the Proper Use", in The Monetary Approach to the Balance of Payments, Jacob Brenkel and Harry Johnson (eds.), London: G. Allen & Unwin, 1976.

Tanzi, Vito, "Inflation, Real Tax Revenue, and the Case for Inflationary Finance: Theory with an Application to Argentina", IMF Staff Papers, Vol. 25 (1978), pp. 417-451.

--, and Mario Blejer, "Inflation, Interest Rate Policy, and Currency Substitution in Developing Economies: A Discussion of Some Major Issues", World Development, Vol. 10 (1982), pp. 781-789.

Turnovsky, Stephen, "The Asset Market Approach to Exchange Rate Determination: Some Short-Run, Stability, and Steady-State Properties", Journal of Macroeconomics, Vol. 3 (1981), pp. 1-32.

--, "Exchange Market Intervention in a Small Open Economy: an Exposition Model", Paper presented at the International Seminar on Recent Developments in Macroeconometric Models (Paris, September 1982).

Tyler, William, "Exchange Rate Flexibility Under Conditions of Endemic Inflation: a Case Study of the Recent Brazilian Experience", in Leading Issues in International Economy Policy, F. Bergsten and W. Tyler (eds.), Mass.: Lexington Books, 1973.

van Wijnbergen, Sweder, "Stagflationary Effects of Monetary Stabilization Policies: A Quantitative Analysis of South Korea", Journal of Development Economics, Vol. 10 (1982), pp. 133-169.

Vaubel, Roland, "International Shifts in the Demand for Money, Their Effects on Exchange Rates and Price Levels, and Their Implications for the Preannouncement of Monetary Expansion", Weltwirtschaftliches Archiv, Vol. 116 (1980), pp. 1-44.

--, Strategies for Currency Unification: The Economics of Currency Competition and the Case of the European Parallel Currency, Kieler Studien No. 156, 1978.

--, "Free Currency Competition", Weltwirtschaftliches Archiv, Vol. 113 (1977), pp. 435-461.

Villegas, Carlos G., Regimen Legal de Bancos, Actualización, Buenos Aires: Ediciones de Palma, 1980.

Viñals, Jose and Frits van Beek, "The Demand for Money in Latin-American Countries, 1964-1978", Paper Presented at XVI Meeting of Central Bank Technicians of the American Continent, San Jose de Costa Rica, November 1979.

Watcher, Susan M., Latin-American Inflation, Lexington Books, 1976.

Whitman, Marina, "Global Monetarism and the Monetary Approach to the Balance of Payments", Brookings Papers on Economic Activity, (3), Washington D.C.: The Brookings Institution, 1976, pp. 491-536.

Williamson, John (ed.), IMF Conditionality, The MIT-press, 1983.

--, (ed.), Exchange Rate Rules: The Theory, Performance, and Prospects of the Crawling-Peg, The McMillan Press Ltd., 1981.

--, "The Crawling-Peg", Princeton Studies in International Finance, No. 50 (December 1965).